ACCA

Paper 1.3

MANAGING PEOPLE

For exams in June 2007

Practice & Revision Kit

In this January 2007 new edition

- We discuss the **best strategies** for revising and taking your ACCA exams
- We show you how to be well prepared for the **June 2007 exam**
- We give you **lots of great guidance** on tackling questions
- We include **genuine student answers** with BPP commentary
- We show you how you can **build your own exams**
- We provide you with **two** mock exams including the **December 2006 exam**

Our **i-Pass** product also supports this paper.

BPP LEARNING MEDIA

First edition 2001
Seventh edition January 2007

ISBN 9780 7517 3334 1 (previous ISBN 0 7517 2550 1)

British Library Cataloguing-in-Publication Data
A catalogue record for this book is available from the British Library

Published by

BPP Learning Media Ltd
BPP House, Aldine Place
London W12 8AA

www.bpp.com/learningmedia

Printed in Great Britain by
Ashford Colour Press Ltd
Unit 600 Fareham Reach
Fareham Road
Gosport, P013 0FW

Your learning materials, published by BPP Learning Media Ltd, are printed on paper sourced from sustainable, managed forests.

We are grateful to the Association of Chartered Certified Accountants for permission to reproduce past examination questions. The answers to past examination questions have been prepared by BPP Learning Media Ltd.

Contents

Question index

The headings in this checklist/index indicate the main topics of questions, but questions often cover several different topics.

Preparation questions, listed in italics, provide you with a firm foundation for attempts at exam-standard questions.

	Marks	Time allocation Mins	Page number Question	Answer
Effective management				
49 Question with analysis: *Scenario:* Leadership styles (12/05)	40	72	71	162
50 Leadership skills and actions (6/04)	15	27	73	165
51 Question with answer plan: Leadership style	15	27	73	167
52 Questions with helping hand: Blake and Mouton (6/05)	15	27	73	168
53 Theory Z (12/02)	15	27	73	169

Part E: Effective communication practices

	Marks	Time allocation Mins	Question	Answer
Interpersonal and communication skills				
54 *Scenario:* Interpersonal skills (6/02)	40	72	74	170
55 Aggressive or assertive? (6/06)	15	27	75	173
56 Communication barriers (6/05)	15	27	75	175
57 Communication flows (12/03)	15	27	75	176
Conflict, grievance and discipline				
58 Question with answer plan: *Scenario:* Managing conflict	40	72	76	177
59 Conflict (6/02)	15	27	76	180
60 Conflict good and bad (12/05)	15	27	76	182
61 Question with helping hand: *Scenario:* Discipline and grievance (6/05)	40	72	77	183
62 Discipline (12/01; 12/04)	15	27	78	186
63 Grievance interview	15	27	78	188
64 Counselling (6/03)	15	27	78	189

Mock exam 1

Questions 65 to 70

Mock exam 2

Questions 71 to 76

Mock exam 3 (December 2006)

Questions 77 to 82

Planning your question practice

Our guidance from page 37 shows you how to organise your question practice, either by attempting questions from each syllabus area or **by building your own exams** – tackling questions as a series of practice exams.

Topic index

Listed below are the key Paper 1.3 syllabus topics and the numbers of the questions in this Kit covering those topics.

If you need to concentrate your practice and revision on certain topics or if you want to attempt all available questions that refer to a particular subject, you will find this index useful.

Syllabus topic	Question numbers
Performance management	18
Person specification	24, 25
Peters and Waterman	6
Recruitment	20, 21, 22
Responsibility	13, 14, 15
Rewards	47, 48
Selection	27, 28, 29, 30
Social responsibility	17
Supervisor	4, 13
Teams	10, 11, 12
Theory X & Y	42, 43
Theory Z	53
Training	20, 32, 33
Tuckman	10, 12

Using your BPP Practice and Revision Kit

Tackling revision and the exam

You can significantly improve your chances of passing by tackling revision and the exam in the right ways. Our advice is based on recent feedback from ACCA examiners.

- We look at the dos and don'ts of revising for, and taking, ACCA exams
- We focus on Paper 1.3; we discuss revising the syllabus, what to do (and what not to do) in the exam, how to approach different types of question and ways of obtaining easy marks

Selecting questions

We provide signposts to help you plan your revision.

- A full **question index**
- A **topic index** listing all the questions that cover key topics, so that you can locate the questions that provide practice on these topics, and see the different ways in which they might be examined
- **BPP's question plan** highlighting the most important questions and explaining why you should attempt them
- **Build your own exams**, showing how you can practise questions in a series of exams

Making the most of question practice

At BPP we realise that you need more than just questions and model answers to get the most from your question practice.

- Our **Top tips** provide essential advice on tackling questions, presenting answers and the key points that answers need to include
- We show you how you can pick up **Easy marks** on questions, as we know that picking up all readily available marks often can make the difference between passing and failing
- We summarise **Examiner's comments** to show you how students who sat the exam coped with the questions
- We include ACCA's **marking guides** to show you what the examiner rewards
- We refer to the **BPP 2006 Study Text** for detailed coverage of the topics covered in each question
- A number of questions include **Analysis** and **Helping hands** attached to show you how to approach them if you are struggling

Attempting mock exams

There are three mock exams that provide practice at coping with the pressures of the exam day. We strongly recommend that you attempt them under exam conditions. **Mock exams 1 and 2** reflect the question styles and syllabus coverage of the exam; **Mock exam 3** is the actual December 2006 exam. To help you get the most out of doing these exams, we not only provide help with each answer, but also guidance on how you should have approached the whole exam.

Passing ACCA exams

Revising and taking ACCA exams

To maximise your chances of passing your ACCA exams, you must make best use of your time, both before the exam during your revision, and when you are actually doing the exam.

- Making the most of your revision time can make a big, big difference to how well-prepared you are for the exam
- Time management is a core skill in the exam hall; all the work you've done can be wasted if you don't make the most of the three hours you have to attempt the exam

In this section we simply show you what to do and what not to do during your revision, and how to increase and decrease your prospects of passing your exams when you take them. Our advice is grounded in feedback we've had from ACCA examiners. You may be surprised to know that much examiner advice is the same whatever the exam, and the reasons why many students fail don't vary much between subjects and exam levels. So if you follow the advice we give you over the next few pages, you will **significantly** enhance your chances of passing **all** your ACCA exams.

How to revise

☑ Plan your revision

At the start of your revision period, you should draw up a **timetable** to plan how long you will spend on each subject and how you will revise each area. You need to consider the total time you have available and also the time that will be required to revise for other exams you're taking.

☑ Practise Practise Practise

The **more exam-standard questions** you do, the **more likely you are to pass** the exam. Practising full questions will mean that you'll get used to the time pressure of the exam. When the time is up, you should note where you've got to and then try to complete the question, giving yourself practice at everything the question tests.

☑ Revise enough

Make sure that your revision covers the breadth of the syllabus, as in most papers most topics could be examined in a compulsory question. However it is true that some topics are **key** – they often appear in compulsory questions or are a particular interest of the examiner – and you need to spend sufficient time revising these. Make sure you also know the **basics** – the fundamental calculations, proformas and report layouts.

☑ Deal with your difficulties

Difficult areas are topics you find dull and pointless, or subjects that you found problematic when you were studying them. You mustn't become negative about these topics; instead you should build up your knowledge by reading the **Passcards** and using the **Quick quiz** questions in the Study Text to test yourself. When practising questions in the Kit, go back to the Text if you're struggling.

☑ Learn from your mistakes

Having completed a question you must try to look at your answer critically. Always read the **Top tips guidance** in the answers; it's there to help you. Look at **Easy marks** to see how you could have quickly gained credit on the questions that you've done. As you go through the Kit, it's worth noting any traps you've fallen into, and key points in the **Top tips** or **Examiner's comments** sections, and referring to these notes in the days before the exam. Aim to learn at least one new point from each question you attempt, a technical point perhaps or a point on style or approach.

☑ Read the examiners' guidance

We refer throughout this Kit to **Examiner's comments**; these are available on ACCA's website. As well as highlighting weaknesses, examiners' reports as often provide clues to future questions, as many examiners will quickly test again areas where problems have arisen. ACCA's website also contains articles by examiners which you **must** read, as they may form the basis of questions on any paper after they've been published.

☑ Complete all three mock exams

You should attempt the **Mock exams** at the end of the Kit under **strict exam conditions**, to gain experience of selecting questions, managing your time and producing answers.

How NOT to revise

☒ Revise selectively

Examiners are well aware that some students try to forecast the contents of exams, and only revise those areas that they think will be examined. Examiners try to prevent this by doing the unexpected, for example setting the same topic in successive sittings or setting topics in compulsory questions that have previously only been examined in optional questions.

☒ Spend all the revision period reading

You cannot pass the exam just by learning the contents of Passcards, Course Notes or Study Texts. You have to develop your **application skills** by practising questions.

☒ Audit the answers

This means reading the answers and guidance without having attempted the questions. Auditing the answers gives you **false reassurance** that you would have tackled the questions in the best way and made the points that our answers do. The feedback we give in our answers will mean more to you if you've attempted the questions and thought through the issues.

☒ Practise some types of question, but not others

Although you may find the numerical parts of certain papers challenging, you shouldn't just practise calculations. These papers will also contain written elements, and you therefore need to spend time practising written question parts.

☒ Get bogged down

Don't spend a lot of time worrying about all the minute detail of certain topic areas, and leave yourself insufficient time to cover the rest of the syllabus. Remember that a key skill in the exam is the ability to **concentrate on what's important** and this applies to your revision as well.

☒ Overdo studying

Studying for too long without interruption will mean your studying becomes less effective. A five minute break each hour will help. You should also make sure that you are leading a **healthy lifestyle** (proper meals, good sleep and some times when you're not studying).

How to PASS your exams

☑ Prepare for the day

Make sure you set at least one alarm (or get an alarm call), and allow plenty of time to get to the exam hall. You should have your route planned in advance and should listen on the radio for potential travel problems. You should check the night before to see that you have pens, pencils, erasers, watch, calculator with spare batteries, also exam documentation and evidence of identity.

☑ Select the right questions

You should select the optional questions you feel you can answer **best**, basing your selection on the topics covered, the requirements of the question, how easy it will be to apply the requirements and the availability of easy marks.

☑ Plan your three hours

You need to make sure that you will be answering the correct number of questions, and that you spend the right length of time on each question – this will be determined by the number of marks available. Each mark carries with it a **time allocation** of **1.8 minutes**. A 15 mark question therefore should be selected, completed and checked in 27 minutes. With some papers, it's better to do certain types of question first or last.

☑ Read the questions carefully

To score well, you must follow the requirements of the question, understanding what aspects of the subject area are being covered, and the tasks you will have to carry out. The requirements will also determine what information and examples you should provide. Reading the question scenarios carefully will help you decide what **issues** to discuss, **techniques** to use, **information** and **examples** to include and how to **organise** your answer.

☑ Plan your answers

Five minutes of planning plus twenty-five minutes of writing is certain to earn you more marks than thirty minutes of writing. Consider when you're planning how your answer should be **structured,** what the **format** should be and **how long** each part should take.

Confirm before you start writing that your plan makes **sense,** covers **all relevant points** and does not include **irrelevant material.**

☑ Show evidence of judgement

Remember that examiners aren't just looking for a display of knowledge; they want to see how well you can **apply** the knowledge you have. Evidence of application and judgement will include writing answers that only contain **relevant** material, using the material in scenarios to **support** what you say, **criticising** the **limitations** and **assumptions** of the techniques you use and making **reasonable recommendations** that follow from your discussion.

☑ Stay until the end of the exam

Use any spare time to **check and recheck** your script. This includes checking you have filled out the candidate details correctly, you have labelled question parts and workings clearly, you have used headers and underlining effectively and spelling, grammar and arithmetic are correct.

How to FAIL your exams

☒ Don't do enough questions

If you don't attempt sufficient questions on the paper, you are making it harder for yourself to pass the questions that you do attempt. If for example you don't do a 15 mark question, then you will have to score 50 marks out of 85 marks on the rest of the paper, and therefore have to obtain 68% of the marks on the questions you do attempt. Failing to attempt all of the paper is symptomatic of poor time management or poor question selection.

☒ Include irrelevant material

Markers are given detailed mark guides and will not give credit for irrelevant content. Therefore you should **NOT** braindump all you know about a broad subject area; the markers will only give credit for what is **relevant**, and you will also be showing that you lack the ability to **judge what's important.** Similarly forcing irrelevant theory into every answer won't gain you marks, nor will providing uncalled for features such as situation analyses, executive summaries and background information.

☒ Fail to use the details in the scenario

General answers or reproductions of old answers that don't refer to what is in the scenario in **this** question won't score enough marks to pass.

☒ Copy out the scenario details

Examiners see **selective** use of the right information as a key skill. If you copy out chunks of the scenario which aren't relevant to the question, or don't use the information to support your own judgements, you won't achieve good marks.

☒ Don't do what the question asks

Failing to provide all the examiner asks for will limit the marks you score. You will also decrease your chances by not providing an answer with enough **depth** – producing a single line bullet point list when the examiner asks for a discussion.

☒ Present your work poorly

Markers will only be able to give you credit if they can read your writing. There are also plenty of other things that will make it more difficult for markers to reward you. Examples include:

- Not using black or blue ink
- Not showing clearly which question you're attempting
- Scattering question parts from the same question throughout your answer booklet
- Not showing clearly workings or the results of your calculations

Paragraphs that are too long or which lack headers also won't help markers and hence won't help you.

Using your BPP products

This Kit gives you the question practice and guidance you need in the exam. Our other products can also help you pass:

- **Learning to Learn Accountancy** gives further valuable advice on revision
- **Passcards** provide you with clear topic summaries and exam tips
- **Success CDs** help you revise on the move
- **i-Pass CDs** offer tests of knowledge against the clock
- **Learn Online** is an e-learning resource delivered via the Internet, offering comprehensive tutor support and featuring areas such as study, practice, email service, revision and useful resources

You can purchase these products by visiting www.bpp.com/mybpp.

Visit our website www.bpp.com/acca/learnonline to sample aspects of Learn Online free of charge.

Passing 1.3

Revising 1.3

1.3 is not an easy paper, because of the breadth and detail of topics potentially covered by the exam – and the fact that you only get a choice of four out of five optional questions: only one 'weak' area allowed...

The examiner, Dr John Ball, has warned very strongly against question-spotting (trying to predict the topics that will be included in the exam). He reinforces the point by occasionally setting very detailed topics among broader ones; repeating topics (and sometimes questions) as well as introducing topics not previously examined; and varying the topics set as scenario questions.

But there's some good news, too. Dr John Ball has been the examiner for this paper for many years. The style of his questions is consistent, and familiar – and the good news is, that he isn't a 'tricky' examiner!

Each paper is designed to be a realistic test of candidates' theoretical knowledge (gained by study and revision) *and* ability to select and apply that knowledge thoughtfully in the exam (gained by question practice and exam technique). The question terms and topics are nearly always clear and precise, letting you know exactly what the markers will be looking for.

Dr Ball regularly contributes concise, helpful articles to *Student Accountant* – and these are often a guide to at least one of the topics that will come up in the following exam. (Don't be tempted to over-rely on this – but use it to focus one area of your revision: it is designed to get you into the habit of scanning useful information sources!)

Although his marking schemes (included in this Kit) are typically very brief – as befits clear, simply structured questions which may have a range of acceptable answers – Dr Ball provides helpful feedback in his examiner's reports, indicating areas of misunderstanding that need clearing up, and points of exam technique that have been neglected. This is great advice, and we'll cover the main points in our notes to questions in this Kit.

Topics to revise

You really can't limit your revision by question-spotting. Remember, you only get one optional question to leave out in the exam. No areas appear to be 'off-limits' for compulsory scenario questions, and a wide range of topics has been tested in the paper as a whole.

That said, exams over the years suggest that the following areas of the syllabus are 'favourites', and your revision therefore needs to cover them particularly well.

- The nature of management and supervision (including the work of named theorists in the area such as Mintzberg, Fayol and Weber)
- Organisation structure (including specific structural types and models)
- Groups and teams (including Belbin's team roles and Tuckman's group development model)
- The procedures, tools and techniques of recruitment and selection (in detail, and often focused on potential confusions of terminology, like the difference between job description and person specification)
- Training methods, and the advantages of training for the organisation and the individual
- Theories of motivation (including a range of named models), with an awareness of their value and limitations
- Leadership styles (including named models) and skills
- The importance of communication and interpersonal skills, communication barriers and how they can be overcome
- Conflict, its causes and effects
- Discipline and grievance procedures

Dr John Ball has said that the topic of personal development will *not* be examined again under this syllabus, so – while it's a useful topic to understand for your own professional development, it needn't be a revision priority.

In your revision, focus on:

- Ensuring that you understand and can clearly distinguish between related (potentially confusing) terms: extrinsic/intrinsic rewards; job analysis/job evaluation; authority/responsibility and so on. These are often the focus of exam questions, and present both pitfalls – and opportunities for easy marks.
- Ensuring that you can describe the work of named theorists/writers, attribute them to the right authors (and spell their names correctly!) *and* cite the strengths and weaknesses of their model, where this is covered in the Study Text.
- Ensuring that you can outline a systematic approach to Human Resource Management issues such as appraisal, training, recruitment/selection and discipline. Dr Ball maintains that sound procedure in these areas important for fair and ethical treatment of people – as well as efficient management. Use the procedural frameworks as a revision checklist: could you say more about each element, if asked?

Question practice

Question practice under timed conditions is essential, so that you can get used to the pressures of answering exam questions in the **limited time** available. You need to practise the key exam techniques of selecting, interpreting and answering questions – *and* allocating your time between the different requirements in each question (essential to gaining the marks available). Our list of recommended questions includes both the longer Section A (scenario) questions and Section B (essay) questions: try and do a mix of questions in full, to get used to their different demands.

Passing the 1.3 exam

Displaying the right attitude

1.3 is a 'wordy' subject, without the clear 'right' and 'wrong' answers you can achieve in the other papers at this level. That doesn't mean that you can waffle your way to a pass in your sleep, but there are often some easy marks to be had.

The keys to passing this paper are:

- **Demonstrating preparation**. You can't rely on 'common sense'. The questions are often factual, and you are expected to be able to cite, explain and apply supporting theories (some of them specifically named in the question) and background knowledge.
- **Time management**. Section A should take 72 minutes *maximum*, and each of the four Section B questions should take 27 minutes. This has to be non-negotiable: you can't get more than the maximum marks for each question, however long you spend on it – but you'll get *no* marks for questions (or question parts) you don't have time to attempt.
- **Demonstrating thought**. You need to show that you haven't thrown points together at random. Plan your answers so that they have a coherent structure which reflects the requirements of the question. Use section headings to highlight this structure for the markers.

Avoiding key weaknesses

We give details of Dr Ball's comments and criticisms throughout this Kit. These don't vary much from exam to exam: the same weaknesses keep cropping up, to Dr Ball's disappointment. These may seem like basic points, but they regularly lose students marks! Candidates repeatedly:

- Fail to read the questions carefully enough
- Fail to answer the question requirements precisely enough
- Fail to prepare sufficiently for the exam – substituting vague guesses and assumptions for an informed understanding of theory and practice
- Fail to organise answers neatly and systematically – either running answers into one another on the page or scattering them haphazardly through the answer book
- Write out portions of the scenario as answers to Section A questions (which wastes time and gains no marks)
- Write the same for part (a) and part (b) of a question (whereas, if the examiner has used sections, it's precisely because the requirements are *different*...)

You will enhance your chances significantly if you avoid these mistakes.

Choosing which questions to answer first

Dr Ball's comments for this paper have repeatedly noted that students who left the compulsory question until last appeared, due to poor time management, to have 'rushed' their answers – missing out on vital marks.

If, having underlined the topic and instruction keywords of all the questions on the paper, you feel relatively comfortable with Question 1, it would be a good idea to attempt it early in the exam: get it out of the way! If you feel less confident, you may prefer to start with your **strongest question** from Section B, to boost your confidence and recall – and then go back to Question 1.

Tackling questions

Try and get used to a step-by-step approach, along the following lines.

Step 1 Check the rubric, highlight all instructions – and ensure that you obey them! For example, Dr Ball has highlighted the importance of ticking the boxes on the front of the answer book, to indicate which questions have been attempted.

Step 2 Read the whole paper through, underlining or highlighting:

- The **instruction key words** in the 'required' section of each question: these are the words that tell you what to do ('critically discuss', 'describe', 'produce a report', 'list six factors')
- The **topic key words** in the 'required' section of each question: these are the words that tell you exactly what the question is *about.*

Step 3 Check the **mark allocations** for each question part: this indicates how many mark-worthy points you need to make on each topic (as well as helping you allocate time, once you start your answers)

Step 4 Identify Section B questions you know you will be able to answer reasonably strongly (or identify the one Section B question that you will want to leave *out*, as your weakest area).

Step 5 Decide which question to tackle first (see below).

Tackling the Section A question

Start by allocating your time. Allowing time to read the scenario through carefully, and to jot down answer plans, you have about 65 minutes to allocate between the 40 marks available: a 10 mark question part should take about 16 minutes; a 5 mark question part about 8 minutes…

Tackle the question parts in order: they often build on each other, which helps you to avoid duplicating material, enables you to build up to more challenging parts – and refreshes your memory of the topic as you go.

Step 1 Check your highlighted topic/instruction key words to 'prime' your attention

Step 2 Re-read the scenario, highlighting key words that are relevant to the requirements.

Step 3 Plan your answer. Jot down the key points or headings that occur to you. Check them against the topic and instruction keywords for relevance. Then number them, or rewrite them as a checklist for writing your answer.

Step 4 Write your answer, sticking carefully to your time allocation. Aim for one fully-stated definition, fact or discussion point per mark available, and relate your points specifically to the scenario wherever possible.

> Dr Ball has published a very useful article on answering the scenario question (in *Student Accountant*, August 2006): we have reproduced it in fulfil (with kind permission of the ACCA) at the end of this section.

Choosing Section B questions

Section B questions mostly require factual descriptions or explanation, so your 'least favourite' or 'weakest' question will depend mostly on your revision: which topics you have covered and recall most strongly. You may, for example, simply not recall a topic in sufficient detail to be confident of finding 15 marks' worth to say about it – in which case, that's the one to leave out.

If you find more than one such question, check the topic/instruction keywords and mark allocations. They may well jog your memory of the topic (which is partly why they're there). They will also enable you to assess how many marks you are confident of getting for each question, bearing in mind the marks available for different question parts.

Gaining the easy marks

The bad news is that the only easy marks on this paper are the ones you've earned through study and revision. The good news is that if you've *done* the study and revision, there are plenty of easy marks – if you read and answer the question accurately!

- If in doubt, define the key terms, or the issue posed by the question: this should be worth some basic marks to start with.
- Work through the precise requirements of the question, paying particular attention to instruction/topic key words ('six causes of...', 'four symptoms of...'). This is where the bulk of the marks are found. If a 12-mark question part asks for six factors, you know you can gain the first six marks by identifying the six factors – and the other six marks by describing or explaining them (or whatever the question has asked you to do).
- Name a model/writer/theorist (accurately), or give an example, if asked to do so: this in itself is worth a mark.
- For Section A questions, relate your points back to the scenario eg using the name of the manager or organisation; focusing on the problems/issues raised; and making sure your comments are relevant to the size/structure/culture/industry of the organisation concerned.

Answering the scenario question

Practical application

The exam for Paper 1.3 is divided into two sections, the first of which is based on a scenario and requires candidates to apply the ideas learned in the syllabus to a particular situation. Although there is now a collection of past papers, which students can refer to in their revision, answering the scenario question in the exam appears to remain a challenge for students.

It is important for students to understand the purpose of the scenario question. It is there to test whether candidates can apply their knowledge of people management theory to the environment described in the scenario. There are a number of fundamental issues to remember when attempting the scenario question.

- Do not simply describe the events and the issues raised – this is the most common mistake.
- As the scenario demands knowledge of the topics being tested, guesswork and personal experience is simply not enough to answer the question.
- The scenario requires the application of ideas and theories learned during the course of candidates' studies.
- Candidates are required to show that they understand the way in which the topics addressed in the scenario are linked to one another.

The scenario is designed to test candidates' skill in applying knowledge in a practical way. Each scenario includes topics from across the syllabus, and therefore tests whether candidates are able to identify both the causes of problems and appropriate solutions. The scenarios are very precisely written, and great care is taken with words and construction so that well-prepared candidates can identify the issues, theory, or idea being presented and then develop a solution.

When answering the scenario question, the first and obvious step is to read the scenario very carefully – then to read it again and look for the clues. The questions that follow can then be addressed using a three-step approach: 'what does the theory say?', 'what does the evidence (from the scenario) say?', and 'what do you say?' (the appropriate response).

As with the scenario, the questions are carefully constructed. In every case, the response to the scenario is divided into a number of sub-questions, which begin by checking understanding (often asking for a description of a particular theory or idea), before asking candidates to discuss and apply an appropriate response. In addition, students should note that the marks allocated to each sub-question indicate the level of detail required, and length of answer expected for each part. So, to answer the scenario question, a step-by-step approach is recommended.

Begin by considering the relevant theory – what is the 'ideal'? This part of the question often carries the most marks, and invariably asks either for a theory based on a particular writer (eg Herzberg or Handy) or on a specific topic (eg organisational structure). The next step is to examine the evidence in the scenario. Having identified the theory or topic, what does the scenario say about it? Are there problems or issues that a correct understanding and application of the theory identified can resolve? Very often, the question will require a further step, for example, a description of the advantages or disadvantages of a particular approach. At this point, always remember that your answer must relate to the scenario.

Candidates should avoid the following practices when answering the scenario question:

- Do not waste time re-writing the scenario (or parts of it) in your answer. Refer to people and events in the scenario, but only as part of your answer.
- Do not waste time underlining or highlighting parts of your answer – simply write in narrative form.
- Attempt all parts of the question – remember, the marker cannot allocate marks for work that is not presented.

Remember to read feedback on previous papers. This gives an excellent indication of good and bad practice in answers to specific scenarios. The feedback for the June 2006 exam session is published in the October issue of *Student Accountant.*

Recent exams

Format of the paper

		Number of marks
Section A:	Compulsory scenario question	40
Section B:	Choice of 4 out of 5 essay questions (15 marks each)	60
		100

Time allowed: 3 hours

Section A consists of a brief scenario with one question worth 40 marks, comprising a range of 6-7 requirements each carrying 5-10 marks. Candidates should **apply** relevant theoretical knowledge for the main areas of the syllabus to the **information contained within the scenario**.

Section B consists of five essay-type questions, assessing knowledge acquired from all five main areas of the syllabus. Each question carries 15 marks and candidates must attempt **four** questions.

There are no calculations involved, and candidates should note that the answers in Section B **must be presented in essay form** (BPP emphasis). Candidates need to show conceptual understanding of the detail of the topic, not just listing points. Candidates should be aware that although the course is made up of a number of discrete topics, examination questions may well require the integration of more than one of these topics.

Additional information

The Study Guide provides more detailed guidance on the syllabus.

Analysis of recent papers

The analysis below shows the topics which have been examined in the current syllabus.

December 2006

Section A (compulsory)

1 Case study, based on the role and skills of external counsellors and the advantages of counselling.

Section B (4 questions from 5)

2 Organisational objectives: Drucker's eight classifications
3 Recruitment and selection
4 Appraisal interviews
5 Motivation theory
6 Good communication

Examiner's comments were not available at the time of going to print.

This paper is Mock exam 3 in this Kit.

June 2006

Section A (compulsory)		*Question in this Kit*
1	Case study based on management, supervision and delegation issues	13
Section B (4 questions from 5)		
2	Organisational structure; Mintzberg's five components	2
3	Selection interviews (one-to-one and panel)	28
4	Methods of training	33
5	Maslow's hierarchy of needs theory and its application	45
6	Aggressive and assertive behaviour	55

Examiner's comments. Overall a marked improvement in both the pass rate and knowledge displayed by candidates. Candidates who displayed appropriate written communication skills scored highly.

December 2005

Section A (compulsory)		*Question in this Kit*
1	Case study, based on leadership styles	49
Section B (4 questions from 5)		
2	Mintzberg's view of management	5
3	Recruitment and selection (application forms)	27
4	Personal development plan	35
5	Reward systems	48
6	Conflict	60

Examiner's comments. Overall, a disappointing performance. This was mainly due to (a) making assumptions about issues rather than demonstrating factual understanding, and (b) carelessness in reading the examination questions and considering the appropriate answer. Candidates who had studied and prepared for the exam did well.

June 2005

Section A (compulsory)		*Question in this Kit*
1	Case study, based on disciplinary and grievance procedures	61
Section B (4 questions from 5)		
2	Leadership (Blake and Mouton's Managerial Grid)	52
3	Recruitment (job descriptions and person specifications)	25
4	Selection (references)	30
5	Motivation (definition of terms)	44
6	Good communication	56

Examiner's comments. The general approach to the whole exam was disappointing. One main problem was that candidates do not take enough care in reading questions properly. Also, some candidates tended to produce answers as lists rather than providing the required discussion or explanation. The compulsory scenario question was not particularly well-answered and there was some indication that a lot of candidates left it until last.

December 2004

Section A (compulsory)		*Question in this Kit*
1	Case study, based on groups, team membership and team development	10
Section B (4 from 5)		
2	Organisational culture	7
3	Job analysis	23
4	Stages in recruitment and selection	21
5	Job enrichment, job enlargement and job rotation	47
6	Employee discipline	62

Examiner's comments. Some answers were presented in a general form and indicated guesswork and assumptions, rather than an understanding of theory and practice. However, candidates showed improvement in reading the question carefully.

June 2004

Section A (compulsory)		*Question in this Kit*
1	Case study, based on appraisal systems and interviews	38
Section B (4 questions from 5)		
2	Management by Objectives	19
3	Selection testing	29
4	Training benefits and methods	Mock 1 (q4)
5	Leadership skills and action centred leadership	59
6	Discipline and disciplinary action	Mock 1 (q6)

Examiner's comments. The examiner noted improvement in candidates' more careful reading of questions and timing/structuring of answers according to marks available for each question point.

December 2003

Section A (compulsory)		*Question in this Kit*
1	Case study, based on Herzberg, culture and training	42
Section B (4 questions from 5)		
2	Tom Peters ('excellence')	6
3	Recruitment advertising	26
4	Coaching, mentoring, evaluating training	36
5	Content theory (motivation); McGregor Theory X/Y	43
6	Directions and patterns of communication	57

Examiner's comments .Some candidates answered questions based on individual experiences, guesses or assumptions, with little reference to theory, application of theory, or evidence of study. Students must learn to consider which theory, ideas and practices underpin each exam question.

Candidates lost marks through: (a) failing to read the question carefully enough (eg discussing Maslow when the question specifically referred to Herzberg); and (b) failing to allocate their time according to the marks available (giving overly long answers for parts carrying low marks and overly short answers for parts carrying high marks).

June 2003

Section A (compulsory)		*Question in this Kit*
1	Case study, based on communication and committees	Mock 1 (q1)
Section B		
2	Performance management	18
3	Selection interviews	28
4	Health and safety policies, hazards	41
5	Tuckman's stages of team development	12
6	Counselling in the workplace	64

Examiner's comments. Candidates still appear to answer questions on the basis of personal experiences or general guesswork, rather than applying the theory and practice, covered by the syllabus, to the question. There was some evidence of wider reading (citing named authors) – but not as much as there should be. Candidates were advised to tackle answers systematically, rather than breaking them up and scattering them through the answer booklet: apart from demonstrating disorganisation, this makes it all too easy to miss a question.

December 2002

Section A (compulsory)		*Question in this Kit*
1	Case study, based on introduction of equal opportunity/discrimination policies	31
Section B (4 questions from 5)		
2	Theory Z management approach	53
3	Internal recruitment, external recruitment and recruitment consultants	22
4	Learning cycle and learning styles	37
5	Motivation: process theory, equity theory	46
6	Good communication and barriers to communication	Mock 2 (q6)

Examiner's comments. Answers continue to lack background theoretical knowledge, failing to present and test the theories and ideas required by the questions: it is vitally important to show evidence of learning. Particularly disappointing was the **confusion** of theories, ideas and terminology: suggesting that Theory Z was part of Theory X and Y, for example, or failing to distinguish accurately between content and process theories of motivation.

Detailed comments on each question are provided with the answer to each question as they appear in this Kit.

June 2002

Section A (compulsory)		*Question in this Kit*
1	Case study, based on assertive/aggressive/passive behaviour and the need for effective interpersonal skills	54
Section B (4 questions from 5)		
2	Fayol's managerial functions; roles of supervisor/manager	4
3	Authority, responsibility; effective delegation	15
4	Stages in planning for recruitment	Mock 2 (q3)
5	Definition, causes and characteristics of conflict	59
6	Teams and groups; team success; Belbin's team roles	11

Examiner's comments. The examiner regretted candidates' apparent lack of preparation and exam technique, given the fact that all questions related closely and straightforwardly to syllabus topics. In particular, candidates failed:

- To read the question carefully (for example in distinguishing between 'Describe', Explain' and 'Identify')
- To structure or focus answers according to the requirement of the question
- To demonstrate reading and/or understanding of theories (rather than relying on assumptions and personal experience)

Detailed comments on each question are provided with the answers to each question as they appear in this Kit.

December 2001

	Section A (compulsory)	*Question in this Kit*
1	Case study, based on change from functional to matrix organisation structure	3
	Section B (4 questions from 5)	
2	Blake and Mouton managerial grid	Mock 2 (q5)
3	Person specification and job description	25
4	Performance appraisal: benefits and methods	Mock 2 (q4)
5	Motivation: content theory and Maslow	Mock 1 (q5)
6	Discipline and disciplinary procedures	62

Examiner's comments. Substantially, as for June 2002. Detailed comments on each question are provided with the answers to each question as they appear in this Kit.

Exam update

Technical update

If you have been studying with the 6/06 edition of the BPP *Managing People* Study Text you will already be up to date for developments up to June 2006.

Articles published since then which are of direct relevance to the syllabus are listed below.

'Answering the scenario question', Dr John Ball, *Student Accountant,* August 2006.

'Counselling and the workplace', Dr John Ball, *Student Accountant,* September 2006.

Examiners often base exam questions on articles which have appeared in *Student Accountant.* You would therefore be well advised to review this publication, either in print or on-line.

Useful websites

The websites below provide additional sources of information relevant to your studies for *Managing People.*

- www.ft.com

  The Financial Times website provides information about current international business and management issues.

- www.accaglobal.com

  The ACCA's website, featuring a student section with relevant technical articles and examiner feedback.

- www.bpp.com/learningmedia

  Our website provides information about BPP products and services, with a link to the ACCA website.

answering the scenario question
relevant to Professional Scheme Paper 1.3

technical

practical application

The exam for Paper 1.3 is divided into two sections, the first of which is based on a scenario and requires candidates to apply the ideas learned in the syllabus to a particular situation. Although there is now a collection of past papers, which students can refer to in their revision, answering the scenario question in the exam appears to remain a challenge for students.

It is important for students to understand the purpose of the scenario question. It is there to test whether candidates can apply their knowledge of people management theory to the environment described in the scenario. There are a number of fundamental issues to remember when attempting the scenario question:

- Do not simply describe the events and the issues raised – this is the most common mistake.
- As the scenario demands knowledge of the topics being tested, guesswork and personal experience is simply not enough to answer the question.
- The scenario requires the application of ideas and theories learned during the course of candidates' studies.
- Candidates are required to show that they understand the way in which the topics addressed in the scenario are linked to one another.

The scenario is designed to test candidates' skill in applying knowledge in a practical way. Each scenario includes topics from across the syllabus, and therefore tests whether candidates are able to identify both the causes of problems and appropriate solutions. The scenarios are very precisely written, and great care is taken with words and construction so that well-prepared candidates can identify the issues, theory, or idea being presented and then develop a solution.

When answering the scenario question, the first and obvious step is to read the scenario very carefully – then to read it again and look for the clues. The questions that follow can then be addressed using a three-step approach: 'what does the theory say?', 'what does the evidence (from the scenario) say?', and 'what do you say?' (the appropriate response).

The scenario is designed to test candidates' skill in applying knowledge in a practical way. Each scenario includes topics from across the syllabus, and therefore tests whether candidates are able to identify both the causes of problems and appropriate solutions.

As with the scenario, the questions are carefully constructed. In every case, the response to the scenario is divided into a number of sub-questions, which begin by checking understanding (often asking for a description of a particular theory or idea), before asking candidates to discuss and apply an appropriate response. In addition, students should note that the marks allocated to each sub-question indicate the level of detail required, and length of answer expected for each part. So, to answer the scenario question, a step-by-step approach is recommended.

Begin by considering the relevant theory – what is the 'ideal'? This part of the question often carries the most marks, and invariably asks either for a theory based on a particular writer (eg Herzberg or Handy) or on a specific topic (eg organisational structure). The next step is to examine the evidence in the scenario. Having identified the theory or topic, what does the scenario say about it? Are there problems or issues that a correct understanding and application of the theory identified can resolve? Very often, the question will require a further step, for example, a description of the advantages or disadvantages of a particular approach. At this point, always remember that your answer must relate to the scenario.

Candidates should avoid the following practices when answering the scenario question:

- Do not waste time re-writing the scenario (or parts of it) in your answer. Refer to people and events in the scenario, but only as part of your answer.
- Do not waste time underlining or highlighting parts of your answer – simply write in narrative form.
- Attempt all parts of the question – remember, the marker cannot allocate marks for work that is not presented.

Remember to read feedback on previous papers. This gives an excellent indication of good and bad practice in answers to specific scenarios. The feedback for the June 2006 exam session will be published in the October 2006 issue of *student accountant*.

John Ball is examiner for Paper 1.3

Syllabus mindmap

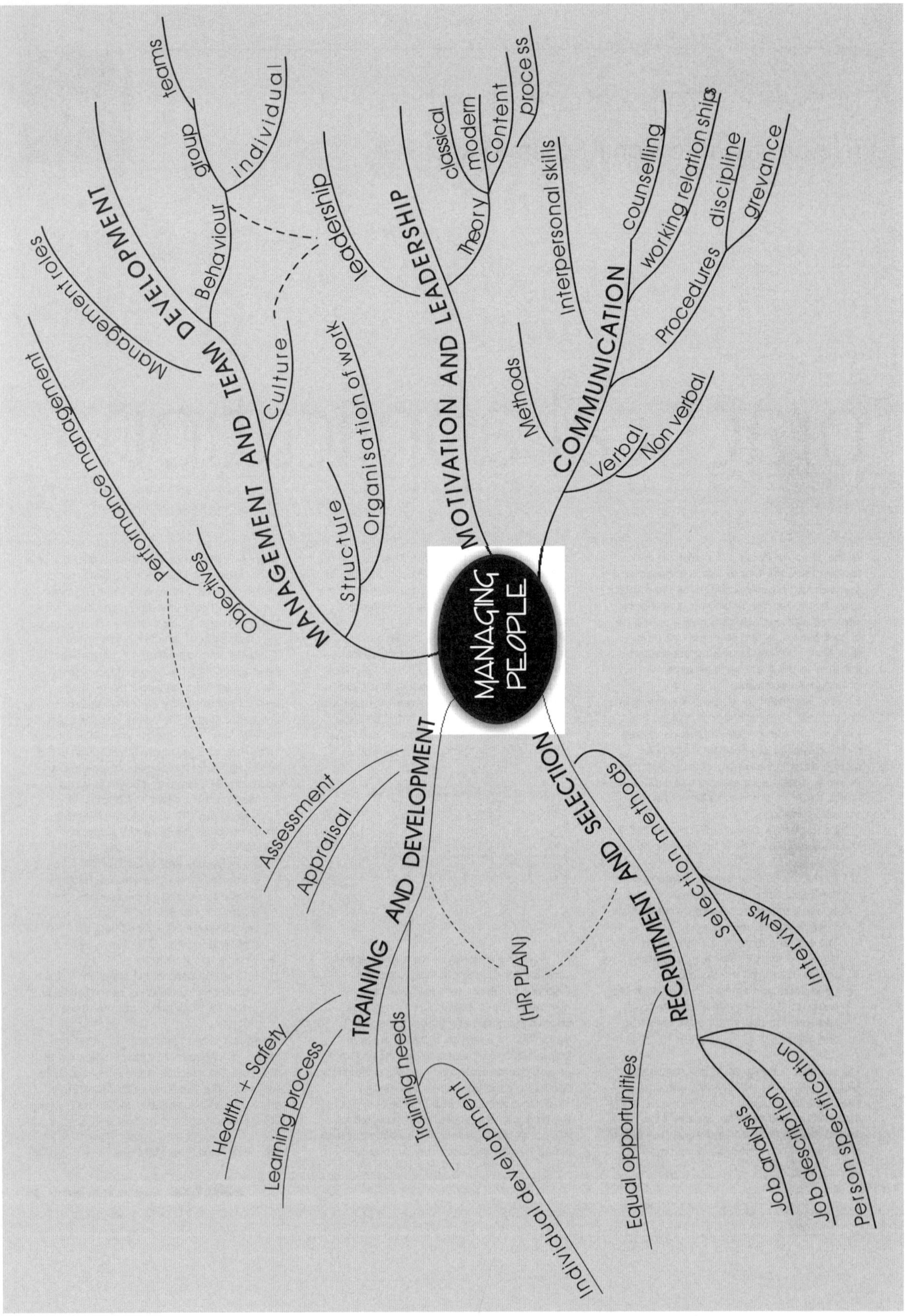

Planning your question practice

Planning your question practice

We have already stressed that question practice should be right at the centre of your revision. Whilst you will spend some time looking at your notes and Paper 1.3 Passcards, you should spend the majority of your revision time practising questions.

We recommend two ways in which you can practise questions.

- Use **BPP's question plan** to work systematically through the syllabus and attempt key and other questions on a section-by-section basis
- **Build your own exams** – attempt questions as a series of practice exams

These ways are suggestions and simply following them is no guarantee of success. You or your college may prefer an alternative but equally valid approach.

BPP's question plan

The BPP plan below requires you to devote a **minimum of 30 hours** to revision of Paper 1.3. Any time you can spend over and above this should only increase your chances of success.

Step 1 **Review your notes** and the chapter summaries in the Paper 1.3 **Passcards** for each section of the syllabus.

Step 2 **Answer the key questions** for that section. These questions have boxes round the question number in the table below and you should answer them in full. Even if you are short of time you must attempt these questions if you want to pass the exam. You should complete your answers without referring to our solutions.

Step 3 **Attempt the other questions** in that section. For some questions we have suggested that you prepare **answer plans** rather than full solutions. Planning an answer means that you should spend about 40% of the time allowance for the questions brainstorming the question and drawing up a list of points to be included in the answer.

Step 4 Attempt **Mock exams 1, 2 and 3** under strict exam conditions.

Syllabus section	2007 Passcards chapters	Questions in this Kit	Comments	Done ☑
Revision Period 1 *The organisation of work*				
Formal organisation structures	1	[1]	Key question: answer in full for a good foundation in this area of the syllabus.	☐
		2	A useful test of your understanding of structural factors, including a popular model: do an answer plan.	☐
		[3]	Key question: answer in full, allocating your time carefully. A good example of a varied scenario question with theory *and* application elements.	☐
Revision Period 2 *The role of management and supervision*				
The role of the manager	2	4	An opportunity to think through some management theory: worth an answer plan.	☐
The role of the supervisor		5	Useful practice in recalling the detail of a named model or theorist: do an answer plan.	☐
		6	Useful practice in recalling another named model or theorist: do an answer plan.	☐
Revision Period 3 *Group behaviour: organisation culture*				
Organisation culture	3	[7]	Key question: answer in full. An opportunity to display knowledge of one popular model. (Make sure you know what culture is and how it manifests itself *before* focusing on this example.)	☐
		8	A more general survey of the role of culture in organisations. Worth attempting in full if you have time.	☐
		9	A highly structured question: good practice for checking your answer planning. Worth attempting in full if you have time.	☐
Revision Period 4 *Individuals, groups and teams*				
Groups and teams	4	[10]	Key question: answer in full, allocating your time carefully. A typical scenario question with theory *and* application elements. A great overall revision of groups and teams.	☐
		11	A useful test of some basic knowledge in this area. Do an answer plan: if you have time, expand to a full answer.	☐
		[12]	Key question: answer in full. Tuckman is one of those models that is frequently tested: note the difference between addressing it in scenario form (question 10) and essay form (question 12).	☐

Syllabus section	2007 Passcards chapters	Questions in this Kit	Comments	Done ☑
Revision Period 5 *Authority, power and delegation*				
Authority and power	5	13	Key question: answer in full. This question usefully crosses syllabus topics, and specifically requires you to relate your answer back to the scenario: excellent practice for scenario questions.	☐
		14	Useful practice in structuring an answer to an unstructured question; do a careful and detailed answer plan, and expand to a full answer if you have time.	☐
Delegation	5	15	Worth an answer plan to recheck your basic terminology (exam pitfall!) and knowledge areas. Again: note the difference in requirements from question 13: good practice in reading questions carefully.	☐
Revision Period 6 *Performance objectives and targets*				
Objectives	6	16	Key question: answer in full. Parts (b) and (c) – and the distinction between them – deserve careful thought.	☐
		17	Social responsibility is an important new topic: do an answer plan to fix the key points in your mind.	☐
Performance management	6	18	Read the question introduction and key words carefully, so that you focus your answer correctly. A useful overview: do an answer plan.	☐
		19	Worth an answer plan if you haven't already tackled management by objectives in question 18.	☐
Revision Period 7 *Recruitment*				
Recruitment	7	20	Key question: Answer in full. This covers a range of HRM topics, including recruitment planning, job description, person specification, selection, training and development. Excellent practice in drawing material from across the syllabus. (Come back to this question later in your revision programme if you need to.)	☐
Recruitment procedures		21	A useful overview of recruitment and selection: remember that a systematic approach is important for both efficiency and equity. Do an answer plan.	☐

Syllabus section	2007 Passcards chapters	Questions in this Kit	Comments	Done ☑
Recruitment procedures	7	22	An example of a structured 15-mark question on a very specific set of topics. Do an answer plan, ensuring you have enough points to earn the marks!	☐
		23	Pay attention to the terminology (exam pitfall!) to focus your answer on the tight topic. Worth a full answer if you have time.	☐
		24	This may seem like a minor syllabus topic – but it comes up regularly. A useful guide to how much *detailed* knowledge is required. Do an answer plan, and expand if you have time.	☐
		25	Worth doing an answer plan. Note the different requirements of this question and question 24 in the same area: a useful comparison to develop your ability to read questions carefully.	☐
		26	Specific use of topic and instruction keywords in this question; analyse carefully before attempting an answer plan.	☐
Revision Period 8 *Selection*				
Selection procedures	8	27	An example of how a 'minor' topic may be set, requiring an awareness of systematic procedure: do an answer plan.	☐
		28	A popular exam topic: do an answer plan.	☐
		29	It's important that you cover all the *alternatives* to interviews, as a selection tool: do an answer plan.	☐
		30	Another 'minor' aspect of procedure, and good practice in working systematically to earn the marks available: do an answer plan.	☐
Revision Period 9 *Diversity and Equal Opportunities*				
Equal opportunities	9	31	Key question: answer in full. A useful overview of various areas of equal opportunity and diversity. (As a bonus exercise, see if you can name 3 areas of discrimination *not* covered by the question.)	☐

Syllabus section	2007 Passcards chapters	Questions in this Kit	Comments	Done ☑
Revision Period 10 *Employee development and training*				
Development and training	10	[32]	Key question: answer in full. This is essential practice not only in answering scenario questions, but in formatting your answer as requested: in this case, as a report. An excellent review of your knowledge in key areas.	☐
		33	This is a highly structured and detailed test of your knowledge of specific training methods, and ability to avoid terminology pitfalls: worth an answer in full, if only to check your definitions.	☐
		34	Part (a) is a typical 'advantages/disadvantages' question – but in this case, it poses a particular challenge. Do an answer plan.	☐
		35	The examiner has indicated that this topic won't be set again under this syllabus: you may like to attempt an answer plan, just for extra exam technique practice.	☐
		36	A useful reminder to distinguish terms carefully (exam pitfall) and to revise in detail. Do an answer plan.	☐
The learning process	10	37	A useful review of two specific learning models. Do an answer plan – and expand to a full answer if you have time.	☐
Revision Period 11 *Appraisal and competence assessment*				
Appraisal		[38]	Key question: answer in full. A good review of the full range of issues in appraisal. Remember to *apply* your knowledge to the scenario.	☐
		39	A useful check that you are up-to-date. Do an answer plan, bearing in mind the underlying structure of the question (3 approaches).	☐
Revision Period 12 *Health and safety*				
Healthy and safety	12	40	A straightforward question: do an answer plan. Note that this is only one area of occupational health and safety. (As a 'bonus' exercise see if you can list other areas for potential questions on OHS.)	☐
		[41]	Key question: answer in full. A straightforward question but one which allows you to utilise some of your practical knowledge. Note the requirement to discuss *policy* in part (b) – not just operational measures!	☐

Syllabus section	2007 Passcards chapters	Questions in this Kit	Comments	Done ☑
Revision Period 13 *Motivation at work*				
Motivation	13	42	Key question: answer in full. Motivation almost invariably comes up in one aspect or another. This is a useful topic overview in scenario format, and good practice in analysing instruction key words.	☐
		43	The distinction between 'process' and 'content' theory is basic and often tested – as are Theory X and Y. Do an answer plan.	☐
		44	A useful test of your ability to *identify* (and then explain) a key theoretical model. Do an answer plan.	☐
		45	A broad opportunity to explain a very popular model – with the challenge of evaluating its application in practice. Typical interest of this examiner: worth an answer in full (paying attention to time/mark allocation) if you have time.	☐
		46	A challenging question on a highly specific topic area. Worth expanding to a full answer if you have time – if only to ensure you have 15 marks' worth of material!	☐
		47	Note the requirement to both *define* and *explain*. Since the question introduction says 'There is often confusion…' don't fall into the trap yourself! Check your answer plan carefully.	☐
		48	An example of a question founded solely on understanding your terminology! Do an answer plan.	☐
Revision Period 14 *Effective leadership*				
		49	Key question: answer in full. An example of a very detailed theory-and-application question that will really test your revision and mark-earning skills.	☐
Leadership	14	50	Good practice in both showing general knowledge (without waffling) *and* addressing specific named writers: do an answer plan.	☐
		51	Key question: answer in full. Good practice in tackling unstructured discussion question: make sure you give a detailed and balanced ('critically discuss') answer.	☐
		52	A review of a highly specific model: do an answer plan and check the details carefully when you review the solution. Note the requirement to discuss the theory's *usefulness*: you should approach this in a balanced way.	☐
		53	A review of another highly specific model: do an answer plan and appraise whether you have enough material for 15 marks. Make sure you know your Theory Z from you Theory X and Y!	☐

Syllabus section	2007 Passcards chapters	Questions in this Kit	Comments	Done ☑
Revision Period 15 *Interpersonal and communication skills*				
Interpersonal skills	15	54	Key question: answer in full. A particularly challenging scenario question, focusing on the detailed application of specific theory.	☐
		55	A relatively straightforward question on a specific area: do an answer plan, noting the difference in requirements from the treatment of the same topic in question 54.	☐
Communication in organisations	15	56	A straightforward question on a key topic area: do an answer plan.	☐
		57	An example of a highly structured question. Worth answering in full as a test of your time management skills!	☐
Revision Period 16 *Conflict, discipline and grievance*				
Conflict	16	58	Key question: answer in full. A comprehensive review of the topic – with challenging requirements to *apply* theory in the scenario given. (Practise resisting the temptation to answer the many questions that *might* have been asked – but weren't...)	☐
		59	The more straightforward version of question 58 for comparison! Do an answer plan.	☐
Conflict		60	A detailed question, expanding a topic touched on in question 58. Note how much more work you have to do for these marks. Do an answer plan to ensure you have enough points to make.	☐
Discipline		61	Key question: answer in full. The examiner's interest in discipline and grievance finally finds full form in a scenario question. Great practice for clearing up terminology confusion and showing systematic procedural awareness.	☐
		62	A straightforward question. Check that your definition of 'discipline' is sufficiently complex. (The identical question was also set in December 2001: this is obviously a key theme so make sure you are on top of it.)	☐
Grievance	16	63	Key question: answer in full. This addresses a specific area of discipline and grievance: good practice in answering the question set.	☐
		64	Another highly structured and specific question: make sure that your answer plan addresses the right topic key words.	☐

Build your own exams

Having revised your notes and the BPP Passcards, you can attempt the questions in the Kit as a series of practice exams. You can organise the questions in the following ways:

- Either you can attempt complete old papers; recent papers are listed below.

	1.3								
	Jun'02	Dec'02	Jun'03	Dec'03	Jun'04	Dec'04	Jun'05	Dec'05	Jun'06
Section A									
1	54	31	Mock 1 (q1)	42	38	10	61	49	13
Section B									
2	4	53	18	6	19	7	52	5	2
3	15	22	28	26	29	23	25	27	28
4	Mock 2 (q3)	37	41	36	Mock 1 (q4)	21	30	35	33
5	59	46	12	43	50	47	44	48	45
6	11	Mock 2 (q6)	64	57	Mock 1 (q6)	62	56	60	55

- Or you can make up practice exams, either yourself or using the mock exams that we have listed below. (Just remember that your Section A must be a scenario question, and the Section B 15 mark essays).

	Practice exams									
	1	2	3	4	5	6	7	8	9	10
Section A										
1	3	10	13	20	32	38	42	49	54	58
Section B										
2	26	29	12	1	2	4	5	8	15	19
3	37	39	22	41	11	14	18	25	27	28
4	50	47	36	45	30	24	23	33	34	41
5	56	55	48	55	43	44	40	46	50	53
6	16	60	63	64	59	62	55	60	7	9

- Whichever practice exams you use, you must attempt **Mock exams 1, 2 and 3** at the end of your revision.

Questions

MANAGEMENT AND TEAM DEVELOPMENT

Questions 1 to 19 cover Management and Team Development, the subject of Part A of the BPP Study Text for Paper 1.3.

1 Organisation structure — 27 mins

All organisations have some kind of formal structure.

Required

(a) What are the purposes of a formal organisation structure? **(5 marks)**

(b) What factors influence the structure of an organisation? **(5 marks)**

(c) Outline five main criticisms of bureaucracy as an organisational form. **(5 marks)**

(Total = 15 marks)

2 Organisation structure: Mintzberg (6/06) — 27 mins

The activities of an organisation have to be managed and co-ordinated to ensure that its objectives are met. The organisation's structure is designed to support this.

Required

(a) What is meant by the term 'organisational structure', often shown as an organisation chart? **(5 marks)**

(b) Explain Mintzberg's five organisational components. **(10 marks)**

(Total = 15 marks)

3 Question with analysis: Scenario: Matrix structure (12/01)

72 mins

Greg Pye is the Chief Executive of a medium sized company that traditionally has been organised hierarchically according to function. After attending a management seminar, he decided to encourage inter-functional departmental co-operation by implementing a matrix structure in the organisation.

Greg agreed that a matrix organisation and cross-functional team working would provide flexibility and enhanced performance to the organisation. However, the Company Secretary drew Greg's attention to some potential drawbacks.

These include the possibility that 'people won't know who they are meant to be reporting to, supervision will be difficult for their line manager who thinks they are working in their teams and team leaders will have no real authority over the team members'.

After speaking to the Company Secretary, Greg began to have a second thoughts about the matrix structure. Greg decides to ask for a more considered view of restructuring the company.

Required

Greg Pye has asked you to explain:

(a) The advantages of the existing hierarchical structure **(13 marks)**

(b) The advantages of introducing a matrix structure **(15 marks)**

(c) How Greg and his management team can address the concerns expressed by the Company Secretary **(6 marks)**

(d) How it might be possible to gain some of the benefits of a matrix structure without fully restructuring the organisation **(6 marks)**

(Total = 40 marks)

3 Question with analysis: Scenario: Matrix structure (12/01)

72 mins

Indicates a *classical* organisation. This will form the basis of your thinking for part (a).

Greg Pye is the Chief Executive of a medium sized company that traditionally has been **organised hierarchically according to function**. After attending a management seminar, he decided to encourage inter-functional departmental co-operation by implementing a matrix structure in the organisation.

Useful keys to advantages of matrix structure: part (b).

Greg agreed that a matrix organisation and cross-functional team working would provide **flexibility and enhanced performance** to the organisation. However, the Company Secretary drew Greg's attention to some potential drawbacks.

Clear limits to the drawbacks you need to *address* in part (c).

These include the possibility that '**people won't know** who they are meant to be reporting to, **supervision will be difficult** for their line manager who thinks they are working in their teams and team leaders will have **no real authority** over the team members'.

After speaking to the Company Secretary, Greg began to have a second thoughts about the matrix structure. Greg decides to ask for a more considered view of restructuring the company.

Required

Greg Pye has asked you to explain:

(a) The advantages of the existing hierarchical structure **(13 marks)**

(b) The advantages of introducing a matrix structure **(15 marks)**

Suggest *solutions* to the three concerns, don't just repeat them!

(c) How Greg and his management team can **address the concerns** expressed by the Company Secretary **(6 marks)**

(d) How it might be possible to gain **some of the benefits** of a matrix structure without fully restructuring the organisation **(6 marks)**

(Total = 40 marks)

This is about *hybrid* organisation with *flexible, cross-functional* elements.

4 Management and supervision (6/02) **27 mins**

Exactly what constitutes the management task is often unclear or misunderstood.

Required

(a) Explain the five main duties of a manager, according to the writer Henri Fayol. **(10 marks)**
(b) Explain the differences between the role of a supervisor and that of a manager. **(5 marks)**

(Total = 15 marks)

5 Mintzberg's managerial roles (12/05) **27 mins**

Research has shown that management involves more than simply giving orders or commands.

Required

(a) Briefly describe Mintzberg's view of the process of management. **(3 marks)**
(b) From Mintzberg's research, identify and describe the three key roles which management appears to fulfil. **(12 marks)**

(Total = 15 marks)

6 Question with helping hand: Excellence (12/03) **27 mins**

All managers need to understand which activities contribute to organisational success.

Required

Briefly describe and discuss Tom Peters' characteristics of successful business. **(15 marks)**

Helping hand. The name of Tom Peters is associated with a number of different interests in the area of organisation, management and leadership.

If you are aware of Peters & Waterman *('In Search of Excellence'),* this might immediately give you ideas for an answer: the eight attributes of 'excellent' companies is a good match for 'characteristics of successful businesses'.

If you can't remember the excellence factors, you may need to think more widely about Peters' work: fortunately, the question isn't too specific! You might then think about ideas such as:

- the importance of cultural values, replacing tight controls
- the use of flexible, horizontal, 'chunked' structures to increase responsiveness
- the need to 'thrive on chaos': create a learning, flexible organisation and leadership.

7 Types of culture (12/04) **27 mins**

All organisations develop a culture which influences the way an organisation's employees behave.

Required

(a) Define and describe what is meant by the term 'culture' in the organisational context. **(3 marks)**
(b) Describe Handy's four cultural types. **(12 marks)**

(Total = 15 marks)

8 Culture **27 mins**

Organisation culture has been defined as the complex body of shared beliefs, attitudes and values in an organisation.

Required

(a) Describe how culture manifests itself, giving examples. **(8 marks)**

(b) Suggest why culture is important to an organisation. **(7 marks)**

(Total = 15 marks)

9 Question with answer plan: Informal organisation **27 mins**

Alongside every formal organisation structure, there is an informal structure.

Required

(a) What is meant by the term 'informal organisation'? **(4 marks)**

(b) What are the benefits of the 'informal organisation' for overall organisational effectiveness? **(5 marks)**

(c) What are the dangers of the 'informal organisation' and how can they be minimised? **(6 marks)**

(Total = 15 marks)

10 Question with helping hand: Scenario: Groups and teams (12/04) **72 mins**

'Rockers' is a small recording studio established four years ago which is owned and operated by a group of twelve people. The group has been working together amicably and successfully for a considerable time.

Neville has been in charge since the beginning and his leadership is valued by all the team's members and the support given to him by Olivia, the second in command. Outgoing and extrovert, she often elaborates on Neville's instructions and deals on his behalf with group members' queries, especially when he is away on business.

Much of the success of the group has been due to Peter, who is creative at problem solving, and Rosalind, who has an encyclopaedic knowledge of sources of supply and information. Another group member, Quentin, is an expert on charts and records and Suki is invaluable at sorting out disagreements and keeping everyone cheerful. The remaining members of the group also fulfil roles which are acceptable to themselves and others.

Recently, Olivia resigned for family reasons. As the workload has been increasing, Neville took it upon himself to recruit four new people to the group. Neville now finds that various members of the original group complain to him about what they are expected to do and about other people's failings. Peter and Rosalind have been particularly helpful to Neville, but have had several serious arguments between themselves and with others.

Required

(a) Describe Tuckman's stages of group development and explain the stage the group was at before and after Olivia's departure. **(15 marks)**

(b) Until the changes, the group worked well together as a team with each member fulfilling a role as identified **by Belbin.**

(i) What role did Olivia play and what are its characteristics? **(5 marks)**

(ii) Name and describe the team roles fulfilled by Neville, Peter, Rosalind, Quentin and Suki. **(10 marks)**

(iii) What problems might arise as a consequence of Olivia's departure and consequently the team role she played? **(5 marks)**

(c) Recommend how Neville should ensure that the group reverts to its former cohesiveness. **(5 marks)**

(Total = 40 marks)

Helping hand. First of all, note that part (a) has two separate requirements. If you tackle the first (describing Tuckman's stages), you'll have a much better chance of identifying *which* of them describes the 'Rockers' group before and after Olivia's departure. Read the question for the clear hints: Tuckman = stages of group development!

In part (b), the examiner again clearly indicates the topic and model he wants addressed. Belbin = team roles! You are given brief but accurate descriptions of the roles played by each member. If you're stuck, it may help to jot down all nine of Belbin's roles and then place the people one by one.

When tackling part (b) (iii), think first about the consequences of losing Olivia's particular role – but also about the consequence of losing *any* role, for the balanced functioning of the team.

For part (c), you already have some hints from part (b) (iii) – but think *practically* in terms of member selection/recruitment and team building. (Remember, you only have 5 marks to earn here.)

11 Team working (6/02) — 27 mins

As organisations become more complex and more demanding, the establishment of teams is increasingly seen as a way of resolving organisational problems or undertaking particular tasks.

Required

(a) In what ways do teams differ from groups? **(4 marks)**

(b) Identify five factors required to ensure team success. **(5 marks)**

(c) From Belbin's model, explain any three roles that members of a team might perform. **(6 marks)**

(Total = 15 marks)

12 Team development (6/03) — 27 mins

An organisation has decided to create a team oriented approach to business.

Required

Describe Tuckman's stages of team development. **(15 marks)**

13 Question with analysis: Scenario: Management, supervision and delegation (6/06) 72 mins

Flavours Fine Foods is a leading producer for the food industry, supplying many of Europe's leading restaurants. Started just five years ago, by brothers Lee and Alan Jones, the organisation has grown from a small company employing five people to a multi-divisional organisation employing 120 people.

The organisation's production facility is divided into three separate departments. Each department has a single manager with supervisors assisting on the production lines. The managers and supervisors, all of whom are aware of their roles, work well together. However, although the organisation has grown, the owners continue to involve themselves in day to day activities and this has led to friction between the owners, managers and supervisors.

As a result a problem arose last week. Alan Jones instructed a supervisor to repair a machine on the shop floor, which he refused to do without confirmation and instruction from his departmental manager. The supervisor's manager, Dean Watkins, became involved and was annoyed at what he saw as interference in his department's activities. Dean told Alan Jones that he "should have come to me first" because although the responsibility for the overall organisation was a matter for the brothers, action taken in the factory was through powers that had been delegated to him and through his authority, as manager. In the argument that followed, Alan Jones was accused of failing to understand the way that the hierarchy in such a large organisation operates and that interference with operational decisions by senior management was not helpful.

As a consequence of this, Alan Jones has asked you to explain to him and his brother the issues behind the dispute to clarify the roles of managers and supervisors and to indicate how and why successful delegation might be achieved.

Required

(a) Explain to Alan Jones the main differences between the work of a manager and that of a supervisor. **(13 marks)**

(b) Explain, in the context of Flavours Fine Foods, what is meant by:

- (i) Responsibility **(4 marks)**
- (ii) Authority **(3 marks)**
- (iii) Delegation **(3 marks)**

(c) To correct the problems at Flavours Fine Foods, explain to Alan Jones:

- (i) The need for delegation **(3 marks)**
- (ii) How effective delegation might be achieved **(6 marks)**
- (iii) Problems with delegation **(4 marks)**
- (iv) How these problems might be overcome. **(4 marks)**

(Total = 40 marks)

13 Question with analysis: Scenario: Management, supervision and delegation (6/06) **72 mins**

> Rapid growth in size and complexity: common cause of structure/ culture problems!

Flavours Fine Foods is a leading producer for the food industry, supplying many of Europe's leading restaurants. Started just **five years ago**, by brothers Lee and Alan Jones, the organisation has **grown** from a small company employing five people to a **multi-divisional organisation** employing 120 people.

> Key problem: useful to refer back to in your answer

The organisation's production facility is divided into three separate departments. Each department has a single manager with supervisors assisting on the production lines. The managers and supervisors, all of whom are aware of their roles, work well together. However, although the organisation has grown, the **owners continue to involve themselves** in day to day activities and this has led to friction between the owners, managers and supervisors.

> Dean (manager) helpfully makes points that should help your answer

> Distinction between operational decisions and senior management decision: useful point for an answer

As a result a problem arose last week. Alan Jones instructed a supervisor to repair a machine on the shop floor, which he refused to do without confirmation and instruction from his departmental manager. The supervisor's manager, Dean Watkins, became involved and was annoyed at what he saw as interference in his department's activities. Dean told Alan Jones that he "should have come to me first" because although the **responsibility for the overall organisation** was a matter for the brothers, action taken in the factory was through powers that had been **delegated** to him and through his **authority, as manager**. In the argument that followed, Alan Jones was accused of **failing to understand** the way that the hierarchy in such a large organisation operates and that interference with **operational decisions** by senior management was not helpful.

> Note the key words and focus your answer

As a consequence of this, Alan Jones has asked you to explain to him and his brother the issues behind the dispute to clarify the roles of managers and supervisors and to indicate how and why successful delegation might be achieved.

Required

(a) Explain to Alan Jones the main **differences** between the work of a **manager** and that of a **supervisor**. **(13 marks)**

> The examiner is deliberately reminding you to *apply* the theory

(b) Explain, **in the context of Flavours Fine Foods**, what is meant by:

(i)	Responsibility	**(4 marks)**
(ii)	Authority	**(3 marks)**
(iii)	Delegation	**(3 marks)**

> Clear keywords in a logical sequence: tackle them precisely and in order

(c) To **correct the problems at Flavours Fine Foods**, explain to Alan Jones:

(i)	The **need** for delegation	**(3 marks)**
(ii)	**How** effective delegation might be achieved	**(6 marks)**
(iii)	**Problems** with delegation	**(4 marks)**
(iv)	How these problems might be **overcome**	**(4 marks)**

(Total = 40 marks)

14 Authority and responsibility — 27 mins

'Authority without responsibility creates tyrants. Responsibility without authority creates martyrs.'

Required

Explain what you would expect to be the results of a mismatch between delegated authority and responsibility in an organisation.

(15 marks)

15 Authority, responsibility and delegation (6/02) — 27 mins

As organisations expand and the number of employees increase there is a need for delegation and clear definitions of levels of authority and responsibility.

Required

(a) Briefly explain what is meant by:

- (i) Responsibility **(2 marks)**
- (ii) Authority **(2 marks)**
- (iii) Delegation **(2 marks)**

(b) Briefly explain the difference between authority and responsibility. **(2 marks)**

(c) Explain how effective delegation can be achieved. **(7 marks)**

(Total = 15 marks)

16 The purpose of objective setting — 27 mins

'Objectives are needed in every area where performance and results directly and vitally affect the survival and prosperity of the business.' (Peter Drucker)

Required

(a) Explain what you understand by the term 'objectives'. **(3 marks)**
(b) What are the organisational purposes of setting objectives? **(4 marks)**
(c) What are the behavioural purposes of setting objectives? **(5 marks)**
(d) Give three examples of organisational objectives. **(3 marks)**

(Total = 15 marks)

17 Social responsibility — 27 mins

'The only justification for social responsibility is enlightened self-interest.' (Milton Friedman)

Required

(a) Explain the benefits to a business of socially responsible policies. **(8 marks)**
(b) List areas in which an organisation might formulate socially responsible and ethical objectives. **(7 marks)**

(Total = 15 marks)

18 Performance management (6/03) **27 mins**

'Performance management' is defined as a means of achieving better results by understanding and managing overall organisational performance.

Required

Describe the five stages typically involved in the process of performance management. **(15 marks)**

19 Management by objectives (6/04) **27 mins**

Your manager has decided to introduce a system of Management by Objectives but is uncertain how to set about it. You have been asked to advise.

Required

Describe the seven key stages that should be followed in a Management by Objectives programme.

(15 marks)

RECRUITMENT AND SELECTION

Questions 20 to 31 cover Recruitment and Selection, the subject of Part B of the BPP Study Text for Paper 1.3.

20 Question with analysis: Scenario: Human resource management **72 mins**

Deborah Williams, the finance director of SMG Ltd, thinks that the staff in the accounts department are overworked and has asked the Human Resource Department for an additional accounts clerk, preferably two.

SMG has no formal procedures or processes to ensure that appropriate and qualified staff are appointed. In the past SMG Ltd has relied on agencies and informal contacts to recruit new employees.

SMG Ltd has recently appointed you as assistant Human Resource Manager. You have been asked to take charge of the situation, to see if Ms Williams has a case and then to manage the new appointments process if the vacancy is approved.

Required

(a) Explain how you would establish whether Deborah Williams has a legitimate case for a new member of staff. **(8 marks)**

(b) Given that the vacancy is approved, discuss the procedure you would take to ensure that a suitably qualified person is recruited. **(10 marks)**

(c) Describe the contents of a job description and person specification for the new accounts clerk. **(7 marks)**

(d) Explain how you would carry out the recruitment and selection of the new clerk. **(10 marks)**

(e) What might be the benefits of ongoing training and development to the clerk and the business? **(5 marks)**

(Total = 40 marks)

20 Question with analysis: Scenario: Human resource management

72 mins

Overwork *may* not be evidence that more staff are needed: part (a)

Deborah Williams, the finance director of SMG Ltd, thinks that the staff in the accounts department are **overworked** and has asked the Human Resource Department for an additional accounts clerk, preferably two.

SMG has no formal procedures or processes to ensure that appropriate and qualified staff are appointed. In the past SMG Ltd has relied on **agencies and informal contacts** to recruit new employees.

Valid recruitment options – but not the only ones!

SMG Ltd has recently appointed you as assistant Human Resource Manager. You have been asked to take charge of the situation, to see if Ms Williams has a case and then to manage the new appointments process if the vacancy is approved.

Absence of procedures. Some form of human resource planning required.

Required

Systematic formal procedure for recruitment.

(a) Explain **how you would establish** whether Deborah Williams has a legitimate case for a new member of staff. **(8 marks)**

(b) Given that the vacancy is approved, discuss the **procedure** you would take to ensure that a suitably qualified person is recruited. **(10 marks)**

(c) Describe the contents of a job description and person specification for the new accounts clerk. **(7 marks)**

This is an *application* of part (b) to a specific vacancy.

(d) Explain **how** you would carry out the recruitment and selection of the new clerk. **(10 marks)**

(e) What might be the benefits of **ongoing training and development** to the clerk and the business? **(5 marks)**

Note the shift of topic!

(Total = 40 marks)

21 Question with answer plan: Systematic approach (12/04)

27 mins

Your employer has realised that a formal recruitment and selection process is required. You have been asked to advise.

Required

Identify and explain the stages involved in recruitment and selection. **(15 marks)**

22 Promote or recruit? (12/02) 27 mins

An organisation is recruiting additional staff and has decided to compare the benefits of appointing existing internal staff with that of appointing external candidates.

Required

(a) Define and describe the advantages of internal promotion. **(5 marks)**

(b) Define and describe the advantages of external recruitment. **(5 marks)**

(c) Describe three factors that should be taken into account when deciding upon whether to use recruitment consultants. **(5 marks)**

(Total = 15 marks)

23 Job analysis (12/04) 27 mins

You have been asked to carry out a job analysis of the employees in the accounts department.

Required

(a) Briefly explain what is meant by the term 'job analysis'. **(3 marks)**

(b) Briefly explain the four stages involved in carrying out a job analysis. **(4 marks)**

(c) Identify and briefly explain the information you would expect to collect during the job analysis investigation. **(8 marks)**

(Total = 15 marks)

24 Job descriptions 27 mins

You have been asked to advise the Accounts Manager on the documentation required for the recruitment of a new Accounts Assistant.

Required

(a) Briefly explain the difference between a job description and a person specification. **(4 marks)**
(b) Describe the contents of a job description. **(5 marks)**
(c) Outline the uses and limitations of job descriptions. **(6 marks)**

(Total = 15 marks)

25 Person specification (12/01; 6/05) — 27 mins

The 'person specification' is a development from the job description.

Required

(a) Explain what is meant by the terms:

(i) Person specification **(4 marks)**
(ii) Job description **(4 marks)**

(b) Briefly describe the way in which a 'person specification' differs from a 'job description'. **(3 marks)**

(c) Describe the purposes for which a person specification might be used. **(4 marks)**

(Total = 15 marks)

26 Job advertisement (12/03) — 27 mins

You have been asked to provide guidelines on the structure and content of an advertisement to be used for the future recruitment of new staff.

Required

(a) What factors need to be taken into account when preparing a recruitment advertisement? **(5 marks)**
(b) Briefly describe five factors which will influence the choice of advertising media. **(10 marks)**

(Total = 15 marks)

27 Application forms (12/05) — 27 mins

Recruitment and selection of potential employees involves a number of different steps, one of which may be the completion of an application form.

Required

(a) Describe the purpose of the application form. **(5 marks)**
(b) Describe the kind of information that the application form should obtain. **(10 marks)**

(Total = 15 marks)

28 Interviews (6/03; 6/06) — 27 mins

All organisations need to recruit new employees. An important step in the process is the selection interview.

Required

(a) Explain the purpose of the selection interview. **(4 marks)**

(b) Explain the advantages and the disadvantages of:

(i) The face to face interview between two people **(6 marks)**
(ii) The panel interview with more than one interviewer. **(5 marks)**

(Total = 15 marks)

29 Selection tests (6/04) 27 mins

Selection testing has become a common method of seeking information about potential employees. Such tests however are subject to some limitations.

Required

(a) Briefly describe the purposes of:

(i) intelligence tests **(2 marks)**
(ii) aptitude tests **(2 marks)**
(iii) competence tests **(2 marks)**
(iv) personality tests **(2 marks)**

(b) Briefly outline four limitations of selection tests. **(7 marks)**

(Total = 15 marks)

30 References (6/05) 27 mins

In addition to the application form and interview, references provide further confidential information about the prospective employee.

Required

(a) Define the purpose of a reference **(3 marks)**
(b) Describe the content of a reference **(5 marks)**
(c) Outline the problems with references **(7 marks)**

(Total = 15 marks)

31 Question with helping hand: Scenario: Equal opportunity (12/02) 72 mins

The supermarket chain 'Food is Us' has decided to tackle prejudice and discrimination in all its stores by establishing a policy applicable to all its stores. As part of this, it is challenging all employees, especially managers, to examine their **attitudes towards people of a different race, sex and ability**.

The reasons for introducing the policy are threefold. Plainly there is **legislation** on discrimination which must be complied with if the company is to avoid the risk of legal action against it. Also, from a marketing point of view, 'Food is Us' wish to be **identified with its customer base** by reflecting the racial diversity of the environments in which it operates. Most positively, the company wants to **develop a workforce which can reflect sufficient diversity** not only to avoid risk and to maintain its current market position, but also produce the initiatives which will develop the company in a successful and sustained manner.

During the course of the coming year, all store employees will be expected to attend an **awareness-raising training** programme. This programme is intended to help employees explore their own attitudes and highlight any prejudices that these employees might have.

The personnel director, Anne Healey, told shop operatives 'we want to make all our front line employees who deal closely with the members of the public aware of any subconscious prejudices that they might have.'

'It is very difficult to quantify the benefits of such specialist training, but it is one of our corporate principles that all people are treated fairly by employees, whether they are customers or work colleagues,' she added.

Initially small groups of employees will attend sessions to raise awareness. These sessions, to be held in-store, will take place during time already set aside for staff training and development.

The new policy is to be an extension of 'Food is Us' current equal opportunities scheme for managers. So far more than 1500 managers have attended one day awareness-raising courses over the past 18 months.

The same course is to be revised and updated following feedback from previous participants and will also be extended to include senior executives for the first time.

Required

With reference to the above scenario:

(a) Equal opportunities encompass many features. For 'Food is Us'

(i) What would be the main features of a sex discrimination policy? **(10 marks)**

(ii) What would be the main characteristics of a race relations policy? **(6 marks)**

(b) Why should an organisation like 'Food is Us' have an equal pay policy? **(6 marks)**

(c) What are the key points of a disability discrimination policy? **(8 marks)**

(d) What is the difference between an equal opportunities policy and a managing diversity initiative within an organisation? **(10 marks)**

(Total = 40 marks)

Helping hand. Parts (a) and (c) require knowledge of the legal framework in your country of study – but it is really addressing what a *policy* involves: what kinds of definitions, statements, explanations and provisions would it require?

Part (b) is about *why* equal pay is important, but also why the organisation needs a *policy* in place to deal with it. Think carefully about whom such a policy is protecting (some hints have been highlighted in bold in the scenario).

Part (d) requires an understanding that 'diversity' refers to a wide range of ways in which *individuals* (not just legal 'categories' of people or minorities) differ.

TRAINING AND DEVELOPMENT

Questions 32 to 41 cover Training and Development, the subject of Part C of the BPP Study Text for Paper 1.3.

32 Scenario: Training — 72 mins

JIK Ltd is a retail chain selling camera equipment and supplies to professionals and the general public. Feedback surveys completed by its customers have recently highlighted customer service problems, including 'ignorant or uninformed staff' and 'indifferent or inattentive staff'.

JIK has traditionally recruited photography enthusiasts to work in its stores and has not so far felt the need to offer training in either technical knowledge or customer service skills. The Manager of one store, Matthew Hlavcek, has been heard to say: 'Photographers know what they want, and they know that they can get it from us. Training is a waste of time and resources.' As the newly-appointed Assistant Manager at Hlavcek's store, you decide that the feedback surveys give sufficient impetus for you to recommend a new attitude to training.

Required

Draft a report for Matthew Hlavcek, outlining the following.

(a) What you consider to be the benefits of training to:

  (i) The organisation **(5 marks)**
  (ii) The individual **(5 marks)**

(b) How you would identify the training needs of staff **(10 marks)**

(c) What methods you would choose to satisfy the training needs of staff **(8 marks)**

(d) How you would carry out evaluation of training methods **(6 marks)**

(e) What you understand by the term 'employee development' **(6 marks)**

(Total = 40 marks)

33 Training methods (6/06) — 27 mins

All organisations require trained employees. However, training can take many forms, some of which are internal to the organisation.

Required

Explain what is meant by the terms:

(a) Computer based training **(3 marks)**
(b) Coaching **(3 marks)**
(c) Mentoring **(3 marks)**
(d) Job rotation **(3 marks)**
(e) Job instruction **(3 marks)**

(Total = 15 marks)

34 Induction — 27 mins

Attitude surveys used among staff in your organisation have highlighted the perception that it is difficult to 'fit in' in the first year of employment. You have been asked to consider introducing formal induction programmes for new recruits.

Required

(a) What are the advantages and disadvantages of formal induction? **(8 marks)**

(b) Suggest a format for a formal induction course. **(7 marks)**

(Total = 15 marks)

35 Personal development plan (12/05) — 27 mins

You have been asked to prepare a personal development plan for new employees.

Required

Explain the three steps involved in the preparation of a personal development plan. **(15 marks)**

36 Coaching and mentoring (12/03) — 27 mins

Training and development programmes form an important part of improving employee skills.

(a) Briefly explain what is meant by the following different types of training and development:

  (i) Coaching **(5 marks)**

  (ii) Mentoring **(5 marks)**

(b) Explain five criteria against which the effectiveness of training might generally be evaluated. **(5 marks)**

(Total = 15 marks)

37 Question with answer plan: Learning theory (12/02) — 27 mins

Modern business organisations require trained employees, but individuals approach learning in different ways.

Required

(a) Briefly describe the four stages in the experiential learning cycle. **(4 marks)**

(b) Describe the four learning styles identified by Honey and Mumford and their implications for training programmes. **(11 marks)**

(Total = 15 marks)

38 Scenario: Appraisal (6/04) **72 mins**

Watkin Williams is a small accountancy practice based in a small British town. The two partners, Reg Watkin and Oscar Williams are supported by a small team of qualified and part qualified accountants, technicians and support staff. The staff consists of five account managers who look after the main clients, a customer liaison manager (whose role it is to look for new clients), four account managers who maintain contact with smaller and newer clients and a support staff of five technicians and four secretaries. The practice is regarded as outgoing and constantly seeking expansion.

The two partners feel that the practice has grown so much that it can no longer be managed in an informal way. Reg Watkin has been studying management in his spare time and suggested to his partner that a staff appraisal scheme should be introduced. He believes that rewards should be related to performance and wants to use the appraisal scheme as the basis for salary increases, annual bonuses and other incentives. Despite the office being very busy and there being substantial demands on staff, the scheme has been active for the last six months, with appraisal interviews being fitted in as time has become available.

The two partners are soon to discuss strategy and amongst other things, intend to discuss the salaries budget for the coming year. However, feedback from the staff has identified a number of problems with the appraisal system. It has been alleged that nobody on the staff knows what appraisals are for, whether they are simply a discussion or a session to ask for more money. Some members of staff regard appraisals as a waste of time and resources since their own performance depends on others' work, how well they perform and the time they are given. The partners are rarely available in the office and are therefore seen as out of touch. Staff members feel that appraisal interviews are a low priority for the partners, who hold them only at short notice when convenient to them. As a consequence, some staff say nothing, others complain and in reality, there has been no follow up to the interviews. The staff now feel that an informal system should be introduced since the formal system has failed because, in their view, it is inappropriate to the organisation.

The partners are concerned about the views of the staff and have commissioned you to report on performance appraisal systems.

Required

(a) Briefly describe the three main components of an appraisal system. **(3 marks)**

(b) Outline the potential benefits of the appraisal from the viewpoint of:

- (i) The employees at Watkin Williams **(5 marks)**
- (ii) The employer – Watkin Williams **(5 marks)**

(c) Describe five main barriers to an effective appraisal system at Watkin Williams. **(5 marks)**

(d) Describe the documentation that should be prepared **before** an appraisal interview. **(8 marks)**

(e) Describe three approaches the partners of Watkin Williams might use for conducting the appraisal interview and explain which method you think might be most beneficial and why. **(9 marks)**

(f) Explain what actions should be taken after the appraisal has been completed. **(5 marks)**

(Total = 40 marks)

39 Trends in appraisal — 27 mins

Appraisal schemes have been criticised as being backward-looking, perfunctory, perpetuating 'top-down' control and irrelevant to performance in the job.

Required

Identify and describe three new approaches to appraisal which may address the issues raised in these criticisms.

(15 marks)

40 The cost of accidents — 27 mins

Newspapers frequently quote statistics showing large numbers of employee hours lost through accidents, and the associated cost to business.

Required

(a) List the potential costs to employers of accidents at work. **(8 marks)**

(b) Outline steps which can be taken to reduce the frequency and severity of accidents. **(7 marks)**

(Total = 15 marks)

41 Health and safety (6/03) — 27 mins

The health and safety of employees has become increasingly a matter for management.

Required

(a) Briefly describe three hazards to health and safety that might be found in the workplace and demonstrate why they are hazards. **(5 marks)**

(b) Briefly describe general policies that an organisation might take to avoid risks in the workplace.

(10 marks)

(Total = 15 marks)

MOTIVATION AND LEADERSHIP

Questions 42 to 53 cover Motivation and Leadership, the subject of Part D of the BPP Study Text for Paper 1.3.

42 Question with analysis: Scenario: Aspects of motivation (12/03) 72 mins

A management consultancy has been employed by Swandiff Local Authority to examine the problems junior staff appear to be having in reaching the performance expected of all staff. The authority employs 8,500 staff in total with 25 senior managers, 123 middle managers and some 2,560 employed at junior management level, mainly supervisors. The authority has evolved into a traditional, bureaucratic, formal governmental type of organisational structure.

The management consultants decided to hold a series of meetings with all levels of management. Initially they found that the junior managers were unhappy with and sceptical about the value of the meetings; 'we've seen it all before' was the main response. After the meetings, the consultants produced a report which identified three main problem areas.

Firstly, it became apparent that the level of morale for all staff was low. Lack of facilities, pressure of work and particularly reductions in available funds appeared to be the main grievance. There appeared however to be a deeper problem, that of mistrust between the staff as a whole and senior management. The mistrust appeared to be more apparent between the senior management and supervisors. The reason for this was unclear.

The second problem appeared to be that the staff as a whole regarded the supervisors as a level of management poor at managing their sections, disregarding or ignoring work practices and performance standards. In response, the supervisors said that their position in general was unclear; there were no clear lines of authority, command or responsibility which allowed them to make decisions for their departments. Some supervisors simply regarded themselves as menial and unrecognised, referring to funding shortages, unrealistic targets, little recognition of their position, no job descriptions and lack of training.

Job security was the third issue. Financial cutbacks and changes in service levels had led to rumours of substantial cutbacks in staff. Rumours were especially strong amongst the junior management. New, younger staff would be better trained to replace supervisors, more adaptable and better able to use computer systems and the latest available software packages.

In all, the problems had shown themselves in high labour turnover, which in addition to the problems already outlined, were blamed on low salaries, little opportunity for personal advancement and poor working conditions.

Required

(a) Using Herzberg's theory of motivation, explain the attitude of the supervisors. **(15 marks)**

(b) What aspects of organisational structure and culture could explain the supervisors' attitude at Swandiff Local Authority? **(10 marks)**

(c) How could re-training supervisors overcome the problems identified in (a) and (b)? **(15 marks)**

(Total = 40 marks)

42 Question with analysis: Scenario: Aspects of motivation (12/03) 72 mins

Structural & cultural implications: part (b).

A management consultancy has been employed by Swandiff Local Authority to examine the problems junior staff appear to be having in reaching the performance expected of all staff. The authority employs 8,500 staff in total with 25 senior managers, 123 middle managers and some 2,560 employed at junior management level, mainly supervisors. The authority has evolved into a **traditional, bureaucratic, formal governmental type of organisational structure.**

The management consultants decided to hold a series of meetings with all levels of management. Initially they found that the junior managers were unhappy with and sceptical about the value of the meetings; 'we've seen it all before' was the main response. After the meetings, the consultants produced a report which identified three main problem areas.

Attitudes of supervisors: parts (a) and (b).Problems due to *hygiene* or *motivator* factors?

Firstly, it became apparent that the level of morale for all staff was low. **Lack of facilities, pressure of work** and particularly reductions in available funds appeared to be the main grievance. There appeared however to be a deeper problem, that of mistrust between the staff as a whole and senior management. The mistrust appeared to be more apparent between the senior management and supervisors. The reason for this was unclear.

The second problem appeared to be that the staff as a whole regarded the supervisors as a level of management poor at managing their sections, **disregarding or ignoring work practices** and performance standards. In response, the supervisors said that their position in general was unclear; there were **no clear lines of authority**, command or responsibility which allowed them to make decisions for their departments. Some supervisors simply regarded themselves as menial and **unrecognised**, referring to funding shortages, unrealistic targets, little recognition of their position, no job descriptions and **lack of training**.

Job security was the third issue. Financial cutbacks and changes in service levels had led to rumours of substantial cutbacks in staff. Rumours were especially strong amongst the junior management. New, younger staff would be better trained to replace supervisors, more adaptable and better able to use computer systems and the latest available software packages.

In all, the problems had shown themselves in high labour turnover, which in addition to the problems already outlined, were blamed on low salaries, little opportunity for personal advancement and poor working conditions.

Two-factor theory Hygiene factors a problem? Any motivator factors?

Required

(a) Using Herzberg's theory of motivation, explain the attitude of the supervisors. **(15 marks)**

(b) What aspects of organisational structure and culture could explain the supervisors' attitude at Swandiff Local Authority? **(10 marks)**

What are the morale-levering aspects of *bureaucracy*?

Start with the problems you identified in (a) and (b). Would training help – if so, how, and how far?

(c) How could re-training supervisors overcome the problems identified in (a) and (b)? **(15 marks)**

(Total = 40 marks)

43 Theories of motivation (12/03) 27 mins

All managers and supervisors need to understand the concept of motivation in the workplace.

Required

(a) Explain the 'content theory' of motivation. **(5 marks)**

(b) Explain what is meant by MacGregor's

(i) Theory X **(5 marks)**
(ii) Theory Y **(5 marks)**

(Total = 15 marks)

44 Hygiene and movitator factors (6/05) 27 mins

An organisation's goals can only be achieved through the efforts of motivated individuals.

Required

Explain what is meant by the following terms:

(a) Hygiene factors **(8 marks)**
(b) Motivators **(7 marks)**

(Total = 15 marks)

45 Maslow (6/06) 27 mins

Your manager has heard of Maslow's hierarchy of needs theory and how it has some relevance to motivational techniques.

Required

(a) Explain Maslow's hierarchy of needs theory. **(10 marks)**
(b) How can Maslow's theory be applied to the motivation of staff? **(5 marks)**

(Total = 15 marks)

46 Equity theory (12/02) 27 mins

Motivation is fundamental to the task of management.

Required

(a) What is meant by the term 'process theory' of motivation? **(5 marks)**
(b) What is meant by the 'equity theory' of motivation? **(5 marks)**
(c) Briefly describe the response an individual might have to feelings of negative inequity. **(5 marks)**

(Total = 15 marks)

47 The job as a motivator (12/04) — 27 mins

There is often confusion between the meanings of 'job enrichment', 'job enlargement' and 'job rotation'.

Required

(a) Define and explain the term 'job enrichment'. **(5 marks)**

(b) Define and explain the term 'job enlargement'. **(5 marks)**

(c) Define and explain the term 'job rotation'. **(5 marks)**

(Total = 15 marks)

48 Rewards (12/05) — 27 mins

Reward systems should involve more than assuming that financial rewards are appropriate in all circumstances.

Required

(a) Explain what is meant by 'intrinsic' rewards. **(3 marks)**

(b) Explain what is meant by 'extrinsic' rewards. **(3 marks)**

(c) Describe any six types of extrinsic reward. **(9 marks)**

(Total = 15 marks)

49 Question with analysis: Scenario: Leadership styles (12/05) — 72 mins

At Williams, Watkins and McDonald investment fund managers, there is a strong emphasis on democratic management. The employees are grouped into teams with a team leader. The team is given sales targets to meet but is allowed to decide how it will go about meeting those targets. The team decides how it will organise work in its own area (ie the physical layout of the area). Alongside each team area there are meeting areas with chairs grouped in a circle. In this area are charts showing the performance of each team. The teams meet to discuss what is going well and what is going badly and to suggest ideas for improvement. The team then has the responsibility for putting their ideas into practice.

Dean Thomas is responsible for the blue team. He is the most recently recruited team leader in the organisation. The blue team has an average age of 26 years. Dean Thomas enjoys bringing his team together every morning for a daily briefing. He gives out the tasks for the day and allows his team to pick and choose their tasks and to discuss any problems with each other before they actually settle down to begin work. Dean tends to be more concerned with maintaining good relations with his team than sometimes with achieving targets. The blue team like Dean's approach, where they can make their own decisions, work on their own and are one of the most cohesive teams in the organisation if not as successful as they should be.

Lee Allen is the green team leader. He is the most experienced team leader. His team of eight members have all been at Williams, Watkins and McDonald for many years. Lee Allen knows that the company policy strongly prefers a more relaxed style of leadership. However, Lee comes from a disciplined background and quite often needs to give orders and demand results when deadlines need to be met or the team appears likely to fail to meet its target. The green team has the best success rate but also the highest absentee rate of all six teams working for Williams, Watkins and McDonald.

Emma Jenkins, a green team member, has complained about Lee Allen's style of leadership and has asked to be moved to the blue team. She feels that she has less input into decision making than she would like.

Required

(a) (i) Identify the four broad styles of leadership described in Tannenbaum and Schmidt's continuum of management style. **(12 marks)**

(ii) Briefly describe the four factors upon which the appropriate management style depends. **(4 marks)**

(b) Using the Tannenbaum and Schmidt model and appropriate evidence from the scenario, identify which of the broad styles of leadership Dean Thomas and Lee Allen demonstrate at Williams, Watkins and McDonald. **(8 marks)**

(c) Explain action centred leadership and justify why Lee Allen's approach can be described as action centred. **(8 marks)**

(d) Using Fiedler's contingency theory of leadership, explain the possible reasons for Emma Jenkins' dissatisfaction as a green team member and her desire to become a blue team member. **(8 marks)**

(Total = 40 marks)

49 Question with analysis: Scenario: Leadership styles (12/05)

72 mins

> Helpful label followed by description of the prevailing WWM style

At Williams, Watkins and McDonald investment fund managers, there is a strong emphasis on **democratic** management. The employees are grouped into **teams** with a team leader. The team is given sales targets to meet but is **allowed to decide** how it will go about meeting those targets. The team decides **how it will organise work** in its own area (ie the physical layout of the area). Alongside each team area there are **meeting areas** with chairs grouped in a circle. In this area are charts showing the **performance** of each team. The teams **meet to discuss** what is going well and what is going badly and to suggest ideas for improvement. The team then has the **responsibility** for putting their ideas into practice.

> Useful details to refer accurately back to the scenario

> Identify people focused style

Dean Thomas is responsible for the **blue team**. He is the most recently recruited team leader in the organisation. The blue team has an average age of 26 years. Dean Thomas enjoys bringing his team together every morning for a daily briefing. He gives out the tasks for the day and **allows his team to pick and choose** their tasks and to discuss any problems with each other before they actually settle down to begin work. Dean tends to be more concerned with **maintaining good relations with his team than sometimes with achieving targets**. The blue team like Dean's approach, where they can make their own decisions, work on their own and are one of the most cohesive teams in the organisation if not as successful as they should be.

> Clues: clearly a different style of leadership

> Note advantages/disadvantages may be useful data

Lee Allen is the **green team** leader. He is the most experienced team leader. His team of eight members have all been at Williams, Watkins and McDonald for many years. Lee Allen knows that the company policy strongly prefers a more relaxed style of leadership. **However**, Lee comes from a **disciplined** background and quite often needs to **give orders** and **demand results** when deadlines need to be met or the team appears likely to fail to meet its target. The green team has the **best success rate** but also the **highest absentee rate** of all six teams working for Williams, Watkins and McDonald.

> Note issue of employee preference for democratic style

Emma Jenkins, a green team member, has complained about Lee Allen's style of leadership and has asked to be moved to the blue team. She feels that she has **less input into decision making** than she would like.

Required

> Key topic for

(a) (i) Identify the four broad styles of leadership described in **Tannenbaum and Schmidt's continuum** of management style. **(12 marks)**

(ii) Briefly describe the four factors upon which the appropriate management style depends. **(4 marks)**

> Use evidence from the scenario

(b) Using the Tannenbaum and Schmidt model and appropriate evidence from the scenario, identify which of the broad styles of leadership **Dean Thomas** and **Lee Allen** demonstrate at Williams, Watkins and McDonald. **(8 marks)**

> Note two requirements

(c) **Explain action centred leadership** and justify **why Lee Allen's approach** can be described as action centred. **(8 marks)**

Support argument with this theory

(d) Using Fiedler's **contingency theory of leadership**, explain the possible reasons for Emma Jenkins' dissatisfaction as a green team member and her desire to become a blue team member. **(8 marks)**

(Total = 40 marks)

50 Leadership skills and actions (6/04) — 27 mins

Your manager has heard of Action Centred Leadership and wishes to involve the department in this idea. You have been asked to explain the idea to your colleagues.

Required

(a) Briefly outline three skills a leader might possess. **(6 marks)**

(b) Briefly explain the term 'action centred leadership'. **(3 marks)**

(c) Describe the three major goals of action centred leadership. **(6 marks)**

(Total = 15 marks)

51 Question with answer plan: Leadership style — 27 mins

'Choosing a leadership style which is entirely appropriate to any given situation is one of the most important skills that an effective manager can possess.'

Required

Critically discuss this statement, giving reasons for your views. **(15 marks)**

52 Question with helping hand: Blake and Mouton (6/05) — 27 mins

An important part of management is understanding the style of leadership.

Required

(a) Explain what Blake and Mouton's Managerial Grid measures **(5 marks)**

(b) Briefly describe the five extreme scores identified by Blake and Mouton **(5 marks)**

(c) Discuss the usefulness of the managerial grid in assessing the attributes of managers **(5 marks)**

(Total marks = 15)

Helping hand. Part (a) should be easy if you know the grid. You may like to draw a quick, neat diagram as part of your description.

Part (b): There are, strictly speaking, four 'extreme' scores – plus one 'in the middle' of the grid. You should recognise this as a reference to the five identified styles. If you recall their 'labels' this will be a good start to 'briefly describing' each score.

Part (c): How does the grid help managers understand their 'leadership style'?

Start by explaining the concept of 'leadership style', and why *it* is relevant to modern managers.

How is the managerial grid (specifically) helpful in identifying areas for improvement in a manager's style?

What are the practical limitations of using the grid? (Think about *any* highly simplified model, which takes into account only two variables ... or any *theoretical* model, for that matter...)

53 Theory Z (12/02) — 27 mins

In seeking organisational success, some managers are adopting a 'Theory Z' approach to managing.

Required

(a) Describe the characteristics of an organisation which uses a 'Theory Z' approach. **(10 marks)**

(b) Are the ideas of 'Theory Z' universally applicable? **(5 marks)**

(Total = 15 marks)

EFFECTIVE COMMUNICATION PRACTICES

Questions 54 to 64 cover Effective Communication Practices, the subject of Part E of the BPP Study Text for Paper 1.3.

54 Scenario: Interpersonal skills (6/02) — 72 mins

Simon Price works as an accounts clerk in a large manufacturing organisation and has worked there for seven years. He is known as an *unassuming* individual who *quietly* goes about his work. Over recent months his workload has *increased dramatically*. Many members of the accounting team have been away from work due to discontentment and Simon **has had to do** their work also.

Simon has **tried explaining** to his line manager, David Lowe, how he and the accounting team feel about the absenteeism and the increase in workload. The feeling amongst the accounting employees is that the manager is **not** *listening and 'is following his own agenda'*. Effective working relationships within the accounting department are now *breaking down.*

Last week Simon Price had influenza and was away from work. He returned on Monday feeling tired and miserable. He has spent the last three days catching up on last week's work in addition to undertaking the work of Sally Simpson, the purchase invoice clerk, who is currently away from work.

It is 15.30 on Thursday and his line manager has just asked him to update the cashbook and reconcile it with the most recent bank statement. At this moment in time Simon is working on inputting sales invoices and has approximately two hours work left on this project. Stopping now would mean that he would have to leave the sales invoicing work and return to it tomorrow. He *really does not want to do the* new task now.

Simon feels that he has enough pressure. He has endeavoured to communicate with David Lowe and although Simon and the accounting department regard David Lowe as possessing poor interpersonal skills, Simon feels that he must now do something.

Required

With reference to the above scenario:

(a) When he communicates his feelings to David Lowe, the line manager, Simon Price needs to distinguish between aggressive and assertive behaviour. In this situation, explain:

  (i) The inappropriateness of aggressive behaviour **(6 marks)**
  (ii) The appropriateness of assertive behaviour **(7 marks)**

(b) Explain whether Simon Price has been displaying passive behaviour. **(6 marks)**

(c) Explain why David Lowe, the line manager, needs to possess effective interpersonal skills. **(6 marks)**

(d) Explain why David Lowe, the line manager, needs effective interpersonal skills in the following specific areas:

  (i) Motivation **(5 marks)**
  (ii) Negotiation **(5 marks)**
  (iii) Team building **(5 marks)**

(Total = 40 marks)

55 Aggressive or assertive? (6/06) — 27 mins

An important part of managing people in a professional organisation is to be able to distinguish between aggressiveness and assertiveness in an employee.

Required

(a) Explain and give examples of aggressive behaviour. **(8 marks)**

(b) Explain and give examples of assertive behaviour. **(7 marks)**

(Total = 15 marks)

56 Communication barriers (6/05) — 27 mins

The accountant communicates information to others in reports and statements. Understanding the nature and importance of communication is therefore an important part of the accountant's role.

Required

(a) Explain the importance of good communication. **(5 marks)**

(b) Describe five major barriers to good communication. **(10 marks)**

(Total = 15 marks)

57 Communication flows (12/03) — 27 mins

Communication is vital in all organisations but requires an understanding of appropriate structures and communication channels and patterns.

Required

(a) Briefly explain the main purposes of the three main formal communication channels in an organisation:

- (i) Downwards **(3 marks)**
- (ii) Upwards **(3 marks)**
- (iii) Lateral or horizontal **(3 marks)**

(b) Briefly explain the characteristics and effectiveness of ANY THREE of the following communication patterns:

- (i) The Circle
- (ii) The 'Y'
- (iii) The Wheel
- (iv) The All Channel **(6 marks)**

(Total = 15 marks)

58 Question with answer plan: Scenario: Managing conflict

72 mins

Sandra Kristensson, Finance Manager of GBH Ltd, has noticed a marked decrease in the Accounts Department's efficiency in the last few months.

The problems appear to coincide with the introduction of the 'Employee of the Month' competition, the recruitment of a new supervisor with a rather abrasive personal style and discussions over the re-allocation of office space. There has been no overt argument over these issues: indeed, staff appear to be communicating less and less.

GBH has recently appointed you as Assistant Human Resource Manager. Sandra Kristensson has asked you to help her diagnose and resolve the problems in her department.

Required

(a) Explain what you think may be happening in the Accounts Department and why. **(10 marks)**

(b) Draft notes on the tactics commonly used in conflict situations:

- (i) By the conflicting parties **(5 marks)**
- (ii) By managers responding to the conflict **(7 marks)**

(c) Explain how you would go about managing the conflict in the Accounts Department. **(10 marks)**

(d) Explain how the conflict in the Accounts Department may be seen as constructive or positive in its results. **(8 marks)**

(Total = 40 marks)

59 Conflict (6/02)

27 mins

Conflict is an inevitable feature of organisations but is rarely recognised or understood.

Required

(a) Define what is meant by conflict within an organisation. **(3 marks)**
(b) Describe causes of conflict. **(7 marks)**
(c) Briefly describe characteristics of conflict which may be observed in the work place. **(5 marks)**

(Total = 15 marks)

60 Conflict good and bad (12/05)

27 mins

Conflict in the workplace is a common feature of organisational and business life.

Required

(a) Under what circumstances can a conflict be constructive? **(5 marks)**
(b) Under what circumstances can a conflict be destructive? **(5 marks)**
(c) Briefly describe five causes of conflict. **(5 marks)**

(Total = 15 marks)

61 Question with helping hand: Scenario: Discipline and grievance (6/05) 72 mins

Oliver Hoppe has been working at Hoopers and Henderson accountancy practice for eighteen months. He feels that he fits in well, especially with his colleagues and has learnt a lot from them. However, he feels that the rules and regulations governing everyday activities and time keeping are not clear.

Oliver does not get on well with his line manager, David Morgan. There appears to be a clash of personalities and reluctance on David Morgan's part to deal with the icy atmosphere between them after David was asked by one of the accounting partners to give Oliver a job. For the past three months Oliver has gone to lunch with his fellow workers and always returned to work with them or before them. In fact they all have returned to work about ten minutes late on several previous occasions. After the third time, Oliver was called into David Morgan's office and given an oral warning about his time keeping.

Oliver was not permitted to argue his case and none of the other staff who returned late were disciplined in this way. On the next occasion the group was late returning from lunch, David Morgan presented Oliver with a written warning about his time keeping.

Yesterday, Oliver was five minutes late returning to work. His colleagues returned after him. David Morgan gave Oliver notice and told him to work until the end of the week and then collect his salary, the necessary paperwork and to leave the practice.

There is a partner responsible for human resources. Oliver has come to see the partner to discuss the grievance procedures against David Morgan for his treatment and about what Oliver regards as unfair dismissal.

Required

(a) Describe the six stages of a formal disciplinary procedure that an organisation such as Hoopers and Henderson should have in place. **(12 marks)**

(b) Explain why Oliver might legitimately feel he has a grievance against his manager and identify which aspects of the formal disciplinary procedure David Morgan did not follow or allow in this case. **(9 marks)**

(c) Describe the main stages of a formal grievance *procedure* that Oliver should now pursue. **(10 marks)**

(d) Describe the three stages of a formal grievance *interview* that Oliver might seek with the appropriate partner at Hoopers and Henderson following the formal procedure. **(9 marks)**

(Total = 40 marks)

Helping hand. In part (a), the reference to H&H is not critical to the answer: all organisations should have a formal disciplinary procedure. So:

- Focus first on the 'six stages of a formal disciplinary procedure': this should bring to mind the stages of progressive discipline.
- Make sure you are clear as to the difference between disciplinary procedure (eg the management of Oliver's poor timekeeping by David) and grievance procedure (such as Oliver might bring against David for unfair treatment).

In part (b), you are being asked how David has unfairly treated Oliver: there's a clear hint to focus on 'which aspects of the formal disciplinary procedure' were neglected: this should direct your attention to the ACAS guidelines.

Part (c) should be straightforward – as long as you recognise that we've now switched from disciplinary procedure to grievance procedure.

Part (d) similarly addresses grievance *interviews:* you should be able to define the process as three stages.

62 Discipline (12/01; 12/04) **27 mins**

Employee discipline is important in achieving organisational success.

Required

(a) What is meant by the term 'discipline' in the organisational context? **(3 marks)**

(b) Describe, in the correct order, the six steps involved in a formal disciplinary procedure. **(12 marks)**

(Total = 15 marks)

63 Grievance interview **27 mins**

A grievance occurs when an individual thinks that he or she has been wrongly treated by colleagues or supervisors. The purpose of formal grievance procedures is to resolve the problem to the satisfaction of all concerned.

Required

(a) Outline the process of a grievance interview. **(10 marks)**

(b) List the matters that should be stated in a formal grievance policy. **(5 marks)**

(Total = 15 marks)

64 Counselling (6/03) **27 mins**

Your manager has been called upon to provide advice, guidance and counselling to employees.

Required

(a) Explain what is meant by 'counselling' in the work place. **(2 marks)**

(b) Describe the skills a manager would require to fulfill the role of the counsellor. **(7 marks)**

(c) Briefly describe three advantages of counselling for the organisation. **(6 marks)**

(Total = 15 marks)

Answers

1 Organisation structure

Text references. These areas are covered in full in Chapter 1.

Top tips. This question is straightforward if you read the topic and instruction key words carefully. In part (a) they are the *purposes* of *formal* organisation *structure* (what is it for?). In part (b) they are the *factors* which *influence* the structure (what 'shapes' it?). In part (c) they are *criticisms* of *bureaucracy*. Get used to rationing yourself to 5 marks' worth of relevant points per part, so that you have time to complete all parts of the question: you will see that we have done this quite deliberately (and 'signalled' the fact that we have made 5 mark-earning points, by numbering them clearly in our answer).

10 marks were available in the December 2003 exam for recognising the problems of bureaucratic structure/culture in a given *scenario*: see question 42 in this Kit

Easy marks. A highly-structured question offers plenty of basic marks: you should be able to get the first 2-3 marks for each part (provided you have read the question accurately). You may note that we have gone for *extra* credit, by discussing some of the *theories* underlying our points and naming key authors in the field. This is a useful habit to get into.

(a) **Purposes of formal organisation structure**

The formal structure of an organisation is designed to provide a framework for the controlled performance of collective goals. This framework is intended to perform the following functions.

(i) **Link individuals and teams** in a consistent network of relationships so that the flow of authority, responsibility and communications can be controlled and predicted.

(ii) **Provide a structure for the allocation of tasks** and accountabilities to individuals and teams within functionally specialised or other forms of organisation.

(iii) **Allocate to each individual or team the authority** required to perform the tasks and accountabilities allocated to them, by virtue of positional or legal power.

(iv) **Co-ordinate and control the objectives, activities and use of resources** of individuals and teams within the organisation, so that overall aims are achieved without gaps or overlaps in accountability or flow of work.

(v) **Facilitate the flow of work**, information and other resources through the organisation by establishing communication channels.

(b) **Factors influencing organisational structure**

There are a number of ways of looking at this question.

(i) Fayol, for example, suggested that organisations should be structured according to certain **universal, rational principles**: division of work (or specialisation), a scalar chain of authority and responsibility, unity of command and unity of direction.

(ii) Mintzberg, on the other hand, suggested that organisations have **different ways** of relating to their work and **different methods of co-ordination** and that organisational preferences in these areas shape the structure.

(iii) A contingency theory of structure suggests that a number of variables influence organis-' structure, including:

- Its age
- Its size and geographical dispersion
- The nature of the task and technology
- The type of personnel employed

- Organisational values and strategies (eg a belief in teamworking or empowerment)
- Environment (eg requiring a flexible, or supporting an inflexible, structure).

(c) **Criticisms of bureaucracy**

(i) The **complexity of decision-making** (eg to obtain the go-ahead for new projects or responses to customer demands) slows down the process, causing delays and rigidity and conflicting with increasing customer demands for flexibility and quick responses.

(ii) **Rigidity.** Behavioural **conformity creates ritualism and formalism**, inhibiting the development of individuals. Individuals may become frustrated and demotivated. Innovation and creativity are restricted.

(iii) **Inflexibility.** Rules and procedures, once internalised, tend not to adapt to changing goals and environmental pressures and can become irrelevant or dysfunctional 'red tape' (Merton).

(iv) **No learning.** The control mechanism (whereby feedback on errors are used to initiate corrective action) is hampered by the rigidity and complexity of communication channels, so that the organisation is unable to learn from its mistakes (Crozier).

(v) Bureaucracies take an **inward-looking orientation**, focused on procedures and rituals ('inputs') rather than customer needs, performance and results ('outputs'): they are therefore incapable of responding without trauma to fast-changing environments.

2 Organisation structure: Mintzberg

Text reference. Chapter 1 discusses formal organisation structure and Mintzberg's components.

Top tips. There are two potential pitfalls in this question.

In part (a), you need to get straight in your mind what the question is referring to as 'organisation structure'. Don't get distracted by the reference to organisation charts: that's not what the question is about, but it tells you to focus on *formal* organisation structure (not informal structure).

In part (b), you have to pay careful attention to the question instruction and topic key words. You are asked to 'explain' – *not* merely to list – the components: you need two marks' worth of detail for each of the five components to earn the 10 marks available (and a diagram, while it may be a useful memory prompter, is not a substitute!).

Then you need to confine yourself to *Mintzberg's* organisational components – not Fayol, or Peters, or Burns and Stalker or any other writer on organisational structure. And you need to confine yourself to Mintzberg's *organisational components* – not his models of organisational types or managerial roles. (In a previous 1.3 paper, the examiner set Mintzberg's managerial roles, and complained that candidates lost marks by writing about his organisational components, or other writers' role theories: this question is clearly designed to ensure that students get the message!)

Easy marks. The basic marks can be earned by defining formal organisation structure and accurately identifying Mintzberg's five components (perhaps using the standard diagram): after that, extra marks are available for expanding on those basic points with relevant explanation.

Examiner's comments.

The examiner was disappointed that many candidates displayed a poor understanding of what is meant by 'organisational structure'. Part (a) was, in general, poorly answered especially since candidates assumed all companies are hierarchical, which they are not. In part (b) good marks were earned by those who had a good understanding of Mintzberg's five organisational components.

Marking scheme

		Marks
(a)	Description of the term 'organisational structure'. (One mark per factor identified)	Up to 5 marks **(Maximum for part (a) 5 marks)**
(b)	Explanation of Mintzberg's five organisational components. (Two marks per component)	Up to 10 marks **(Maximum for part (b) 10 marks)**
		(Total for question 15 marks)

(a) **Organisation structure**

A formal organisation structure is formed by the grouping of people into units (according to common tasks, technology, customers or geography) and the allocation of responsibility and authority for different areas of activity.

This creates a framework which:

- Links individuals in an established network of relationships, so that authority, responsibility and communication can be controlled
- Allocates the tasks required to fulfil organisational objectives in the most efficient and effective way
- Gives individuals and groups (by virtue of their role or position) the authority required to perform the allocated tasks
- Co-ordinates the objectives and activities of different units, to ensure unity of direction
- Facilitates the flow of work, information and other resources through the organisation

It is this formal organisation structure that is depicted in an organisation chart: the 'informal' organisation or social system is much more loose, fluid and spontaneous.

(b) **Mintzberg's five organisational components**

Henry Mintzberg suggests that any organisation can be analysed into five basic structural components, according to how they relate to the work of the organisation.

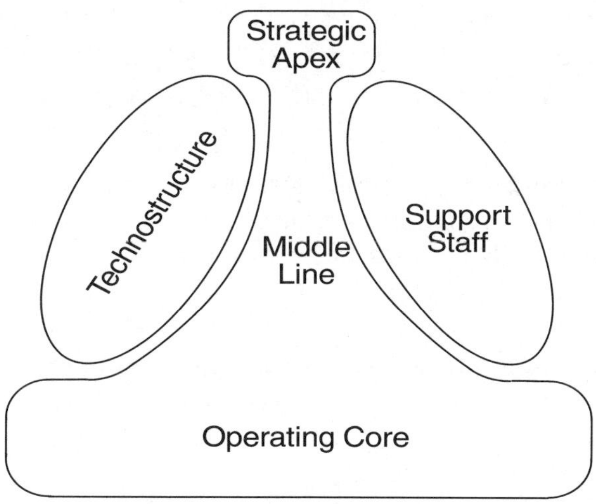

The **strategic apex** (often senior management), sets the organisation's mission and direction, allocates resources and manages the organisation's relationship with its environment.

The **operating core** comprises the units directly involved in the process of obtaining inputs and converting them into outputs (goods and services), via activities such as sales and marketing, purchasing and production.

The **middle line** (middle management) conveys the goals set by the strategic apex to the operating core, and plans, organises and controls the work of the operating core in pursuit of those goals.

The **technostructure** concerns the 'technology' of the organisation (in the sense of work systems and the ways work is organised). It comprises the analysts who design systems in order to standardise work processes and techniques. Examples include quality controllers, financial controllers and HR planners.

Support staff supply ancillary services such as PR, legal counsel, catering or security to the rest of the structure.

The five components will be of different size and importance in different types of organisation: the middle line will be larger in a bureaucracy than in a small entrepreneurial organisation, say.

3 Scenario: Matrix structure

Text reference. Hierarchy and matrix organisation are both discussed in Chapter 1.

Top tips. Careful reading of the question parts, in sequence, should be sufficient to indicate exactly what the examiner wanted. Advantages of the basic hierarchical (scalar chain) model; advantages of a different and more flexible (matrix) structure; ways of overcoming the limitations of this structure; and other ways of obtaining structural flexibility. The mark allocations are an equally useful guide to how much material is required for each question part – and how long each should take you to complete.

Easy marks. The question parts need to be tackled in order, as they follow a logical sequence. Advantages of a 'classical' structure should be straightforward: we have gone for extra credit by citing the main theorist in his area (Fayol), but you needn't have done this. Advantages and disadvantages of matrix structure are also basic – if you spotted that 'the concerns expressed by the company secretary' were simply the disadvantages. Part (d) is more challenging: think through what matrix *offers* (part (b)) – and how else the company could do that...

Examiner's comments. The examiner found it both disappointing and disturbing that candidates failed to understand what was meant by organisational structure; its importance as a communication/authority system; and the different forms it might take. Attempts to fill gaps in knowledge with complicated diagrams, restatements of the question and irrelevant comments did not gain marks.

Marking scheme

		Marks
(a)	Description of the advantages of a hierarchical structure	13
(b)	Description of the advantages of a matrix structure	15
(c)	Description of the way that the problems can be addressed	6
(d)	Description and understanding of a hybrid structure	6
		40

(a) **Advantages of the hierarchical structure**

> Note that we don't just describe hierarchical organisation: we highlight its *advantages*.

Formal organisation structure implies a framework of co-ordinated authority relationships, work flows and communication channels. The current hierarchical structure is modelled on classical principles of organisation (such as those put forward by Henri Fayol), which was explicitly intended to offer the following benefits.

(i) An unbroken line of authority and reporting **relationships**, through the scalar chain of command, ensuring systematic distribution of responsibility and clear accountability to aid managerial control.

(ii) The defined allocation of **responsibilities** for different areas and at different levels, as defined by roles within the hierarchy.

(iii) Division of labour based on functional **specialisation** of departments (and management), which offers efficiencies in standardisation of procedures, equipment sharing and technical proficiency.

(iv) Clear **task distribution**, so that gaps, duplications and other inefficiencies can be avoided or identified.

(v) **Unity of command**: clear command and reporting lines ('one person, one boss'), so that each subordinate knows to whom he or she is accountable.

(vi) **Unity of direction** (one head and one plan for each activity) arising from flow of authority from the management core.

(vii) Strong top-down **decision-making**, from the big-picture perspective of the overall corporate plan – rather than sub unit interests – and backed with clear positional authority.

(viii) An organisation **culture** based on recognition of defined roles, accountability and top-down command. This makes strong leadership possible where necessary (eg in change management).

(ix) A clear framework for training, **development** and succession planning: career 'ladders'.

(x) The **co-ordinating** mechanism of 'cross-over' points in the hierarchy, where managers act as information gatekeepers and liaison officers to integrate the goals and communication of two departments or sub-units.

(xi) Formal channels of **communication**, which ensure and co-ordinate the flow of information to and from those who require it for decision-making.

(b) **Advantages of introducing a matrix structure**

> Starting with a definition gives a solid grounding

Matrix structures essentially 'cross' functional and product/customer/project organisation, with multi-functional team members reporting both to their functional departmental managers and, in matters relating to a given product/customer/project, to the team leader.

The advantages of such an approach may be listed as follows.

> It is always worth referring to a named writer where possible, to demonstrate study...

(i) The removal of **barriers** to direct 'horizontal' communication and work flow from one function to another. According to Tom Peters, this is crucial to effective customer care, since customer experience is primarily horizontal (dealing with different functions in sequence).

(ii) The removal of vertical communication and authorisation channels, speeding up cross-functional **decision-making**. Again, this is considered crucial to responsive customer care, in the face of increasing customer demands for flexibility and speed of service.

(iii) A customer/product focus tends to enhance managers' awareness of the **market**, customer demands and competitive advantage. This in turn should result in both:

- Enhanced product knowledge, and
- More competitive, customer-focused decision-making

(iv) Control over individual products/projects/accounts is improved by de-centralising budgetary control, team member selection, profit centres etc.

(v) Employees develop a tolerance for ambiguity and flexibility, which facilitates organisational **responsiveness** to change.

These points will all be useful when it comes to part (d) – gaining 'some of the benefits' of matrix... The reference to project teams is a good place to start...

(vi) Functional monopolies are broken down, creating a more flexible and quality-supporting **internal customer** orientation.

(vii) There is more direct lateral **communication** between different functions, encouraging co-ordination, problem-solving and ideas generation for innovation.

(viii) Matrix structures are **flexible**: project teams can be put together, amended and disbanded as required, once the working methods and attitudes supporting them are in place.

(ix) There is opportunity to improve inter-disciplinary **co-operation** and knowledge/skill sharing.

(x) Employees may experience greater **participation** in planning and control decisions, as interpersonal management replaces impersonal rules and programmes. This may enhance job satisfaction and commitment.

(xi) Cross-functional experience is useful for employee (and especially management) **development** and training.

(xii) Managers are required to develop **interpersonal skills**, enhancing their 'leadership' (as opposed to 'management') effectiveness.

Such benefits may be available for a medium-sized organisation like Greg Pye's, and are especially desirable in the face of increasing competition and environmental change.

(c) **Addressing potential drawbacks of matrix structure**

Note that we refer our answers to the *scenario* whenever possible.

The Company Secretary has highlighted the main potential drawback of matrix structures: the ambiguity of authority/reporting relationships, which violates the classical principle of unity of command. Greg Pye can address this difficulty essentially by educating and supporting managers and team members to appreciate and adjust to the new structure.

(i) Developing clear reporting systems and guidelines, so that boundaries of authority and reporting relationships are defined for different tasks and situations.

(ii) Establishing regular (formal and informal) communication between functional managers and team leaders, to improve collaboration and co-ordination. This should ensure that functional managers are made aware in advance of the team's demands on staff time. It should also involve them in the product/customer focused decision-making process, reducing resistance.

(iii) Ensuring that managers are willing and able to counsel and coach employees where they need guidance in negotiating conflicts and ambiguities: upward communication must be encouraged.

(iv) Fostering a product/customer focused culture throughout the organisation (by the messages given from the senior management team, rewards, training, selection/promotion criteria and so on). This should restore 'unity of direction' by establishing strong guiding values (Peters and Waterman).

(v) Preparing the ground for matrix structure by establishing multi-functional working groups or task forces to discuss product/customer issues.

(vi) Implementing team development and team building exercises to establish new cross-functional teams.

(d) **Alternative methods of gaining some of the benefits of matrix structure**

We set out clearly the nature of the argument to show our understanding, before tackling the detail that follows from it.

The key benefit of the matrix structure is the flexibility gained from cross-functional ('horizontal') communication and skill-sharing. This can be achieved in various ways without fully restructuring Greg Pye's organisation.

(i) Some units of the organisation could be organised as a matrix (perhaps starting with customer-facing units) while others retain the traditional hierarchical structure. Research and development might, for example, benefit from cross-functional input from marketing and production. Customer service teams would benefit from immediate access to delivery, production and maintenance input. The production department, which relies to a greater extent on standardised procedures, might remain as it is.

(ii) Cross-functional communication, co-operation and co-ordination could initially (or additionally) be improved by other means, such as:

Bullet points can be used to show the examiner that 3 marks-earning points have been made.

- Introducing periodic cross-functional meetings involving selected managers and staff
- Giving key managers responsibility for acting as 'liaison' officers and gatekeepers, specifically to share information across departmental boundaries
- Forming cross-functional product/customer-focused quality circles or task forces which meet regularly to discuss shared concerns, suggestions and topics of interest

4 Management and supervision

Text reference. These issues are covered in Chapter 2.

Top tips. This should have been straightforward, as long as: (a) you recognised the reference to Fayol and were not distracted by the use of the term 'duties' for what are more usually referred to as 'functions' of management; (b) you noted the keyword 'differences' – and did not attempt to describe the role of a supervisor in detail. A useful exercise in answer planning: note that you have to produce 10 marks' worth of material for part (a) (requiring at least some explanation for each of the five functions of management) and only 5 marks' worth for part (b).

Easy marks. If you'd done the revision you should be able to get close to full marks here. Plan for 2 marks' worth of each of Fayol's functions: one to identify each correctly, and one to *explain* what it involves.

Examiner's comments. Some candidates confused their theories and either wrote about Fayol's 'principles of organisation' (division of labour, span of control and so on) or wrote about Mintzberg's managerial roles: read the question carefully and answer the question asked! Surprisingly, too many candidates also failed to appreciate or explain the key difference between management and supervision.

(a) **Fayol's five functions of management**

Fayol classified managerial activity into five key functions, which reflect the classical view of the task of management primarily as controlling resources and processes, rather than people.

(i) **Planning**: determining objectives – and strategies, policies, programmes and procedures for achieving those objectives – for the organisation and its sub-units. Planning is a foundational task in classical management thinking, as it provides purpose, direction and control for the organisation and its resources.

(ii) **Organising**: establishing a structure of tasks which need to be performed to achieve the goals of the organisation; grouping these tasks into jobs for individuals and teams; allocating jobs to sections and departments; delegating authority to carry out the jobs; and providing systems of information and communication, for the co-ordination of activities.

(iii) **Commanding**: giving instructions to subordinates to carry out tasks for which the manager has authority (to make decisions) and responsibility (for performance). It is assumed that subordinates will carry out tasks when commanded or instructed to do so: the more modern concept of managers' motivating and communicating roles was not fully developed in classical theory.

(iv) **Co-ordinating**: harmonising the goals and activities of individuals and groups within the organisation. Management must reconcile differences in approach, effort, interest and timing, in favour of overall (or 'super-ordinate') shared goals.

(v) **Controlling**: measuring and correcting the activities of individuals and groups, to ensure that their performance is in accordance with plans. Deviations from plans are identified and corrected, by adjusting performance or the plans themselves.

(b) **Difference between supervision and management**

As the supervisor's job is a junior management job, the tasks of supervision are similar to those of management, but supervision has **several distinguishing features**.

(i) Supervisors are **usually front line managers**, dealing directly with the levels of the organisation where the basic work is done. They therefore deal with matters such as health and safety at the operational level, while managers may deal with such matters primarily at a strategic or policy-making level.

(ii) Supervisors are the **interface between workers and management**: their subordinates are non-managerial employees, whereas managers may manage lower levels of management.

(iii) Supervisors do not spend all their time on the managerial aspects of the job, as they have their **own technical or operational work to perform**.

(iv) Supervisors monitor and control work by means of day-to-day, frequent and detailed information. Higher levels of management plan and control using longer-term and less detailed information (reporting by exception).

5 Mintzberg's managerial roles

Text reference. Mintzberg's role model is discussed in Chapter 2.

Top tips. The question is helpfully structured to encourage you to write a brief introduction to Mintzberg's views in part (a) – *before* you list or describe the managerial roles. (You won't get marks for duplicating them in parts (a) and (b).) The question stem gives you a hint, by highlighting research (by Mintzberg: remember that the question stem is linked to its requirements!) showing that the real world of management is less systematic than classical management theory had suggested.

Easy marks. If you recall Mintzberg's popular model in detail, you could be confident of some easy marks just by identifying the 10 roles correctly: a brief explanation of what each role involves should be sufficient to justify the additional marks for 'describing' them.

If you hadn't revised this material in detail, easy marks might be hard to come by. You might, therefore, consider using this as your opt-out question (since the other questions are less theoretically specific in their requirements). *don't* be tempted to substitute discussion of Mintzberg's other models (eg components of organisational structure): the question specifically refers to managerial roles.

Examiner's comments. Candidates lost marks for discussing Fayol, or Mintzberg's work on structure: evidence of careless question reading.

Marking scheme

			Marks
(a)	Brief description of Mintzberg's view of the management process		3
(b)	Description and discussion of the three management roles		
	• Interpersonal role (Figurehead, Leader, Liaison)	4	
	• Informational role (Monitor, Disseminator, Spokesperson)	4	
	• Decisional role (Entrepreneur, Disturbance handler, Resource allocatur, Negotiator)	4	
			12
			15

(a) **Mintzberg's view of the managerial process**

Mintzberg's studies and conclusions debunked several myths about managerial work which had arisen from the more theoretical perspective of the classical management school. The classical school suggested that management is a discrete, reflective and systematic process.

In contrast, Mintzberg found that managers are not reflective, systematic planners. Managerial work is disjointed and discontinuous, and managers often have routine duties to perform. Management, rather than being a 'science', is the practice of judgement and intuition, gained from experience in particular situations, and informal (often verbal) interpersonal communication.

Reflecting this complexity, Mintzberg developed a model of the various roles performed by managers across the full range of their functional responsibilities.

(b) **Three key managerial roles identified by Mintzberg**

Mintzberg argued that in their daily working lives, managers fulfil three types of managerial role.

(i) *Interpersonal roles*, based on the manager's formal authority or position in the organisation structure. A manager may act as:

- Figurehead: representing the organisation in the outside world
- Leader: managing human resources
- Liaison: making contacts within the organisation, across functional boundaries

(ii) *Informational roles*, based on the manager's access to upward and downward channels of communication in the organisation, and external networks and contacts. A manager may act as:

- Monitor: gathering information from the environment
- Spokesperson: providing information on behalf of the team or organisation
- Disseminator: passing information on to subordinates and colleagues

(iii) *Decisional roles*, based on the manager's formal authority and access to information, which allow him or her to take decisions relating to the work of the department as a whole. A manager may act as:

- Entrepreneur: evaluating opportunities and initiating projects
- Disturbance handler: responding to problems and conflicts as they arise
- Resource allocatur: deciding where to direct scarce resources
- Negotiator: obtaining resources and decisions in the interests of the team.

6 Excellence

Text reference. The 'excellence' model is covered in Chapter 2.

Top tips. This is an unusually un-structured question. You need to make sure: (a) that you give your answer a clear structure; and (b) that you show that you have made enough valid points to earn 15 marks! The two things go hand in hand. If you could recall all eight of the attributes of 'excellence'. You only had to 'discuss' each briefly: 8 x 2 marks is more than enough! We've added some introductory material – and a 'discussion' of Peter's work. (Note that 'discuss' means 'present a balanced argument'...)

Easy marks. If you didn't know Peter's work, or didn't connect the question with 'excellence', you may have struggled to find any easy marks. However, you could still have talked more generally about Peters' work on culture, horizontal structures, thriving on chaos and other more familiar aspects.

Examiner's comments. This was a very unpopular question, dealing with the relationship between management and culture and organisational success. Candidates either knew the answer or did not. Most of the answers tended to be general in approach and displayed no specific knowledge, or introduced other management writers which were clearly irrelevant.

Marking scheme

	Marks
Description of the thinking behind the characteristics	3
Description of any six of the individual characteristics – 2 marks each	12
	15

Peters and Waterman, in their book *In Search of Excellence*, found that the 'dominance and coherence of culture' was an essential feature of the 'excellent' companies they observed. A 'handful of guiding values' was more powerful than the standard tools of management such as manuals, rule books, budgets, plans, norms and controls formally imposed (and resisted).

The particular characteristics displayed by successful businesses, as identified by Peters, are as follows:

(a) **A bias for action**. The encouragement of an informal, innovative, task oriented culture not based on formal systems

(b) **Close to the customer**. A culture of listening to customers and being very focused on customer service

(c) **Autonomy and entrepreneurship**. The fostering of innovation and the use of product champions where risk taking and original thinking is encouraged

(d) **Productivity through people**. People in the organisation are seen as the basic source of quality. Staff are encouraged and praised, and a team approach is developed

(e) **Hands on, value driven**. The values of the business and its objectives are shared by all the organisation's members, and are held to be very important

(f) **Stick to the knitting**. The organisation grows through internally generated diversification. There is no movement into peripheral markets, or products outside the core business. Things are kept simple.

(g) **Simple form, lean staff**. There are no complicated organisational and management structures. Simple product divisional forms are used.

(h) **Simultaneous loose-tight properties**. Autonomy and responsibility is pushed down the organisation. However, core values such as the control of quality are centralised.

However, the ideas in *In Search of Excellence* have since been criticised, not least by Tom Peters himself.

(a) Some of the companies identified as 'excellent' have stumbled in their business performance, and severe structural/cultural dysfunctions have come to light. This casts doubt on the assumptions underlying the definition of excellence/success.

(b) While strong cultures can be helpful in creating a sense of direction and commitment within an organisation, they can also be dysfunctional. Strong cultures can impede necessary change. (Shared cultural values may be negative, or may focus on the needs of the informal organisation rather than the business.)

(c) The approach is somewhat prescriptive (suggesting 'one best way' to be 'successful'). This runs counter to the insight of contingency theory that successful managerial strategies can only be formulated in the context of a number of organisational and environmental variables.

7 Types of culture

Text reference. Culture, and Handy's model, are discussed in Chapter 3.

Top tips. This is a very clear question, and can be tackled in a straightforward way. Note that in part (a) you are asked to define *and* describe culture: even for 3 marks, you need to show a grasp of some detail! Part (b) clearly requires a description of *Handy's* typology: don't get side-tracked into other areas of the topic!

Easy marks. The first 3 marks should be straightforward – but if 'Handy's four cultural types' did not ring a bell, you should probably not have chosen this as one of your optional questions... If you were able to *identify* the four cultural types, though, you could probably piece together what is meant by 'task' and 'role' culture, and perhaps also 'person' culture. This would gain you the basic marks.

Examiner's comments. This was a very popular question, but candidates either knew the answer or did not. Interestingly in part (b), many candidates used the 'Gods' description (which was acceptable) in preference to the original descriptions. Surprisingly, very few identified the link between culture and organisational structure.

Marking scheme

		Marks
(a)	Explanation of what is meant by the term 'culture' in the organisational context	3
(b)	Description of Handy's four cultural types (3 marks each)	12
		15

(a) **Organisational culture** is the complex body of shared beliefs, attitudes and values in an organisation

Item	Examples
Beliefs and values, which are often unquestioned	Attitude to customers, for example: 'The customer always prefers good quality to a cheaper price'
Customs: acceptable ways of behaviour, sometimes enforced by rules	In the City of London, standard business dress is still taken for granted
Artefacts: tools, buildings office layout	Some companies encourage communication between employees by setting aside spaces for the purpose.
Rituals: formal, repeated behaviour	Sales people might compete with each other, and there is a reward for the salesperson who does best in any period.
Symbols: signs which stand in for other signs	Within the organisation, symbols can represent power; dress, make and model of car, office size and equipment and access to facilities can all be important symbols.

(b) Handy's four cultural types are differentiated by their structures, processes and management methods. These differences are so significant as to create **distinctive cultures** (defined by Harrison), to each of which Handy gave the name of a Greek God.

(i) **Zeus** is the god representing the **power culture**. Power and influence stem from a central source, perhaps the owner-directors or the founder of the business. The degree of formalisation is limited, and there are few rules and procedures. Such a firm is likely to be organised on a **functional** basis.

(1) The organisation is capable of adapting quickly to meet change.

(2) Personal influence decreases as the size of an organisation gets bigger. **The power culture is therefore best suited to smaller entrepreneurial organisations, where the leaders have direct communication with all employees**.

(3) Personnel have to get on well with each other for this culture to work.

(ii) **Apollo** is the god of the **role culture** or bureaucracy. There is a presumption of logic and rationality.

(1) These organisations have a formal structure, and operate by well-established rules and procedures. Individuals are required to perform their job to the full, but not to overstep the boundaries of their authority. Individuals who work for such organisations tend to learn an expertise without experiencing risk; many do their job adequately, but are not over-ambitious.

(2) **The bureaucratic style can be very efficient** in a stable environment, when the organisation is large and when the work is predictable. It would be slow to change.

(iii) **Athena** is the goddess of the **task culture.** Management is seen as completing a succession of projects or solving problems.

(1) The task culture is reflected in project teams and task forces. In such organisations, **there is no dominant or clear leader. The principal concern in a task culture is to get the job done**. Therefore the individuals who are important are the **experts** with the ability to accomplish a particular aspect of the task. Job satisfaction is high.

(2) Performance is judged by **results**.

(3) Task cultures are **expensive**, as experts demand a market price.

(4) Task cultures also depend on **variety**, and to tap creativity requires a tolerance of perhaps costly mistakes.

(iv) **Dionysus** is the god of the **existential** or **person culture**. In the three other cultures, the individual is subordinate to the organisation or task. **An existential culture is found in an organisation whose purpose is to serve the interests of the individuals within it**. These organisations are rare, although an example might be a partnership of a few individuals who do all the work of the organisation themselves (with perhaps a little secretarial or clerical assistance).

(1) Barristers in the UK work through chambers. The clerk co-ordinates their work and hands out briefs, but does not control them.

(2) Management in these organisations is often lower in status than the professionals.

(3) The organisation depends on the **talent of the individuals;** management is derived from the consent of those being managed.

8 Culture

Text reference. These cultural issues are discussed in Chapter 3.

Top tips. Note that this question does not give you any excuse for discussing different types or classifications of organisational culture. It asks you for the ways in which culture manifests or shows itself: some hints are already given in the introduction to the question. It then asks you to suggest why culture is important: it is, in fact, inevitable (every organisation has a culture) but what *effects* – positive or negative – might it have that would lead an organisation to want to *manage* its culture to its benefit.

Easy marks. Part (a) should be straightforward – but don't forget to give *examples*. (Since the examiner has specifically required examples, you will *lose* marks for not providing them. As a general rule, the examiner *likes* to see examples, and gives them credit – as long as the required *theoretical* points are also in place!)

(a) **Manifestations of culture**

Definition

Handy sums up 'culture' as 'that's the way we do things round here'. For Schein, it is 'a pattern of basic assumptions that... have worked well enough to be considered valid and, therefore, to be taught to new members as the correct way to perceive, think and feel'.

Ways in which culture is manifested

(i) **Beliefs, values and attitudes:** for example, values about quality or the customer ('the customer is king'), attitudes towards rules, change, risk ('Slow and steady wins the race') and so on. Attitudes and values will be reflected in the kind of people the organisation employs (their age, education and personality), the degree of delegation and communication and so on.

(ii) **Customs:** acceptable ways of behaving, sometimes enforce by written or unwritten rules. The formality of relationships, dress and ways of speaking are a classic example. Communication and decision-making styles (collaborative or command-and-control) are more complex customs.

(iii) **Artefacts:** visible products and tools through which the organisation expresses its 'style'. The style of the offices or other premises, the corporate identity expressed in letterheads and logos, dress codes, display 'trophies' and so on are visible signs of how the organisation regards itself.

(iv) **Rituals:** formal, repeated behaviours that take on special significance. Organisations may use 'ceremonial' behaviours to open meetings, to congratulate successful performers, to celebrate staff birthdays and so on.

(v) **Symbols:** signs which express values and attitudes. Symbols include the 'badges of status' which are prized in the organisation: a corner office, access to executive facilities, company cars and so on. They may, however, be tied into the mythology of the organisation.

(b) **The importance of culture**

(i) It affects the motivation and satisfaction of employees. A positive culture can encourage commitment to the organisation and its objectives, make employees feel valued and trusted and use 'guiding values' instead of rules.

(ii) It affects the adaptability of the organisation. A positive culture can encourage innovation, acceptable risk-taking, sensitivity to the environment, customer care, willingness to try new methods and technologies and so on.

(iii) It affects the organisation's image in the outside world, and particularly its appeal to potential employees and customers.

(iv) It affects specific areas of operation. 'Macho' cultures, for example, have been shown to encourage unacceptable levels of risk-taking in regard to health and safety.

(v) It creates a predisposition which may undermine attempts at behavioural change. Peters, for example, suggested that IBM's attempts to decentralise were undermined by an essentially bureaucratic culture.

9 Informal organisation

Text reference. This issue is discussed, as a contributor to culture, in Chapter 3.

Top tips. The introduction to the question raises the important point that formal and informal organisations co-exist: managers do not have a choice of whether to have or allow an informal organisation. Understanding and managing the informal organisation (as far as possible) will therefore be valuable. If you correctly identified what was meant by the term 'informal organisation', the rest should be straight forward, but note that part (c) is really two questions in one.

Easy marks. Once you have identified the elements of features of informal organisation (for part (a)), it should be easier to work out what the *benefits* of those features are. (What's helpful about informal communication? Shortcuts? Relationships?) The same process should get you most of the marks for parts (b) and (c)...

Answer plan

It is worth doing a brief answer plan, if only to *ensure* that you've included *all* the question requirements: for example, reminding yourself that there's a second part to part (c).

A simple plan (not too time-consuming) might look like this.

(a) Informal organisation
- Lateral relationships
- Grapevine
- Norms
- leaders

(b) Advantages
- Satisfaction
- Info sharing
- Speed of communication/action
- Flexibility
- Co-ordination

(c) Dangers
- Vs. organisational interests
- Inaccurate info
- Exclusion
- 'Cut corners'

Minimised by
- Meeting social needs
- *Using* elements
- Manager involvement

You should be able to see how this expands to our answer...

(a) **Informal organisation**

Unlike the formal organisation, the **informal organisation** is loosely structured, flexible and spontaneous. It embraces such mechanisms as:

(i) Social relationships and groupings (eg cliques) within – or across – formal structures

(ii) The 'grapevine', 'bush telegraph', or informal communication which by-passes the formal reporting channels and routes

(iii) Behavioural norms and ways of doing things, both social and work-related, which may circumvent formal procedures and systems (for good or ill). New members must 'learn the ropes' and get used to 'the way we do things here'

(iv) Power/influence structures, irrespective of organisational authority: informal leaders are those who are trusted and looked to for advice

(b) **Benefits of the informal organisation**

(i) The meeting of employees' social needs may contribute to **morale and job satisfaction**, with benefits in reduced absenteeism and labour turnover.

(ii) **Knowledge sharing.** The availability of information through informal networks can give **employees a wider perspective** on their role in the task and the organisation, potentially stimulating 'big picture' problem-solving, cross-boundary co-operation and innovation.

(iii) **Speed.** Informal networks and methods may **sometimes be more efficient in achieving** organisational goals, where the formal organisation has rigid procedures or lengthy communication channels, enabling decisions to be taken and implemented more rapidly.

(iv) The directness, information-richness and flexibility of the informal organisation may be particularly helpful in conditions of rapid **environmental change,** facilitating both the mechanisms and culture of anti-bureaucratic responsiveness.

(v) The formation and strengthening of interpersonal networks **can facilitate teamworking and co-ordination across organisational boundaries.** It may reduce organisational politics – or utilise it positively by mobilising effective decision-making coalitions and by-passing communication blocks.

(c) **Managing the informal organisation**

Each of the positive attributes of informal organisation could as easily be detrimental if the power of the informal organisation is directed towards goals unrelated to, or at odds with, those of the formal organisation.

(i) **Social groupings may act collectively against organisational interests**, strengthened by collective power and information networks. Even if they are aligned with organisational goals, group/network maintenance may take a lot of time and energy away from tasks.

(ii) The **grapevine is notoriously inaccurate** and can carry morale-damaging rumours.

(iii) The **informal organisation can become too important** in fulfilling employees' needs: individuals can suffer acutely when excluded from cliques and networks.

(iv) Informal work practices may **'cut corners'**, violating safety or quality assurance measures.

Such dangers can be **minimised** by:

(i) Meeting employees' needs as far as possible via the formal organisation: providing information, encouragement, social interaction and so on

(ii) Harnessing the dynamics of the informal organisation – for example by using informal leaders

(iii) Involving managers in the informal structure so that they support information sharing, the breaking down of unhelpful rules and so on

10 Scenario: Groups and teams

Text reference. All these points are discussed in detail in Chapter 4.

Top tips. We've already given a helping hand. The main requirement is to tackle each question part accurately and systematically. You *must* learn Tuckman and Belbin in full: this is classic question territory!

Easy marks. The first part of part (a) are the easiest marks (probably worth about 10) – as, after that, you have to *apply* the theories to the scenario, without much information to go on. You'd get some marks for describing five Belbin roles and attributing them plausibly to the individuals – even if your labels weren't the same as the examiner had in mind...

Examiner's comments. This was not a difficult question and was in general very well answered. The answer to part (a) required an understanding of group and team development stages, based upon the work of Tuckman. Almost all candidates answered this part correctly.

Marking scheme

			Marks
(a)	Description of Tuckman's stages of group development and explanation of the group stages (2 marks per development stage) 2 marks for identifying the team stage prior to Olivia's departure; 3 marks for identifying the stages the group reverted to after her departure – forming and storming)		15
(b)	Olivia's role and its characteristics	5	
	Description of the team roles (2 marks each)	10	
	Problems after Olivia's departure	5	
			20
(c)	Recommendation on reversion to former cohesiveness		5
			40

(a) Four stages in group development were identified by Tuckman (1965).

Step 1 Forming

The team is just coming together. Each member wishes to impress his or her **personality** on the group. The individuals will be trying to find out about each other, and about the aims and norms of the team. There will at this stage probably be a **wariness about introducing new ideas**. The **objectives** being pursued may as yet be **unclear** and a leader may not yet have emerged. This period is essential, but may be time wasting: the team as a unit will not be used to being autonomous, and will probably not be an efficient agent in the planning of its activities or the activities of others.

Step 2 Storming

This frequently involves more or less open **conflict** between team members. There may be **changes** agreed in the original objectives, procedures and norms established for the group. If the team is developing successfully this may be a fruitful phase as more realistic targets are set and **trust** between the group members increases.

Step 3 Norming

A period of **settling down**: there will be agreements about work sharing, individual requirements and expectations of output. Norms and procedures may evolve which enable)

Step 4 Performing

The team sets to work to execute its task. The difficulties of growth and development no longer hinder the group's objectives.

Step 5 Dorming

This has been suggested as a final stage, when the team becomes complacent and is not really interested any more in the task it was set up to perform. The main goal of this stage tends to be self-preservation.

Before Olivia's departure, the scenario clearly indicates that the group was working well in the performing stage. After her departure and the recruitment of four new members, the group reverted to the forming and storming stages, characterised by wariness (of the new members of the group) disagreements and a failure to work together as well as before. (In an addition to Tuckman's model, this may also be identified as the 'mourning' or 'adjourning' stage of readjustment following change).

(b)

Examiner's comments. Part (b) concerned Belbin's team roles. Section (iii) in particular was poorly answered. The departure of the 'shaper' from the team will have had a damaging effect upon the group and necessitated the recruitment of four new members. Many answers missed this.

(i) Olivia played the central role of the **shaper**. This is one of Belbin's key 'leader' roles. The scenario describes her as dominant, extrovert, passionate about the task, a spur to action.

(ii) The other members fulfilled the following roles.

Co-ordinator	Presides, provides leadership and co-ordinates; balanced, disciplined, good at working with others. This is Neville's role.
Monitor-evaluator	Analytically (rather than creatively) intelligent; dissects ideas, spots flaws; possibly aloof and tactless – but a necessary member of the group. This is Peter's role.
Resource-investigator	Popular, sociable, extrovert, relaxed; source of new contacts, but not an originator; needs to be made use of. This is Rosalind's role.
Implementer	Practical organiser, turning ideas into tasks via scheduling and planning; trustworthy and efficient, but not excitable; not a leader, but an administrator. This is Quentin's role.
Team worker	Most concerned with team maintenance – supportive, understanding, diplomatic; popular but uncompetitive – contribution noticed only in absence. This is Suki's role.

(iii) As Olivia was the shaper, the driving force behind the performance of the team has gone. Her energy and passion for the 'Rockers' group must be found in another team member or a new recruit. Neville is not a leader in the same mould: he is more of an organiser.

As Belbin's model involves eight process roles, which should ideally be balanced and evenly 'spread' in the team, it may be that the team is now seriously lacking the requisite balance of roles: another member may need to adopt the shaper role. At present, the team is strong on people who implement and work with ideas – but it no longer has an initiator or driver of ideas.

(c)

Examiner's comments. Although in many cases this part was answered well, many candidates failed to link the answer to the topic of the scenario. To rebuild team cohesiveness, the vacancy would have had to be identified and filled and the team would once again have to go through the stages of development described in part (a) of the question.

Neville needs to rebuild the team, by playing close attention to Belbin's team roles and identifying where vacancies for the various roles exist (this is in addition to specific skill requirements). All of these roles need to be filled in order for the team to be successful.

The team will need to go through the stages of team development again. Some people may have more than one team role skill, so their best fit needs to be found for the good of the team. Often a team does not work well at all, due to incompatible personalities.

The personalities and goals of the individual members of the team, along with their specific skills, will probably help to determine the group goals, so it is possible that with the recruitment of new members the focus of 'Rockers' may change in some way. This is especially likely to be the case if the group gets a lot bigger (or smaller).

11 Team working

Text reference. All these issues are covered in Chapter 4.

Top tips. In part (b), be careful not to go into too much detail about team roles (Belbin), as you will need to expand on this for part (c). Note, too, that you are only required to describe three of Belbin's team roles in part (c). We have picked three: please check your study text carefully if you chose different ones.

Easy marks. The difference between teams and groups should be straightforward, as should factors in team success. (you may have chosen to cite Woodcock's 'building blocks' of successful teams, for extra credit). Part (c) is only challenging because it requires you to get the roles straight in your head – but then, you only need to sure of *three...*

Examiner's comments. The examiner was surprised that this question was not popular, as it was intended to be straightforward. Common pitfalls included inaccurate reading of instruction key words (eg trying to describe more than three roles in part (c)) and inaccurate reading of topic key words (eg discussing Tuckman instead of Belbin).

Marking scheme

		Marks
(a)	Recognition of different between teams and groups	4
(b)	Team success factors	5
(c)	Explain any three roles (up to 2 marks for each role)	6
		15

(a) **Groups and teams**

A group has been defined as 'any collection of people who perceive themselves to be a group'. It has a sense of identity, acknowledged boundaries and loyalty. A group may also have a defined purpose and leadership, but in a work context, a group is generally understood to be **informal** in its composition, structure and leadership.

A team is a **formal** group, intentionally formed and organised by the organisation, for a task for which they are held responsible. Katzenbach and Smith define a team as 'a small number of people with complementary skills who are committed to a common purpose, performance goals and approach for which they hold themselves basically accountable'. The key differences from a group are therefore:

(i) Formal delegated authority (which may be reflected in appointed leadership)
(ii) Intentional composition to include complementary skills
(iii) Accountability to performance goals

(b) **A variety of factors will contribute to team success**

(i) **Leadership** is probably the most important single factor and the one most often lacking. Good leadership will promote co-operation between team members, motivate the individuals towards the task and ensure that work is properly organised.

(ii) The **task** or **role** of the team must be defined. This can be seen in terms of the objectives set for the leader, since the leader must take responsibility for the team's work.

(iii) The members of the team must possess the **right mix of skills** required for them to perform their roles. To some extent, these can be learned on the job, under the supervision of the leader.

(iv) A proper level of **resources** must be provided, though motivation can overcome many resource deficiencies.

(v) The efforts of the team must be **co-ordinated** with those of the rest of the organisation. To some extent this is a task for the leader, but there must be mechanisms in place to allow sideways communication between team members and other parts of the organisation and to permit proper response to changed circumstances.

(c) **Belbin's team roles**

Belbin argued that a distinction needs to be made between team roles ('a tendency to behave, contribute and interrelate with others at work in certain distinctive ways') and functional roles (job demands). His team role classifications (nine in all) include:

(i) The **Co-ordinator** or **Chairman**. This role contributes by clarifying goals, promoting decision-making and delegating effectively. It is the natural preference of people who are mature and confident, able to act as a communication hub.

(ii) The **Team Worker**. This role contributes by supporting the team maintenance activity which keeps team processes and co-operative working operating smoothly: listening, relationship-building, averting friction, helping to resolve conflict. It is the natural preference of people who are co-operative, mild, perceptive and diplomatic.

(iii) **The Implementer** or **Company Worker**. This role contributes by taking the ideas (provided by Plants and Resource Investigators) and turning them into practical actions. It is the natural preference of people who are disciplined, reliable, conservative and efficient.

12 Team development

Text reference. Tuckman's model is discussed in Chapter 4.

Top tips. If you've been working through the kit, you may be thinking: 'not *another* Tuckman question'! the examiner keeps setting them, because students keep getting them wrong... This is an *unstructured* question, so it's up to you to give your answer structure *and* ensure that you've earned 15 marks. We've added a 'fifth' (non-Tuckman) stage to make mark allocation easy: 5 marks x 3 marks each.

Easy marks. If you've done the revision and planned your answer, these should *all* be easy marks.

Examiner's comments. This was a very straightforward question on a well known theory which attracted very good answers and high marks.

Marking scheme

	Marks
Description of the five stages of team development (3 marks each, including 'dorming')	15

A **team** is formally structured to perform shared task goals: its membership is selected and relatively fixed, and group dynamics are managed in such a way as to facilitate and control performance. While groups can form spontaneously, teams must be 'built' and developed.

Tuckman's stages in group formation

(i) **Forming** is the term given to the first stage, in which members are relatively unknown to each other as a group. Members try to find out about each other and about the aims and norms of the team.

Although each individual wishes to impress his or her personality on the group, there is usually some wariness about introducing new ideas until objectives and dynamics are known. The objective will as yet be unclear and the natural leader of the group may not yet have emerged.

This period is essential in the development of the team, but unproductive in terms of task output.

(ii) **Storming** is the term given to the second stage, in which uncertainty begins to issue in more or less open admission of differences and conflict between members.

There may be political competition for the leadership role, and conflict in the adoption of other team roles (eg those suggested by Belbin). The original objectives, procedures and norms established for the group may be challenged and changed as the team's strengths, weaknesses and needs become clearer.

This can be a fruitful phase of development, as more realistic targets are set, roles are clarified and open communication and trust are established. It may, however, be counter-productive if the team gets stuck in the conflict stage.

(iii) **Norming** is the term given to the third stage, which is a period of settling down. Arising from storming, the group will reach agreements and establish patterns in regard to such matters as working sharing, individual requirements, communication and decision-making processes and output expectations.

Group norms of behaviour and work procedures will evolve: if these are positive, they will enable methodical working to be introduced and maintained in the next phase. Groups can, however, develop negative norms. Constructive norms and dynamics should therefore be facilitated and reinforced.

(iv) **Performing** is the term given to the fourth and final stage in Tuckman's classification, in which the team has resolved its difficulties of roles, conflict and adjustment, and has developed the norms and dynamics required to operate effectively. It can now divert energy from group processes to task performance. The team sets to work to execute its task.

(v) Later writers noted a fifth stage in group development, which (following Tuckman's scheme) they called **dorming**. This is where the team has been performing effectively for some time, and becomes complacent. Little fresh energy is focused on the task – even in the face of change: instead, efforts are devoted primarily to team maintenance and member satisfaction. This reflects the negative effects of group cohesion known collectively as '**group think**'.

13 Scenario: Management, supervision and delegation

Text references. Chapter 2 discusses the roles of manager and supervisor. Responsibility, authority and delegation are covered in Chapter 5.

Top tips. Write an answer plan for part (a) of this question, which is relatively unstructured: bear in mind that your answer should be almost as substantial as a whole essay question, for 13 marks. Parts (b) and (c) are very highly structured, which is helpful – but also makes it very obvious if you waffle or don't answer the precise question requirements. You will need to be disciplined about dividing your time according to the marks available.

Note how explicit the examiner has been about the need to relate each of your answers to the situation at Flavours Fine Foods. Each time you make a theoretical point (eg about the need for delegation), use FFF as an illustrative example (eg the problems Alan Jones is experiencing through failing to delegate). This is a useful approach to any scenario question: look carefully at how we've used it in our answer.

Easy marks. These are all mainstream syllabus topics, so as long as you've avoided the very basic pitfalls of confused terminology, you should be able to get good marks – particularly since, for parts (b) and (c) it should be easy to get the first couple of marks for each subsection: they all add up!

Examiner's comments.

Generally well answered but many answers still failed to properly address the question asked. Too many answers failed to provide an adequate explanation of the work of the manager.

Marking scheme

			Marks
(a)	Explanation of the differences between the manager and supervisor		
	Five marks for the manager		
	Eight marks for the supervisor		
	(One mark for a specific reference to the *interface* role)		Up to 13 marks
			(Maximum for part (a) 13 marks)
(b)	Explanation of:		
	(i)	Responsibility	Up to 4 marks
	(ii)	Authority	Up to 3 marks
	(iii)	Delegation	Up to 3 marks
			(Maximum for part (b) 10 marks)
(c)	Explanation of:		
	(i)	The need for delegation	Up to 3 marks
	(ii)	Achieving effective delegation	Up to 6 marks
	(iii)	Problems with delegation	Up to 4 marks
	(iv)	How to overcome problems	Up to 4 marks
			(Maximum for part (c) 17 marks)
			(Total for question 40 marks)

(a) **Differences between management and supervision**

The roles of manager and supervisor reflect the hierarchy or 'scalar chain' of command in most formal organisation structures: in other words, they reflect the flow of decision-making responsibility down from the top of organisation to different tiers or levels of management.

Note that we clearly relate roles to the scenario

Alan Jones' role as senior manager differs in this respect from **Dean Watkins'** role as departmental manager, which in turn differs from that of his front line **supervisors**. Alan's focus will primarily be strategic (big picture, long term direction of Flavours Fine Foods), while Dean's will primarily be tactical (medium-term planning and control over his production department) and the supervisor's will be operational (day-to-day implementation of plans).

We use a named theory in support of our answer

The work of a manager can be described in various ways. Classical organisation theorists (such as **Henri Fayol**) described it terms of five functions: planning, organising, co-ordinating, controlling and commanding (what we might today call 'leading' or motivating people). The supervisor can be seen as the lowest level of management, carrying out these functions at the most detailed, operational, day-to-day level.

Clear focus on the differences, as the question requires

The **distinctive features** of the supervisory role, however, are as follows.

Note how we use the scenario to provide illustrative examples of key points

(i) The supervisor is a 'front-line' manager, dealing with the daily bread-and-butter work of the production lines. (S)he will deal with matters such as time-keeping, allocating work to team members and machines, and ensuring that health and safety rules are followed. **Dean** (the manager) might deal with similar issues but at a higher and broader level: setting plans, budgets and targets.

(ii) The supervisor will not spend all his or her time on the managerial aspects of the job: time will be spent doing technical/operational work (like repairing and operating the machines).

(iii) A supervisor is a gatekeeper or filter for communication between managerial and non-managerial staff: in this case, between shop floor workers and the departmental manager, Dean. This includes both upward communication (conveying reports and suggestions) and downward (conveying plans and instructions).

(iv) A supervisor monitors and controls work by means of day-to-day, frequent and detailed information: higher levels of management plan and control using longer-term, less frequent and less detailed information, which must be 'edited' or selected and reported by the supervisor.

(b) **Responsibility** is the obligation a person has to fulfil a task (s)he has been given. The term is used in different ways:

- Dean is responsible *to* Alan, in the sense that he must report to him about the production department's performance in line with the company's objectives. Another word for this is 'accountability'.
- Dean is responsible *for* the results achieved by the production department, in the sense that he is required to ensure that objectives are met.

We draw out key issues with reference to the hints given in the scenario

It may be argued that ultimate responsibility is held at the top of the organisation: Alan is, indeed, responsible to the owners of the company, for the **overall performance** of the organisation. However, the principle of delegation (discussed below), means that being 'responsible' for performance does not necessitate '**doing everything yourself**'.

Evidence of deeper reading indicating an excellent student

Authority is a person's legitimate right to do something, or to ask someone else to do it and expect it to be done. **French and Raven** related this to 'position power': the authority that comes from a position in the management hierarchy of an organisation. Alan has the authority to make strategic decisions on behalf of Flavours Fine Foods. However, Dean has been given (by delegation) authority

Note that we give 3 marks' worth *without* using material needed for part (c)

to make the decisions that affect his department. Dean has the right to make decisions within the scope of the authority given to him as a production manager.

Delegation is the process whereby a superior gives a subordinate part of his or her authority to make decisions. It enables authority to 'flow' down the organisation – precisely so that senior managers like Alan do *not* have to be involved in the more detailed running of operations. This creates a 'chain' of command, whereby authority flows down and reports flow back up: by issuing instructions direct to the supervisor, Alan has by-passed a key link in the chain (Dean), and trespassed on the authority which has been delegated to Dean.

Again, we 'personalise' basic theory to the scenario

(c) **The need for delegation**

It is important for managers like **Alan** to delegate because:

- There is a limit to the workload an individual manager can carry out effectively, especially in a growing organisation where increasing technical and managerial specialisation is required: Alan can't do all the work of FFF himself!
- Managers need time to focus on their higher-level tasks: by being over-involved in minor operational issues, Alan may be neglecting his role as strategic planner, figurehead and direction-setter for the organisation.
- Delegated authority contributes to the job satisfaction and development of lower levels of management, which is partly why failure to delegate (or ineffective delegation) is causing frustration.

How effective delegation can be achieved

Bullet points highlight the number of mark-worthy points – but are still in full English (not 'notes')

Effective delegation depends on a balance of control/support (so that people know exactly what is required and are equipped and empowered to do it) and backing off (so that people can show genuine discretion and initiative in the area of authority given to them). It involves:

- Clearly specifying performance: setting out the goals and standards expected of the subordinate. Alan and his brother should have set out clear objectives and success criteria for Dean and the other production managers.
- Formally assigning and agreeing responsibilities: FFF appears to have a clear and workable organisation structure, on paper.
- Allocating the resources and authority to fulfil the responsibilities: there are no identified problems at FFF in this respect.
- Backing off and allowing the subordinate to perform the delegated tasks. This is the key area in which Alan and Lee are delegating ineffectively, as seen by the perception that they are 'interfering' with day-to-day decisions and activities of their managers.
- Maintaining contact, to review progress made, make constructive criticism and be available to give help and advice if required. Alan and Lee have perhaps misunderstood the nature of this 'controlling' function, and have continued to intervene directly in work and decisions.

Problems with delegation

Many managers fail to delegate, for various reasons. In the case of FFF, the most likely reasons for failure to delegate effectively are perhaps that:

- Alan and Lee lack understanding of what delegation involves, the need to back off and to observe the chain of command, and the frustration their interference causes. This leads in turn to a lack of delegation skills.

You might back this up with Handy's 'trust-control dilemma' to show extra study

- Alan and Lee do not really trust their managers: they may still feel that FFF is 'their' business, and that nobody understands its operational needs the way they do. **Lack of trust** leads to the attempt to exercise tighter control.
- The company has grown so fast, Alan and Lee have not really got to grips with the role of senior/general management: they are still thinking in terms of the hands-on direct involvement appropriate to the early days of FFF.
- Alan and Lee may feel threatened by a perceived loss of control over 'their' business, perhaps even feeling threatened by the competence and succession potential of managers like Dean.

We draw on other syllabus areas, to make practical, realistic suggestions

How problems can be overcome

A first step has already been made in educating Alan and Lee in the nature and process of delegation: a similar programme may usefully be extended to all FFF managers. This could be reinforced by implementing regular **upward appraisal**, so that subordinates can freely give feedback to their superiors on the quality of their delegation.

In order to increase their trust in departmental managers (and sense of control), Alan and Lee should agree clear performance objectives, standards and accountabilities with them, and ensure regular, open communication of performance feedback. This would also create an agreed framework within which managers would retain discretion to make their own decisions.

The formal communication mechanisms of FFF may need to be improved, role descriptions developed, and the new organisation structure set out clearly in an organisation chart. Such measures would help everyone to understand their respective roles and responsibilities, and the correct communication/authority channels to pursue.

Alan and Lee should be encouraged to focus on their general management roles: to consider new strategies to consolidate and capitalise on FFF's growth, to develop new business or products, to investigate further international markets and so on.

14 Authority and responsibility

Text reference. All these issues are covered clearly in Chapter 5.

Top tips. The introduction to this question gives you a guideline for your answer. Authority without responsibility means that authority can be exercised in an irresponsible way. Responsibility without authority is frustrating and stressful, because the person is accountable for events over which he has no control. This is an unstructured question, which you may find harder to plan than a structured one: start by defining your terms, and ensure that you include sufficient content to warrant 15 marks.

As a framework, we suggest the following marking guide, which might also act as your answer plan.

Marking scheme

		Marks
(a)	Definition of authority and responsibility	2
(b)	Definition of a 'mismatch' between them	1
(c)	Effects of mismatch (2 marks each: 1 for identifying effect; 1 for explanation)	12
		15

This marking scheme was produced by BPP.

Delegated authority is a person's formal right to perform tasks and make decisions, which is passed down the scalar chain of command. **Responsibility is the level of performance and results for which that person is formally accountable** to his superiors.

A mismatch between the two would be defined as a situation where an individual has authority which exceeds his responsibility (that is, he is allowed to do things without being called to account for the results) or has responsibility without authority (that is, he is called to account for events over which he has no effective control).

If the formal organisation structure fails to make responsibility commensurate with authority (and vice versa) there will be **two main effects**.

(a) **Managers not held accountable** for their authority may exercise that authority in a **capricious or irresponsible way,** which will not necessarily be to the benefit of the organisation. Even if they have the best interests of the organisation at heart, they may take unacceptable risks, because the consequences of decisions will not rebound on them.

(b) Managers who are held accountable for aspects of performance which they have no authority to control are placed in an impossible situation and will become frustrated, stressed, demoralised and demotivated. Performance (and hence, potentially, that of the team) is likely to suffer.

There will also be **spin-off effects**.

(c) **The organisation will fail to learn from its mistakes if accountability fails to operate effectively.** If a superior has delegated authority to a subordinate but fails to make him accountable, the superior will (rightly) be made responsible for any problems arising from the subordinate's errors of judgement – but the problem will not necessarily be effectively analysed and solved. The control mechanisms of the organisation depend on accountability.

(d) If a superior does not give a subordinate enough **authority** to do a job, and the subordinate holds him accountable for failure to do the job properly, there is likely to be conflict. There will thus be two problems: likely failure in the task (because of inadequate resources to complete it effectively) and an on-going lack of co-operation, trust and respect in the work team.

(e) **The management style 'leave alone and zap' has found to be a major cause of work stress**, and such a style may be reflected in a failure to delegate adequate authority ('leave alone') followed by holding the subordinate to account ('zap').

(f) **Subordinates may complain that they have insufficient authority** to perform the tasks for which they are responsible, but this may be based on misperceptions. Subordinates may be demanding an impracticable degree of autonomy, or may misunderstand the nature of delegation. They may also 'feel' more responsible for results than their actually accountabilities indicate. Subordinates may not understand the extent to which work depends on co-ordination with other departments: final authority over a project may lie outside the department and not be within the power of the manager to delegate. The consequences of a perceived mismatch of authority and responsibility might therefore be a lack of co-ordination, inter-departmental territorial disputes and unofficial empire building.

15 Authority, responsibility and delegation

Text reference. All these issues are discussed in Chapter 5.

Top tips. This should have been straightforward, but you really had to make sure that you distinguished clearly and correctly between terms (a surprisingly common exam pitfall)! This is an example of a highly-structured question: note how much material you can (and are expected to) produce to earn 2 marks. It also illustrates another classic exam technique point: make sure you read question key words (*'how* effective delegation can be achieved') carefully.

Easy marks. Definitions of terms (part (a)) *should* be easy marks, setting you up for part (b) – although you need to ensure that your answer to part (b) doesn't just repeat what you've said in part (a)! You should then be able to earn at least the first few marks on delegation – particularly if you use the delegation sequence/cycle as a guide ('how to…').

Examiner's comments. Some candidates failed to recognise that part (c) was about how to achieve effective delegation – *not* why effective delegation was important (or any other variant).

Marking scheme

				Marks
(a)	(i)	Definition/understanding of responsibility	2	
	(ii)	Definition/understanding of authority	2	
	(iii)	Definition of delegation and understanding of its importance in formal organisations	2	6
(b)		Description of the differences between authority and responsibilities		2
(c)		Explanation of how effective delegation can be achieved		7
				15

(a) **Definition of terms**

(i) **Responsibility** expresses the obligation a person has to fulfil a task which (s)he has been given. A person is said to be responsible *for* a piece of work when he or she is required to ensure that the work is done. The same person is said to be responsible *to* a superior when he or she is given work by that superior: in this sense, the term 'accountable' is often used.

(ii) **Authority** expresses the right of a person to do something, or to ask someone else to do it and expect it to be done. Authority is another term for position or legitimate power, as it embodies the ability to do something, formally conferred by the holder's position in the organisation hierarchy.

(iii) **Delegation** expresses the process whereby a person gives to another person part of their own authority to undertake tasks or make decisions. This is commonly a 'downward' process in the scalar chain of command, with the delegation of authority by a superior to a subordinate, but there is also upward delegation (where a decision is referred to a superior).

(b) **Difference between authority and responsibility**

Other than the direct difference in the meaning of the terms themselves, there are key practical differences between authority and responsibility.

(i) The purpose of authority is to give a manager legitimate control over subordinates and resources, while the purpose of responsibility is to control managerial activity.

(ii) Authority can be delegated, but responsibility cannot. A manager may give subordinates the authority to carry out a task, but (s)he remains responsible (and accountable) for the results.

(c) **Achieving effective delegation**

Delegation is not easy and many managers are reluctant to delegate. Effective delegation can be achieved by:

(i) Clearly specifying performance: the goals and standards expected of subordinates

(ii) Taking into account the knowledge, skills and experience required to fulfil the task – and how far subordinates fulfil those requirements

(iii) Formally assigning tasks to subordinates, requiring their formal agreement and clear understanding.

(iv) Allocating adequate and appropriate resources and authority to subordinates to enable them to carry out the delegated tasks at the expected level of performance

(v) Setting clear accountabilities and reporting procedures, including what variances from plan should be reported, what decisions should be referred and so on.

(vi) 'Backing off' and allowing the subordinate to perform the delegated tasks, without over-controlling the process.

(vii) Maintaining contact, to review progress made, give constructive feedback and be available for help and advice if requested.

16 The purpose of objective setting

Text reference. This topic is covered in Chapter 6.

Top tips. This is another highly structured question, so your answers to the various parts can be brief – but time management may be an issue: you will need to use your prioritising and summarising skills. Part (a) allows you to distinguish between qualitative 'aims' and quantifiable 'objectives': resist the temptation to write about SMART objectives, which is not strictly relevant. Parts (b) and (c) ask you to distinguish between the benefits of objective-setting to the *organisation* and the effects of objective-setting on *individual behaviour*: motivation, learning and so on. Part (d) offers wide scope for specific answers: ours are suggestions only.

(a) **Objectives**

Objectives are operational, quantitative goals: desired results or outcomes which can be expressed in quantitative or numerical terms. Objectives can thus be distinguished from 'aims', which are non-operational, qualitative goals. There is likely to be a hierarchy of objectives, with a primary corporate objective (in business, usually profitability) and secondary or subordinate objectives (in areas such as market share or position, product development and so on).

(b) **Organisational purposes of objective-setting**

Objectives focus the energies of the organisation on its priorities for survival and prosperity. Objectives enable management to:

(i) Implement the corporate mission, by outlining what needs to be achieved

(ii) Publicise the direction and goals of the organisation to managers, staff and other stakeholders, so that they know where their efforts should be directed and how their own interests can be integrated with those of the organisation

(iii) Appraise the validity of strategic decisions, by assessing their effectiveness in achieving stated objectives

(iv) Assess and control actual performance, as objectives can be used as targets and yardsticks of achievement

(c) **Behavioural purposes of setting objectives**

People are 'purposive': they act in pursuit of particular goals. Goals or objectives influence what we perceive (because we filter out anything that is irrelevant to our goals), what we learn (because we modify our behaviour in order to meet our goals more effectively in future) and what we do (because we are motivated to behave in ways that meet our goals). Clear objectives help individuals to:

(i) Plan and direct their effort towards those objectives

(ii) Monitor their performance against objectives and adjust (learn) where required

(iii) Experience the reward of achievement, once objectives have been reached

(iv) Feel that their tasks have meaning and purpose, an important element in job satisfaction

(v) Experience the incentive (motivation) of a challenge: the need to expend energy and effort in a particular direction in order to achieve something

(vi) Avoid the de-motivation of impossible, unclear or inadequately rewarded tasks

(d) **Examples of organisational objectives**

(i) Specific targets for profitability, return on capital employed or earnings per share

(ii) Specific targets for market share or growth in market share

(iii) Specific targets for product development, investment in research and development or innovation

(iv) Specific targets for productivity, reductions in the cost per unit of output or quality improvements

(v) Specific targets for human resource utilisation and development, increases in employee retention or skill levels

17 Social responsibility

Text reference. This topic is covered, as a key corporate objective, in Chapter 6.

Top tips. This is a provocative question. The concept of 'enlightened self interest' is based on Friedman's assertion that the only responsibility of a business organisation (as opposed to a public sector one) is profit maximisation for the wealth of its owners over the long term. Business organisations do not have the luxury of being 'enlightened' purely for the sake of society, although they recognise society as stakeholders in the business. This argument underpins part (a): beware of citing social responsibility as a Good Thing in purely ideological terms, however you feel about it. Part (b) offers the opportunity to list many possible areas of concern and interest, of which our suggestions are only a sample: make sure that you include some specifically **ethical** objectives (such as eliminating bribery) as well as **socially responsible** ones (such as environmental conservation).

Easy marks. The easiest marks here are probably in part (b) – because there are plenty of examples you will be aware of. Part (a) is more challenging, though. The only way in is to think: what does being known for social responsibility do for an organisation (like The Body Shop)? What would being known for ethical or social *irresponsibility* do to an organisation (like Euron)?

(a) **Business benefits of social responsibility**

Socially responsible policies benefit the business in the following ways.

(i) Employee benefits over the statutory minimum may aid **the organisation in attracting, motivating and retaining high-quality staff,** particularly in times of competition for scarce skills.

(ii) Social responsibility reflects fashionable issues of concern among consumer and labour groups. Policies may be part of:

- The **product/service brand** of the organisation, attracting the trust and support (and therefore business) of like-minded consumers (as, for example, in the case of The Body Shop) and investors
- The **employer brand** of the organisation, positioning it as an ethical, trustworthy and people-friendly employer, enabling it to attract and retain skilled labour

(iii) Offering customer benefits, added value or quality may be perceived as socially responsible, but is also a powerful source of **customer loyalty**. Retaining customers, and gaining their repeat business, is far more cost effective than winning new customers.

(iv) **Sponsorship may also be perceived as socially responsible** in supporting the cultural, sporting or educational life of the community, but it is also an opportunity to raise brand awareness and exercise public relations activities.

(v) Sustainable economic and environmental practices are **investments in the prosperity of the business,** protecting working relationships, resource and investment streams over the long term.

(b) **Areas for socially responsible and ethical objectives**

Social responsibility

(i) Environmental impact study, waste management, ecology and conservation and so on
(ii) Product labelling, compensation to customers under Fair Trading legislation and so on
(iii) Health, safety, welfare, employment protection and consultation provisions for staff
(iv) Donations, sponsorships and staff secondments to charitable and community causes
(v) Supporting suppliers (especially in developing countries)

Business ethics

(i) Treatment of women, ethnic minorities and other disadvantaged groups in employment

(ii) Sustainable and ethical business and investment practices overseas (not exploiting cheap labour or resources, not investing in illegal or unethical businesses)

(iii) Policies on bribes, transparency and disclosure of conflicts of interest

(iv) Ethical contracts management (tendering, exploitation of contract labour)

The Body Shop and Johnson & Johnson are two examples of businesses which have positioned themselves as ethical leaders in their markets.

18 Performance management

Text reference. This topic is discussed in Chapter 6 (and raised again in the appraisal context in Chapter 11).

Top tips. The main exam pitfall in this area is confusing 'performance management' with something else – like appraisal or management by objectives. Fortunately, the examiner has clearly defined it for us – without giving any detail that would help with the answer... Jot down the elements of performance management to ensure you've got *five* stages.

Easy marks. If you couldn't recall five stages, this probably wouldn't be one of your first choices for your optional question. Don't despair too easily, though. 5 stages = 3 marks each. Even if you recalled 3 stages, this would be worth attempting – and might jog your memory of the other two...

Examiner's comments. This was not a popular question. It was designed to test candidates' knowledge of a contemporary approach to linking management and organisational success, that of performance management. Surprisingly few candidates were aware of this idea. Answers tended to be general in approach and showed no knowledge of the subject, with many discussing Fayol's management functions or performance appraisals.

Marking scheme

	Marks
Description of process of performance management (3 marks per step of process, five steps)	15

Performance management is an approach to performance appraisal and development which is designed to integrate individual, team and organisational goals in order to facilitate both employee commitment and business performance. The aim is for accountants (and other managers) to enable people to realise their potential and to maximise their contribution to the organisation.

The **process of performance management** may be described as five steps.

Step 1 Identify and describe the key functions, competencies, targets and standards required for job performance. This should be derived from the goals and objectives set out for the performance unit, which in turn should be derived from the corporate plan of the business as a whole.

Note. One of the purposes of performance management is to encourage awareness of the mission, goals and objectives of the enterprise: individual performance targets should be based on detailed annual plans underpinned by a clear strategic direction.

Step 2 Define realistic standards and conditions of performance, specific and measurable performance indicators and skill/competency requirements for the job. Taking advantage of input from job-holders as to the nature and requirements of the job, this should result in a mutually acceptable and understood definition of what is expected of the individual or team, in the form of a performance agreement.

Step 3 Draw up a detailed performance and development plan with the collaboration and agreement of the individual or team concerned. This is essentially a problem-solving action plan, detailing:

(i) Areas of performance identified as requiring improvement
(ii) Areas in which the job holder would benefit from training
(iii) Specific improvements that could be investigated or implemented
(iv) Areas in which there is potential for future development

Step 4 Monitor, evaluate, discuss and adjust performance on a continual basis.

Regular reviews of performance are used as opportunities to exchange feedback, in order to:

(i) Identify problems or opportunities and plan control action

(ii) Reinforce successful performance (with praise, recognition, enlarged responsibility, bonus rewards and so on)

(iii) Adjust work plans or targets

(iv) Identify the need for coaching, training or other inputs

Step 5 Review performance at the end of the agreed period (say, annually).

Actual performance is evaluated against the agreed performance plan (by methods akin to traditional appraisal: reports, interviews and so on.) However, this is again to be seen as a forward-looking, problem-solving, opportunity-planning activity, centred on on-going improvement.

19 Management by objectives

Text reference. MbO is covered in Chapter 6.

Top tips. Even if you were not aware of the work of Drucker, McGregor or Humble in this area, you should have recognised 'Management by Objectives' as an approach to integrating organisational and individual objectives. This is an unstructured question – but the seven stages will give a clear structure to your answer, You may like to think about some introductory material: Fayol's classical concept of the scalar chain and how plans and objectives need to 'cascade' down the organisation hierarchy, say; or Peters' and Waterman's ideas about 'simultaneous loose-tight' controls by setting clear objectives...

Easy marks. If you didn't know 'Management by Objectives' well enough to jot down '7 key stages', this might not have been your choice of optional question. If in doubt, you'd need to count how many stages you *could* describe, earning about 2 marks each...

Examiner's comments. This was a very unpopular question. Candidates either knew the answer or did not. Most answers tended to be general in approach, showing no knowledge of the subject or introducing other writers such as Fayol, Waterman, Peters and others.

Marking scheme

	Marks
Description of seven stages in a Management by Objectives programme (2 marks per stage, with extra mark for using examples)	15

Management by objectives (MbO) is a comprehensive approach to setting objectives, targets and plans. MbO is a scheme of planning and control which provides co-ordination of:

- Short-term plans with longer-term plans and goals
- The plans (and commitment) of junior with senior management
- The efforts of different departments with the organisation' s overall strategy

The essential features of the approach are:

(1) Define the **main areas of responsibility** for each individual and department. This might include individual targets and time schedules, for example

(2) Agree with each manager **defined areas of activity**, which will make a quantifiable and measurable contribution to achievement of the plans for the department, branch or company as a whole

(3) Clarify with each manager the **performance standards** to be achieved, and the **means of measurement**. These should conform to corporate and divisional objectives, but each manager should contribute to the process of agreeing performance standards, so as to win his or her commitment to them and what constitutes effective performance

(4) Define the **key result areas** (related to step 3)

(5) Set up an **action plan** with built-in review periods. Having agreed annual plans for each division, with key tasks identified and performance indicators established for each team and individual manager within the division, managers can then identify:

(i) **Policies**: ie guides to making decisions which are in keeping with corporate objectives;

(ii) **Financial budgets**: ie a statement in money terms of a plan to achieve certain objectives. Financial budgets *are not the objectives themselves.*

(6) Have a systematic **performance review** of each manager's results, comparing them with step 1.

(7) **Revise the objectives** as necessary and then set up for the next period as a new sequence. Each division should make a monthly operating report, measuring actual results against key performance indicators. There should also be similar quarterly and annual reviews, after which new divisional plans would be prepared.

20 Scenario: Human resource management

Text references. This question covers topics in recruitment (Chapter 7), selection (Chapter 8) and induction planning (Chapter 10).

Top tips. This question covers the entire process of recruitment and selection from HR planning to HR development – a very substantial portion of the syllabus. Part (a) required you to think carefully about Deborah's situation. Managers have to think how matters can be done better. Before taking on a new member of staff, it would seem logical to see other ways in which this activity can be resourced. Parts (b), (c) and (d) refer more to the 'knowledge' in the syllabus.

Easy marks. It may look as if the easier marks falls in parts (c) and (e), but it is essential to try and tackle scenario question parts systematically, in order to avoid confusion and duplication. Follow our analysis carefully for the 'way in' to the more difficult parts.

Marking scheme

			Marks
(a)	Identification of general background	4	
	Identification and description of job analysis	4	
			8
(b)	Description of formal process (one mark per step)		10
(c)	Contents of job description for this vacancy	4	
	Contents of person specification for this vacancy	3	
			7
(d)	Explanation of procedure involved in the recruitment and selection of the new clerk (max. two marks for each stage)		10
(e)	Recognition and description of benefits (one mark each)		5
			40
	This marking scheme was produced by BPP		

(a) **Deborah's case for a new staff member**

Staff are a major element of **cost** and headcount should be subject to careful control. In a large, mature organisation with established procedures and methods, the **human resource plan** or establishment document would lay down the staff requirements for the accounts department.

Permission to recruit would depend on either a member of staff having left (staff **turnover**), or the **expansion of the department's task**. The latter might result from organisational growth or, particularly in the case of an accounts department, from the increasing burden of government-imposed work, as with the maintenance of working time records, for instance. Where the task had expanded, the human resource plan would have to be amended.

However, SMG Limited 'has no formal procedures or processes' for recruitment and, therefore, reference to an agreed establishment is not possible. It will be for Deborah Williams to demonstrate just why she thinks that the accounts staff are overworked before recruitment is authorised.

Another way would be to look to see if the accounts department can be run more efficiently. An examination of its procedures would be extremely time consuming and probably beyond the capacity of a human resources specialist. However, it may be possible to carry out a job analysis in broad terms if the department is not too large. This would attempt to measure the volume and nature of the work flowing through the office by collecting information from four sources:

- Documentation, such as forms and instructions
- Interviews with managers and supervisors
- Interviews with job holders
- Observation

If it is found that this is not possible, the **fall-back position would be for Deborah Williams to justify the recruitment in concrete terms**. However, because Deborah Williams is a **director** of the company, a recently appointed assistant manager in HR would find it difficult to demand such a justification. A suitable procedure would probably have to be established by agreement among the directors: perhaps Deborah has the authority anyway.

(b) **Procedures to ensure suitably qualified applicants**

Step 1 Obtain agreement that there is a vacancy – already presupposed from the question.

Step 2 Clearly detail the total mix of tasks to be carried out in the department, including work that is not being done owing to lack of resources.

Step 3 Assess whether current employees have the competences currently to carry out all the tasks, or whether these can be developed.

Step 4 Assess whether the current allocation of work amongst employees genuinely reflects their competences. Could there be greater job specialisation?

Step 5 Assess the future needs of the department in terms of the quality and nature of competences required.

Step 6 Identify the mix of training and resourcing needs necessary to carry out the department's task.

Step 7 Develop or revise job descriptions based on the roles currently performed in the department. Existing members of staff will welcome clear descriptions of what is expected of them if roles are to change.

Step 8 Develop person specification as the basis of the recruitment and selection process, based on the job descriptions and required competences which are going to be met by recruitment.

Step 9 Develop plan for recruitment and selection of new staff, if this is the preferred way of matching the resource and competences of the department with the work expected of it.

It is worth noting the overlap between parts (b) and (d) without falling into the trap of repeating the same points!

Step 10 Implement the plan (see part (d) of this answer).

The process involves two types of company policy.

(i) The procedures manual, which deals with the steps gone through, any legal requirements (guaranteeing conformance with equal opportunities legislation)

(ii) The human resources plan, which details the overall requirements for employees, investment in training and so on.

The difference between a job description and person specification is basic exam territory: ensure that you describe their respective contents accurately.

(c) **Job description and person specification**

The difference between a job description and person specification is basic exam territory: ensure that you describe their (respective) contents accurately.

A **job description** is a statement of the tasks, responsibilities and working relationships making up a job. At lower levels it will concentrate on the specification of duties, but at managerial levels it is likely to be written in broader terms dealing with scope and responsibilities. It forms an important part of the documentation needed by a complex organisation, since, in combination with other job descriptions, it defines how work is done.

A **person specification** details the personal qualities, abilities, qualifications and experience required of the holder of a job. A job description is useful in several human resource management contexts, including recruitment, appraisal and career development. A person specification, on the other hand, is rarely useful for anything other than recruitment.

Since it is rare to find a perfect fit between any job and its holder, the task of recruitment is eased if the job description is divided into core and peripheral elements. This allows the features of the person specification to be divided into those that are essential and those that are merely desirable. This split makes it easier to select the best person for the job when no ideal candidate applies.

We have given a lengthy answer for 10-marks: you might make the same 10 points more briefly, *or* cover 5-6 points at this length. (examples attract marks too.)

(d) **Recruitment and selection of the clerk**

The recruitment and selection process is based on the needs of the department, and the state of the labour market. There are a number of different steps. Once it has been decided that recruiting a new member of staff (rather than redeploying current members) is the right course then the following steps should be taken.

Step 1 Obtain job description, which details job content, responsibilities, and the job's relation to other positions in the department, authorisation limits. It might be phrased in more general terms as an accountability profile.

Refer your answer to the specific vacancy mentioned in the scenario when giving examples

Step 2 If a person specification has not yet been drawn up, identify the type of candidate suitable for the job, noting essential attributes (eg for an accounts clerk post, the firm may require a candidate with the ACCA's Certified Accounting Technician qualification), desirable attributes (eg experience in a similar **company**) and contra-indications (ie matters that would rule out the candidate, for example no work experience at all).

Step 3 Identify appropriate media for recruitment. To reach the right people, the firm has to find the right medium.

The firm could use a **recruitment agency** to suggest suitable candidates already on their books, to or the firm may choose to **advertise**.

Step 4 Place the advertisement in suitable **publications** (such as newspapers, professional journals). The firm might also use **government employment offices** (job centres, in the UK). Moreover, firms are increasingly advertising on the **Internet**, either on their own websites or via recruitment services (often owned or run by newspaper groups) such as workthing.com.

Step 5 Review application forms/CVs received. As a matter of courtesy all applicants should receive a reply; some may be rejected out of hand; others may be told that their application has been received and is being reviewed.

Step 6 Shortlist desirable candidates and contact them to arrange interviews. Write to unsuccessful candidates.

Step 7 Interviews

Most firms use the interview as the heart of their recruitment procedures even though it is not reliable as a predictor of job performance. It does enable a firm to assess some of the candidate's interpersonal skills. A mixture of open and closed questions should be used.

Step 8 Tests

A variety of tests can be employed, often relating to the task to be done. This may be of limited relevance to an accounts position where work experience can be validated. However, it should be possible to assess basic numeracy.

Step 9 Make offer, subject to references

References are of limited value, but they can be used to check the candidate's basic honesty (eg in seeing that the candidate's past employment history is truthful, that the candidate worked in a the positions and over the timescales mentioned).

Step 10 Induction

When the new employee starts, he/she needs to become familiar with the firm.

Note that the question asked for *both* types of benefit

(e) Both training and development are likely to offer benefits to the **individual** and to the **organisation**.

(i) Increased job competence makes the organisation more efficient.

(ii) It also reduces stress on the individual and is a source of pride and competence and hence of motivation.

(iii) Organisational flexibility and learning are is enhanced when staff are well trained, since they can deputise for absent colleagues and adapt rapidly to new procedures and other changing circumstances.

(iv) A programme of personal development contributes to succession and promotion planning, for the benefit of organisational continuity and individual self-actualisation.

(v) Individuals may become more employable. This improves their job security within the organisation and their prospects elsewhere if they wish to move.

21 Systematic approach

Text references. Procedures in recruitment and selection are overviewed in Chapter 7, and covered in detail in Chapters 7 and 8.

Top tips. The examiner often focuses on systematic, procedural overviews of recruitment and/or selection, because these are essential for efficiency and fairness in practice. This is an unstructured question, so you need to build structure in. Allowing 1 mark each for identifying and 1-2 for explaining, you need to address at least 7-8 stages. (Note that this question covers recruitment *and* selection: all the way to the job offer.) Don't be tempted to pick 7-8 stages you know well – like job description, interviews etc: try and find 7-8 stages that describe the *whole* process. You'll need to plan your answer carefully: see below.

Easy marks. Once you've planned the stages you're going to discuss, the answer becomes straightforward, as each point is fairly basic.

Examiner's comments. Although in general this question was answered well with many candidates displaying excellent knowledge of the requirements of recruitment and selection, there were some surprising approaches. Too many missed out the importance both of the job description and the person specification.

Answer plan

1	Aim of recruitment and selection procedure	
2	Job description	recruitment
3	Person specification	
4	Job advertisement	
5	Applications	selection
6	Interviews	
7	Testing	
8	Offer	

Marking scheme

	Marks
The seven stages in recruitment and selection (up to 3 marks for each stage)	15

The main aim of recruitment and selection is to match the correct candidate to the post. The first step is the identification of the vacancy.

Typical **recruitment procedures** upon identification of a vacancy will commence with the **job description** for the vacant post, which is a statement of the component tasks, duties, objectives and standards expected of the job holder. It will also detail basic facts such as the job title, location and reporting structure.

A **person specification** is also required. This is a reworking of the job description in terms of the kind of person needed to do the job. It may cover areas such as aptitude, intelligence or communication skills.

The next step is the preparation and publication of **advertising information** which will attract the attention and interest of potentially suitable candidates. It must give a favourable (and accurate) impression of the job and organisation, and equip those interested so that they are able to make an attractive and relevant application. The advertisement must, in other words, encourage an element of 'self selection' by providing enough information (for example on salary, work details, desired qualifications) to deter those who would either not be asked for an interview, or who would not accept the job even if it were offered. Any advertisements must sustain the organisation's reputation in the labour market.

The advertisement may be placed in a newspaper, relevant journal or job centre. Alternatively, a recruitment consultant may be used.

The selection process follows on from the recruitment process and the first step is to deal with responses to the job advertisement. This might involve sending **application forms** to candidates. Some companies are content to simply review CVs. The advantages of application forms are that they provide a mechanism for comparison and screening, as they are specifically designed for the requirements of the recruiting company. It asks specific questions on age, qualifications etc, but also probes deeper with 'tell me more' questions such as 'Why do you think Megacorp plc should recruit you?' The candidate should be given space to elaborate on these type of questions, as they provide vital information about the candidate's suitability.

Application forms are sorted, and this allows early weeding out of unsuitable applicants. Shortlisted candidates are then invited for **interview**, the most important stage in the process and the one which is relied upon most by companies when they are recruiting. The interview gives the organisation a chance to assess applicants (and particularly their interpersonal communication skills) directly, and gives applicants a chance to learn more about the organisation, the people and the working environment. Interviews must make all applicants feel that they have been given fair treatment, whether they get the job or not.

To this end, candidates must be put at their ease and given the opportunity to learn about the job. They must be asked broadly the same questions. Responses have to be evaluated in an objective way, perhaps by employing a points system. For example, points may be given for demonstrating examples of leadership, meeting deadlines, dealing with conflicts etc.

As well as interviews, some organisations employ supplementary **selection tests**. Tests of intelligence, aptitude, personality and proficiency are fairly common, but care is needed in interpreting results as it is difficult to avoid cultural or gender bias. Tests should be standardised and reliable.

Following this will be the **offer** of a position, including the taking up of references and the issuing of a formal contract that the successful candidate must sign to indicate acceptance of the terms. Unsuccessful candidates should also be dealt with courteously, and thanked for their application.

22 Promote or recruit?

Text reference. This topic is specifically covered in Chapter 7.

Top tips. Note that the question stem refers to 'appointing external *candidates'* – not consultants: parts (a) and (b) refer to the 'promote or recruit?' choice. Only part (c) introduces the third option of using consultants.

Easy marks. This should be a straightforward question, if you've covered the topic area: it is highly structured, with clear instruction key words ('*define* and *describe...*' 'describe *three* factors') and topic key words ('advantages of *internal promotion*', 'advantages of *external recruitment* ').

Examiner's comments. This question attracted good answers – although the descriptions in part (c) were sometimes too brief, being presented in one or two words. Take note: 'describe' is not the same as 'identify' or 'list'!

Marking scheme

		Marks
(a)	Description of the advantages of internal recruitment	5
(b)	Description of the advantages of external recruitment	5
(c)	Description of three factors	5
		15

(a) **Advantages of internal promotion**

(i) **Cost-effectiveness.** If internal staff have the skills and attributes required to fill a vacancy (or the potential to develop them at reasonable time and cost), it will be more cost-effective to promote from within – especially if the relevant skills and attributes are scarce in the external labour pool.

(ii) **Performance prediction**. Management will be familiar with an internal promotee, his or her performance record and potential, while an external recruit will be a relatively unknown (and therefore riskier) quantity.

(iii) **Shorter induction**. An internal promotee will be familiar with the culture, objectives, procedures and personnel. This cuts down the lead time for effective performance, where an external recruit may require extensive induction.

(iv) **Staff development**. Internal promotion is evidence of the organisation's willingness to develop people's careers, which may build commitment and loyalty.

(v) **Succession planning**. Internal promotion may form part of a systematic succession plan which maintains managerial continuity and individual performance improvement over time.

(b) **Advantages of external recruitment**

(i) **Skill availability and cost-effectiveness**. If internal staff lack the skills and attributes required to fill a vacancy, and there is a long lead time to develop them, it may be quicker and more cost-effective to recruit a suitably qualified person from the external labour pool.

(ii) **Cultural change**. Insiders may be too socialised into the prevailing culture to see faults or be willing to change.

(iii) **Flexibility and innovation**. Organisations in fast-changing fields may require new people with wider views, fresh ideas and competitor experience.

(iv) **Response to labour turnover**. Jobs characterised by constant labour turnover can be swiftly filled from the external labour pool without the destabilising effect of further internal moves.

(c) **Factors in deciding whether to use recruitment consultants**

Specialist recruitment consultants or agencies may be contracted to perform some external recruitment tasks on the organisation's behalf. The decision of whether this is appropriate will depend on a number of factors, including:

(i) Whether there is a need for **impartiality** which can only be filled by an outsider trained in objective assessment. If fresh blood is desired in the organisation, it may be a mistake to have insiders selecting clones of the common organisational type, or perpetuating the biased perceptions of recruiting managers.

(ii) The balance of **specialist contacts, expertise and knowledge**. There may (or may not) be sufficient recruitment expertise available within the organisation to attract suitable candidates and make optimal selection decisions. A given consultant may (or may not) have sufficient expertise in a specialist area of the organisation's activity. (This may raise additional considerations such as the **time** required to brief consultants effectively and the **acceptability** of an external consultant's decision within the organisation.)

(iii) The **supply of skills**. If there is a large and reasonably accessible pool of labour from which to fill a post, and there are ready channels for reaching the target labour pool (such as professional journals), the use of specialists may not be required. If extensive contacts are required, consultants may be helpful. (This raises an additional key consideration: **cost**.)

23 Job analysis

Text reference. This topic comes under recruitment planning, in Chapter 7.

Top tips. The main pitfalls to this question are: (a) the highly specific topic key words for each part; and (b) resisting the temptation to write too much for parts (a) and (b) and run out of time for part (c), where the bulk of the marks are. Tackle part (a) *carefully* (make sure you know the answer) and the rest should follow.

Easy marks. Once you've highlighted the key words, (*what, stages* and *information*), this should be straightforward – although you would probably not choose this as your optional question if you weren't confident that you knew job analysis in detail.

Examiner's comments. This was a popular question but was often poorly answered. Job analysis is an important selection document, required prior to many other documents used in people management. Job analysis is about the content of the job and not about the person who occupies that position. Too many answers missed this fundamental point.

Marking scheme

		Marks
(a)	Brief description of the term 'job analysis'	3
(b)	Brief description and discussion of the four stages (1 mark each)	4
(c)	Description and discussion of the information expected (1 mark each)	8
		15

(a) **Job analysis** is: 'the process of collecting, analysing and setting out information about the content of jobs in order to provide the basis for a job description and data for recruitment, training, job evaluation and performance management. Job analysis concentrates on what job holders are expected to do.' (Armstrong)

(b) A job analysis has to be done systematically – that is why it is called an analysis – as the purpose is to obtain facts about the job. Therefore the job analysis involves the use of a number of different techniques to gather the data. The stages should be:

Step 1 Obtain documentary information such as procedures manuals and written instructions

Step 2 Ask managers about more general aspects such as the job's purpose, the main activities, the responsibilities involved and the relationships with others.

Step 3 Ask the job holders similar questions about their jobs – perceptions might differ.

Step 4 Observe the job holders to see what they actually do.

(c) **Information that might be obtained from a job analysis**

Information	Comments
Purpose of the job	This might seem obvious. However, it has to be set in the context of the organisation as a whole.
Content of the job	The detailed duties and responsibilities of the job.
Accountabilities	The results for which the job holder must account to his or her manager.
Performance criteria	These are the criteria which measure how good the holder is at the job.
Responsibility	This denotes the importance of the job. For example, a person running a department and taking decisions involving large amounts of money is more responsible that someone who only does what he or she is told.
Organisational factors	Who does the job holder report to directly or on grounds of functional authority?
Developmental factors	Relating to the job, such as likely promotion paths, if any, career prospects and so forth. Some jobs are 'dead-end' if they lead nowhere.
Environmental factors	Working conditions, security and safety issues, equipment

24 Job descriptions

Text reference. These issues are covered in detail in Chapter 7.

Top tips. Job analysis, job description and person specification are the bread and butter of exam questions on recruitment and selection: make sure you can define and distinguish between the terms (correctly!) and that you have a good grasp of the basics like process or content, uses and limitations. (In these topics, always ask yourself: are we talking about measuring/defining the *job* or the *person*? This is usually the key to getting the terms right!) Note that part (c) actually has *two* requirements: uses *and* limitations. Don't get complacent when you encounter a question you know lots about, however: you need all the more to pay attention to mark allocation and related time allocation.

Easy marks. You should be able to get good marks under your belt for parts (a) and (b). Don't try to draw out those parts of your answer though: you can't get more marks than are available – and you'll need time to think about part (c). The first requirement should give more easy marks so you're almost there!

(a) **Difference between a job description and a person specification**

A **job description** is a profile of the job or (in the context of recruitment) of the vacancy to be filled. A **person specification** (or personnel specification) is a profile of the kind of person the organisation should recruit or develop for a given job or vacancy: it sets out the attributes a job holder requires to perform a job satisfactorily.

The difference between the two documents is basically that a person specification focuses on the qualities of the person which will fulfil the requirements of a position, while the job description focuses on the requirements themselves: one is person-centred, the other job-centred. In addition, the person specification involves the organisation's aspirations for an 'ideal' or 'desirable' level of performance in the job, while the job description describes tasks and responsibilities.

(b) **Content of a job description**

(i) Job title and department.

(ii) Reporting relationships: the person to whom the job holder is responsible.

(iii) Job summary: outlining the major functions and tools, machinery and special equipment used.

(iv) Job content: a list of the tasks or duties that constitute the job, including degrees of difficulty or responsibility involved.

(v) The extent (and limits) of the jobholder's authority and accountabilities.

(vi) The relation of the job to other positions, including superior and subordinate positions and liaison with other departments.

(vii) Working terms and conditions (hours, pay rates, special conditions of the job), development opportunities and so on.

(c) **Uses and limitations of job descriptions**

Job descriptions are most commonly used in the following circumstances.

(i) In recruitment, to define the skills and qualifications required by the vacancy, as a basis for screening, interviewing and testing applicants.

(ii) In job evaluation, for establishing wage rates.

(iii) In induction, training, appraisal and development: to highlight the scope and functions of the job, training needs, lines of potential development and so on.

Townsend (*Up the Organisation)* suggested that **job descriptions are of limited use**.

(i) They are only suited for jobs where the work is largely repetitive and predictable.

(ii) Management jobs are likely to be constantly changing as external influences impact upon them, so a job description is constantly out of date.

(iii) Difficulties arise when job descriptions are taken too literally, and cause demarcation disputes and costly over-manning practices.

A job description is a static 'snapshot' of a job at a given time: it requires flexibility and constant, negotiated revision. It must also be remembered that job descriptions are 'the map' – not 'the territory': they are designed as a tool for management, not a constraint.

25 Person specification

Text reference. These issues are covered in detail in Chapter 7.

Top tips. This should have caused you little difficulty, as long as you had done your revision. Perhaps the trickiest aspect of the question is avoiding using, in your explanations of the terms (part (a)), information that you will need in order to distinguish between them (part (b)): check that your answer to part (b) is worth three marks – without duplicating part (a) or being unduly short.

Easy marks. This should be fairly basic.

Examiner's comments. This question was popular and well answered, although the practical application of the concepts (part (c)) appeared to be a weaker area for some candidates.

Marking scheme

				Marks
(a)	(i)	Description/understanding of person specification	4	
	(ii)	Description/understanding of job description	4	
				8
(b)		Recognition of differences		3
(c)		Description of purposes		4
				15

(a) **Definitions**

(i) A '**person specification'** (or personnel specification) is a written statement of the attributes required by a jobholder in order to perform a given job or role satisfactorily. It describes the attributes which are essential, desirable and contra-indicated (undesirable) in the individual(s) to be recruited or developed for the role.

Popular frameworks include:

- Alec Rodger's **Seven Point Plan**, which draws selectors' attention to candidates' physical attributes, attainments, general intelligence, special aptitudes, interests, disposition and circumstances
- J Munro Fraser's **Five Point Pattern**, which highlights impact on others, acquired knowledge, innate abilities, motivation and adjustment
- Systematic **competence** definitions

(ii) A '**job description**' is a written statement of those facts which are important in a job regarding the duties and responsibilities and their organisational and operational interrelationships. It is the output of (formal or informal) job analysis.

Typical **content** includes: a job title and department; reporting relationships; a job summary; detailed job content; the extent of the role's authority and accountabilities; the relation of the job to other positions; and working terms and conditions.

With the erosion of bureaucratic organisation, such comparatively rigid definitions of duties and role demarcations are becoming less relevant: role and person specifications are more flexible in allowing multi-skilling, teamworking and similar approaches.

(b) **Difference between the two**

A job description is a profile of the **job** or (in the context of recruitment) of the vacancy to be filled. A person specification is a profile of the kind of **person** the organisation should recruit or develop for a given job, role or vacancy.

The person specification involves the organisation's aspirations for an 'ideal' or 'desirable' level of performance in the job, while the job description describes basic tasks and responsibilities.

Person specifications are also regarded as more flexible, especially where jobs cannot easily be defined in terms of standard or repeated tasks: for example, in managerial and professional roles.

(c) **Purposes of a person specification**

Person specifications are used in human resources management:

(i) In **human resource planning**, to define the skills and attributes required by the organisation

(ii) In **recruitment**, to guide the formulation of candidate requirements for recruitment advertising

(iii) In **selection,** most obviously, to guide selectors in assessing candidates against the requirements of the vacancy (or the human resource plan as a whole, for general recruitment)

(iv) In **performance appraisal** and **development planning**, to assess employees against the optimum requirements of their current roles; to assess their potential to be transferred or promoted to other roles; and to determine training/ development needs

26 Job advertisement

Text reference. This is covered in Chapter 7.

Top tips. Part (a) of this question is quite general and leaves you plenty of scope: try and spread your guidelines across issues of objectives, content, presentation and so on. Remember not to discuss media in detail here, as this is the topic of part (b).

Easy marks. This is a straightforward bookwork question, which you may be able to answer substantially from personal experience and common sense if you need to. (Bear in mind that a similar question might be set for a particular vacancy – eg for an accounts clerk...) Use practical examples for extra credit.

Examiner's comments. This was a popular question, designed to test candidates' understanding of the importance of the recruitment advertisement. A surprising number, however, failed to understand the wider issues beyond the contents of an advertisement. Few answers recognised the role of the advertisement in pre-selection and presenting an image of the organisation.

Marking scheme

		Marks
(a)	Description of factors to consider	5
(b)	Choice of medium – 5 factors, 2 marks each	10
		15

(a) **Preparing a recruitment advertisement**

The object of recruitment advertising is to **attract** suitable candidates and **deter** unsuitable candidates. It thus needs to take into account the **job, the person and the organisation.**

The organisation should have identified its own recruitment needs early on in terms of the skills it needs. These are outlined in the job description.

The **job description** will form the basis of the ad. A job description sets out the purpose of a job, where it fits in the organisation structure, the context within which the job holder functions and the principal accountability of job holders and the main tasks they have to carry out.

In many cases, the title of the job gives a good idea of what is involved. For example, 'credit controller' is a standard position within the industry.

The person preparing the ad will also have a good idea of the **type of person** – experience, qualifications, character – that he/she is looking for. This is sometimes set out in the person specification.

A **person specification**, also known as a job or personnel specification, sets out the education, qualifications, training, experience personal attributes and competences required of a job holder.

Other considerations for the ad

(i) **Concise**, but comprehensive enough to be an accurate description of the job, its rewards and requirements.

(ii) **Attractive** to the maximum number of the right people.

(iii) **Positive and honest** about the organisation. Disappointed expectations will be a prime source of dissatisfaction when an applicant actually comes into contact with the organisation.

(iv) **Relevant and appropriate to the job and the applicant**. Skills, qualifications and special aptitudes required should be prominently set out, along with special features of the job that might attract – on indeed deter – applicants, such as shift work or extensive travel.

(b) **Choice of advertising medium**

(i) **The type of organisation**. A factory is likely to advertise a vacancy for an unskilled worker in a different way to a company advertising for a member of the Institute of Personnel and Development for an HRM position.

(ii) **The type of job**. Managerial jobs may merit national advertisement, whereas seem-skilled jobs may only warrant local coverage, depending on the supply of suitable candidates in the local area. Specific skills may be most appropriately reached through trade, technical or professional journals, such as those for accountants or computer programmers.

(iii) **The cost of advertising**. It is more expensive to advertise in a national newspaper than on local radio, and more expensive to advertise on local radio than in a local newspaper etc.

(iv) The **readership and circulation** (type and number of readers/listeners) of the medium, and its suitability for the number and type of people the organisation wants to reach.

(v) The **frequency** with which the organisation wants to advertise the job vacancy, and the duration of the recruitment process.

27 Application forms

Text reference. Application forms are covered, as a tool of selection, in Chapter 8.

Top tips. This question could be answered plausibly from common sense and personal experience: indeed, it is difficult to see how you could demonstrate more theoretical learning in this area.

Easy marks. The challenge, in order to pick up the easy marks offered, is to give your answer some structure: in particular, to address the specific requirements of the two question parts.

Having gained the easy marks, there is the additional challenge of extending your answer – without 'waffling' – to earn the 15 marks available. The ACCA's own very brief suggested answer shows that this is not easy to do: we provide a longer answer to show how maximum marks could more clearly be earned. If you get a question like this, where you're not sure there are sufficient points to be made to earn the marks, we recommend that you jot down an answer plan.

Examiner's comments. Too many candidates gave the same answer to part (a) and (b), or based their answers purely on personal experience and assumptions, without considered thought about an important document. In part (b), careless question reading led to time-wasting discussion of what the form '*contains*' instead of what information it is designed to '*obtain*' (from applicants).

Marking scheme

		Marks
(a)	Description of application form's purpose (1 mark per item to max of 5)	5
(b)	Description of the information obtained by the application form (1 mark per item to max of 10)	10
		15

(a) **Purpose of an application form**

Recruitment and selection are a key function in human resource management, and a well-designed and utilised application form can be instrumental in:

(i) Enabling the organisation to gather **systematic** (sufficient and accurate) information about prospective candidates to enable initial screening of suitable and unsuitable applications

(ii) Ensuring the **relevance** of candidate information to the organisation and position available, supporting more efficient sifting of job-relevant information by recruiters and selectors

(iii) Gathering data about candidates in a **standardised** manner (where appropriate), to support administrative efficiency, valid comparison (between candidates and against person specifications) and perceived fairness

(iv) Forming (along with other recruitment documentation) the basis for subsequent **selection procedures**, such as interviewing and selection testing.

(v) Offering easily-stored **data** for future human resource planning, appraisal of selection procedures and so on.

(b) **Information obtained by an application form**

Because of their varied uses, a wide range of relevant information may be gathered, including:

(i) Basic personal and contact details, such as: name and title, address and other contacts (phone or e-mail), age and nationality. This information enables the organisation to pursue contact with the applicant and begin to assess suitability (although care must be taken not to discriminate on the basis of characteristics such as age, gender or nationality).

(ii) Relevant attainments: educational and vocational qualifications, membership of professional/vocational bodies, positions held. Some attainments may be essential in order to fulfil a position, while others (such as having completed a computer course) may be generally helpful.

(iii) Employment experience, attainments and terms, such as: previous employers, positions held, key roles/responsibilities undertaken; and current employment terms and conditions (where relevant). This may take the form of a factual history, or the candidate may be invited more freely to describe challenges met, strengths and weaknesses in their past performance and so on.

(iv) Leisure interests and personal development activities. These may indicate relevant aptitudes (such as leadership or problem-solving), but may also include a self-assessment of the candidate's broader 'fit' with the job and the organisation, career orientation/ambitions and so on.

(v) Health and other issues (where relevant). Some positions may, for example, require health checks, licences (eg driving), visa eligibility (for overseas work) and so on.

The nature of the organisation and position being applied for will influence the extent to which this information is gathered as factual data, or as a form of self-expression and self-appraisal by the candidate. More subjective/expressive information takes longer to process, and is not generally required for mass or standardised applications.

28 Interviews

Text reference. Chapter 8 covers selection interviews.

Top tips. Tackle part (a) from both the organisation's *and* the interviewee's perspective, to get 4 marks' worth of complexity into your answer. Part (b) helpfully defines the different interview forms for you – but this is still a detailed area. Structure your answer carefully (advantages *and* disadvantages) to demonstrate that you are not just waffling on the basis of personal experience!

Easy marks. The first four marks should be straightforward, but you needed to have done your revision to find sufficient detail to do really well in part (b). (Note how we've numbered our points to keep track of them – and signal clearly to the examiner that we've earned the available marks!)

Examiner's comments. This was a popular question and there were some good answers. A surprising number of candidates in part (a) failed to describe the purposes of the interview and some failed to appreciate the wider issues, such as the need for fair treatment and the opportunity for giving a favourable impression of the organisation. In part (b), most candidates recognised the advantages and disadvantages of face-to-face and panel interviews – but it was surprising how many candidates thought that a panel interview consisted of one interviewer and a panel of candidates!

Marking scheme

			Marks
(a)	Explanation of the purpose of the selection interview		4
(b)	Explanation of, and the advantages and the disadvantages		
	(i) The face to face interview	6	
	(ii) The panel interview	5	
			11
			15

(a) **Purposes of the selection interview**

The purpose of the selection interview is to support the identification of suitable candidate(s) for employment, as defined by the human resource plans of the organisation. Within this purpose, selection interviews may be used to:

(i) Allow the organisation to assess applicants (and particularly their interpersonal skills) against selection criteria.

(ii) Inform applicants in detail about the job and organisation, in order to enable self-selection.

(iii) Give a positive impression of the organisation, to support its employer brand and general corporate image. A particularly important part of this will be to ensure that all candidates are given fair treatment.

(b) (i) **Face to face interviews**

A face-to-face interview is an individual or one-to-one interview, in which each candidate is questioned by an appropriate officer of the organisation: usually, his or her prospective superior or an HR specialist. ('Face to face' may also be distinguished from a one-to-one telephone interview.)

The advantages of such interviews are their potential for:

(1) **Direct** face-to-face communication, allowing the use and interpretation of non-verbal cues (grooming, posture, facial expression, gestures) in the interview process.

(2) Establishing **rapport** between candidate and interviewer. One to one communication allows a less stressful and more natural 'conversational' style, if this is what the interviewer wishes to create and observe.

(3) More **focused questioning**, given a single interviewer's strategy and direction, and a single focus of attention.

The disadvantages of such interviews are their potential for:

(1) **Lack of specialist knowledge** on the part of the single interviewer, who may not be effective in assessing the candidate across the range of selection criteria.

(2) **Biased decision-making**, because the perceptual selection or distortions of the single interviewer are not balanced by other judgements.

(3) The **manipulation of the interview by the candidate**, who may exploit the potential for rapport, and detect gaps in the interviewer's knowledge which makes it possible for the candidate to cover up weaknesses.

(ii) **Panel interviews**

Panel interviews consist of two or more people who together interview a single candidate.

Most commonly, a panel would consist of an HR specialist and a department manager, as well as a technical specialist if required.

The advantage of panel interviews are their potential to:

(1) **Save the organisation time and money** where a series of interviews and follow-up discussions would otherwise be required to assess all relevant selection criteria.

(2) Allow relevant specialists to **assess the candidate simultaneously** and share information immediately. This should facilitate a more objective, well-rounded assessment.

The disadvantage of panel interviews are their potential to:

(1) **Fragment the interview** and make it more difficult to control, with more random and varied questions being asked without a single strategy or purpose behind them. This may be needlessly disorienting for the candidate.

(2) **Apply added pressure** to the candidate, since they tend to be more artificial and stressful than one-to-one interviews, with less interpersonal rapport.

(3) Fragment the assessment of the candidate, since **panel members will have different perceptions**. While this may balance individual bias, it may also compound it.

29 Selection tests

Text reference. Selection testing is discussed in Chapter 8.

Top tips. You really need to think through the names of the different types of test, to ensure that you can *distinguish* between them. Note that you are being asked about their *purposes* (what are they designed to measure – and why would this be useful for selection?). For part (a) the limitations are well documented: remember that you are only asked for *four*, but just *listing* them won't be enough for 7 marks.

Easy marks. If you have covered this area, you shouldn't have any difficulty.

Examiner's comments. This was a popular question and attracted some good answers. Too many answers seemed to be based upon guesswork or a fundamental misunderstanding of the differences between the types of test, which are deliberately constructed to test particular attributes. Too many answers addressed the question as if it were about interviews, and some even gave the same answer for all four tests. In an indication of not reading the question properly, some confused the word 'attitude' for 'aptitude'.

Marking scheme

		Marks
(a)	Brief description of each type of test (2 marks each)	8
(b)	Outline of limitations of each type (1 mark per point)	7
		15

(a) In some job selection procedures, an interview is supplemented by some form of **selection test.**

(i) **Intelligence tests** are tests of **general intellectual ability.** They typically test memory, the ability to think quickly and logically, and problem solving skills.

Most people have experience of IQ tests and the like, and few would dispute their validity as good measure of **general** intellectual capacity. However, there is **no agreed definition of intelligence**.

(ii) **Aptitude tests.** Aptitude tests are designed to **measure** and predict an individual's potential for performing a job or learning new skills.

- **Reasoning**: verbal, numerical and abstract
- **Spatio-visual ability**: practical intelligence, non-verbal and creative ability
- **Perceptual speed and accuracy**: clerical ability
- **'Manual' ability**: mechanical, manual, musical and athletic

(iii) **Competence tests.** These tests are perhaps the most closely related to an assessor's objectives, because they **measure ability to do the work involved**. An applicant for a typist's job, for example, might be given a dictation tape and asked to type it.

(iv) **Personality tests.** Personality tests may measure a variety of characteristics, such as an applicant's skill in dealing with other people, his ambition and motivation or his emotional stability.

The validity of such tests has been much debated, but is seems that some have been shown by research to be valid predictors of job performance, so long as they are used **properly.**

(b) **Limitations of testing**

(i) There is not always a direct relationship between ability in the test and ability in the job: the job situation is very different from **artificial test conditions**.

(ii) The **interpretation of test results is a skilled task**, for which training and experience is essential. It is also highly subjective (particularly in the case of personality tests), which belies the apparent scientific nature of the approach.

(iii) Additional difficulties are experienced with particular kinds of test. For example:

(1) An aptitude test measuring arithmetical ability would need to be constantly revised or its content might become known to later applicants.

(2) Personality tests can often give misleading results because applicants are often able to guess which answers will be looked at most favourably.

(3) It is difficult to design intelligence tests which give a fair chance to people from different cultures and social groups and which test the **kind of intelligence** that the organisation wants from its employees: the ability to **score highly in IQ** tests does not necessarily correlate with desirable traits such as mature **judgement** or **creativity**. It merely tests mental ability.

(4) Most tests are subject to the effects of coaching and practice if known about in advance.

(iv) **It is difficult to exclude bias from tests**. Many tests (including personality tests) are tackled less successfully by women than by men, or by some candidates born overseas than by indigenous applicants because of the particular aspect chosen for testing.

30 References

Text reference. References, as a tool of selection, are covered in Chapter 8.

Top tips. You could make a good effort at this question using common sense and past experience, if you read the question carefully. Don't confuse purposes (part (a): What a reference is for) and content (part (b): What's *in* a reference).

Easy marks. This is one of those questions you just have to work through systematically, avoiding duplication. It's a relatively minor topic in Selection – but not difficult, if you think carefully.

Examiner's comments. This was not a popular question, and almost every answer provided was either confused, missed the point, or provided irrelevant detail. The clear misunderstanding of the role of references is both surprising and worrying – almost all employers in every sector will seek references before a prospective employee is offered a post.

Marking scheme

		Marks
(a)	Description of the purpose of a reference	3
(b)	Description of the content of a reference	5
(c)	Outline of the problems with references	7
		15

(a) **Purpose of a reference**

References are a **selection tool** designed to support other sources of information about candidates, in order to help the organisation to fulfil its human resource plans.

(i) **Checking and confirming** personal and employment-related data provided by the candidate in a résumé or interview.

(ii) Seeking **credible third-party assessments** of the candidate's attributes and employability.

(b) **Content of a reference**

The content of a reference will depend on the form in which it is requested or obtained: whether it is solicited or unsolicited, obtained by telephone interview, standard form or letter requesting specific information.

It will also depend on the relationship between the candidate and the person giving the reference: a personal reference speaks to general character, while an employer reference speaks to job-related facts and assessments.

Typical content of a standard employment reference might include:

(i) The **title** of the job held, and its main duties and responsibilities
(ii) The **dates** of employment
(iii) **Pay/salary** earned at leaving
(iv) **Education**/training attainments
(v) **Reason for leaving** (where relevant)
(vi) A **general assessment** of performance, job-relevant attributes and employability

(c) **Problems with references**

References, by themselves, score very low on **predictive validity** scales such as Smith and Abrahamsen's. They are not a reliable guide to future job performance. While they are useful for confirming factual information provided by candidates, they are of limited value for a number of reasons.

Opinions about a candidate's character and personal attributes may **unreliable** because of:

(i) **Biased** judgement, whether favourable or unfavourable to the candidate

(ii) Charity (**withholding detrimental remarks** in order to avoid prejudicing future employment opportunities)

(iii) The withholding of negative opinions for fear of being **actionable for libel** if opinions prejudice a candidate's standing in the employment market. (In fact, references are legally privileged in this respect, as long as they are factually correct and devoid of malice)

(iv) **Ill-preparedness** to give a specific or factually-confirmed reference (for example, if a reference is sought by telephone without prior warning)

References from a past employer may also be of limited usefulness.

(i) They represent a single, potentially biased viewpoint

(ii) The candidate's performance in one job and organisation will not necessarily be transferable to another, with a different work group, environment and management style.

(iii) Unchecked assumptions may be made about the candidate on the basis of reference facts. For example, the assumption that frequent employment changes are due to lack of focus (rather than circumstance) or that the candidate will want to maintain a previous salary level (whereas he may be motivated by other factors).

Personal references are of little direct relevance to the job and are inevitably subject to positive bias, being selected by the candidate.

31 Scenario: Equal opportunity

Text reference. Discrimination and diversity issues are covered in detail in Chapter 9.

Top tips. This is a challenging question, as it gives an unusually lengthy scenario, and requires an unusually high degree of application to the scenario (clearly indicated: 'For Food is Us...', 'Why would an organisation like Food Is Us...'). Note that part (b) is about the purpose and importance of equal pay policy (instruction key word: '*Why should* an organisation...?').

Easy marks. There are straightforward marks to be gained for recognising the main features of sex discrimination, race relations and disability policies (based on law and any elements of best practice of which you are aware).

Examiner's comments. This question was designed to test an important area of people management – and to reflect the ACCA's own ethical policies. Candidates tended to offer generalised statements on the need not to discriminate – rather than substantive content on the basis of the policies specifically referred to in the question – or offered comment on their own experiences, rather than analysing and referring to the case study. Some candidates were, however, lead astray by the market-focused comments in the case study, and focused their answers on customers, rather than employees and managers – who are the basis of HR policies.

Marking scheme

		Marks
(a)	Description of the main features of a sex discrimination policy	10
	Description of the main features of a race relations policy (Maximum for part (a) 16 marks)	6
(b)	Reasons for an equal pay policy (Maximum for part (b) 6 marks)	6
(c)	Description of key points of policy and means of discrimination (Maximum for part (c) 8 marks)	8
(d)	Discussion and recognition of the differences (Maximum for part (d) 10 marks)	10
		40

(a) **Main features of a sex discrimination policy**

Food Is Us should have a sex discrimination policy which clearly sets out the following points.

(i) A statement that sex discrimination is unacceptable within the firm, as it is: unethical; illegal (under UK law); detrimental to the firm's employer brand; and detrimental to the firm's brand, market position and future prosperity.

(ii) A definition of the issues related to *sex* discrimination including: sex, marital status and sex change (Sex Discrimination Act 1986) and sexual orientation (Employment Equality Regulations 2003); Equal Pay (Equal Pay Act 1970 and amending regulations); and sexual harassment. It should be emphasised that sex discrimination affects men as well as women.

(iii) A definition of 'discrimination' in its various forms, as covered in relevant legislation and Codes of Practice.

- Direct discrimination, where one interested group is treated less favourably than another. For Food Is Us, an example might be giving recruitment preference to single people.
- Indirect discrimination, where a practice is fair in form, but discriminatory in operation. For Food Is Us, an example might be a height requirement (for the purposes of shelf-stacking) which would favour men over women.
- Victimisation, whereby a person is penalised for giving information or taking action in pursuit of a claim of discrimination.

(iv) Explanation of key areas to which the obligation of non-discrimination applies, including: advertisements, recruitment and selection programmes, access to training, promotion, provision of benefits, disciplinary procedures, redundancy and dismissal.

(v) Clear statement of intent, in regard to: publicising the policy; monitoring performance (with suitable indicators); awareness training to be provided (and to whom, as Food is Us extends its scheme); and disciplinary procedures (including recourse available to victims, and the role of the Equal Opportunities Commission).

Main features of a race relations policy

Food is Us should have a race relations policy which clearly sets out the following points.

(i) A statement that race discrimination, like sex discrimination, is unacceptable within the firm, for the same reasons.

(ii) A definition of the issues related to *race* discrimination including colour, race, nationality and ethnic or national origin (Race Relations Act 1996) and religious beliefs (Employment Equality Regulations 2003).

(iii) A definition of 'discrimination' in its various forms (as for sex discrimination) as covered in relevant legislation and Codes of Practice.

(iv) Explanation of key areas to which the obligation of non-discrimination applies (as for sex discrimination), with acknowledgement of the requirement for larger public organisations (like Food Is Us) to draw up detailed plans for achieving racial equality in all employment practices (Race Relations (Amendment) Act 2000).

(v) Clear statement of intent, in regard to improving performance (as for sex discrimination), with additional focus on the need for sensitivity in monitoring the ethnic origins of employees and the role of the Commission for Racial Equality.

(b) **Reasons for developing an equal pay policy**

An organisation like Food Is Us, like any other employer, should have an equal pay policy in order to:

(i) Ensure compliance with the Equal Pay Act (1970) and Equal Pay (Amendment) Regulations 1984, which entitle a woman to equal pay for 'work of equal value' to that of a man in the same establishment.

(ii) Ensure compliance with the Equal Opportunities Commission Code of Practice on Equal Pay (used by Employment Tribunals), which covers definitions, pay systems, methods of identifying discrimination, job evaluation methods and a model policy.

(iii) Avoid the costs and negative public relations (potentially affecting its image in its labour and consumer markets) of equal pay claims.

(iv) Enable it to attract and retain high quality (and diverse) human resources, as a fair and ethical employer.

(v) Position it as an ethical and diverse organisation – appealing to an equally diverse customer base (particularly women, who are still disproportionately represented among supermarket shoppers).

(c) **Key points of a disability discrimination policy**

A disability discrimination policy should make clear statements on the following points.

(i) A disabled person is defined as a person who has a physical or mental impairment that has a substantial and long-term (more than 12 months) adverse effect on his or her ability to carry out normal day to day activities. Severe disfigurement is included, as are progressive conditions such as HIV, even though the current effect may not be substantial.

(ii) The 'effect' of disability may be wide, including mobility, manual dexterity, physical co-ordination, and lack of ability to life or speak, hear, see, remember, concentrate, learn or understand or to perceive the risk of physical danger.

(iii) The Disability Discrimination Act 1995 makes it unlawful for organisations like Food Is Us (more than 20 employees) to discriminate against a disabled person: in deciding who to interview or employ, or in the terms of an employment offer; in opportunities for promotion, transfer, training or other benefits; and by dismissal or any other disadvantage.

(iv) The employer has a duty (and is willing) to make reasonable adjustments to working arrangement or to the physical features of premises where these constitute a disadvantage to disabled people (for example, disabled toilets, ramp access, wide supermarket aisles).

(d) **Difference between equal opportunities policy and managing diversity initiative**

The concept of 'managing diversity' is based on the belief that the individual differences on which organisations currently focus, under equal opportunities, are crude and performance-irrelevant classifications of the most obvious differences between people. They should be replaced by a genuine understanding of the ways in which individuals differ.

Diversity in employment, as a concept, goes further than equal opportunities. The ways in which people meaningfully differ in the work place include not only race and ethnicity, age and gender, but personality, preferred working style, individual needs and goals and so on.

Effective managers seek to understand the job-relevant ways in which their staff differ. A 'managing diversity' orientation implies the need to be proactive in managing the needs of a diverse workforce in areas (beyond the requirements of equal opportunity and discrimination regulations) such as:

(i) Tolerance of individual differences

(ii) Communicating effectively with (and motivating) ethnically diverse work forces

(iii) Managing workers with increasingly diverse family structures and responsibilities

(iv) Managing the adjustments to be made by an increasingly aged work force

(v) Managing increasingly diverse career aspirations/patterns and ways of organising working life (including flexible working)

(vi) Confronting issues of literacy, numeracy and differences in qualifications in an international work force

(vii) Managing co-operative working in ethnically diverse teams.

32 Scenario: Training

Text reference. All the points for an answer can be found in Chapter 10.

Top tips. Although this scenario covers training and development, it also examines your skills at written communication: note that you are asked to provide your answer in draft report format, and that it will need to be a persuasive report in order to overcome your Manager's negative attitudes to training. This is a highly structured question with detailed topic and instruction key words: part (a) asks for **benefits** of training; part (b) asks for a method of **identifying** training **needs** (not for training needs themselves); part (c) asks for recommendations on training **methods and media** (appropriate to the scenario); part (d) asks for a method of **evaluating** training; and part (e) for a definition of **development** (which is not just the same as training). Make sure you have answered all the questions as set – *and* refer specifically back to the scenario details where possible!

Easy marks. Pick up the basic marks for format by ensuring that you've headed your report appropriately: basic report structure should suffice. Then work through each of the requirements accurately and systematically: these should all be familiar topics.

Marking scheme

			Marks
Report format/structure		0-2	
(a)	Benefits of training to the organisation (1 mark each)	5	
	Benefits of training to the individual (1 mark each)	5	
			10
(b)	Overall appraisal of training needs	3	
	Steps of systematic analysis	6	
	Recognition of need for process	1	
			10
(c)	Training methods (2 marks each, including suitability to scenario)		8
(d)	Methods of evaluating training (1 mark each)		6
(e)	Definition of development: career/personal	3-5	
	Activities involved in development	3-5	
			6
This marking scheme was produced by BPP			40

REPORT: TRAINING AND DEVELOPMENT AT JIK LTD

Prepared by: Your Name, Assistant Store Manager
For: M Hlavcek, Store Manager

Purpose: To consider the implications of recent customer feedback surveys and the need for systematic staff training in order to retain customer loyalty and competitive edge.

I **THE BENEFITS OF TRAINING**

Recent customer feedback has suggested that the levels of technical and product knowledge and customer service skills of our staff are:

(a) Inadequate to meet customer expectations
(b) Impacting on the satisfaction and loyalty of customers

While it is acknowledged that training is no substitute for strategic staff selection, and that it bears:

Benefits for the organisation	**Benefits for the individual**
Increased skills, knowledge and incompetence: enhanced job performance	Enhanced competence: sense of achievement, self-esteem and security
Continuous improvement of the skill base, and greater employee retention: adding value to the human assets of the business	
Enhanced workforce flexibility and potential for management succession	Opportunities for greater contribution to customer satisfaction and business success, which are a source of job satisfaction
Better customer service, leading to customer retention (which is more cost-effective than winning new customers)	Opportunities for increased rewards and career development
Fewer purchase returns, complaints, service queries and so on (which waste time and resources)	Opportunities to extend own interests and skills in photography
Less need for detailed staff supervision and managerial intervention in problems	Knock-on effects of training needs analysis: potential improvements in work methods, supervisory style and so on.

II **IDENTIFYING TRAINING NEEDS**

We do not propose that indiscriminate training be given, with a waste of time and resources. Specific training needs, relevant to JIK's customer care and business requirements, could be identified as follows.

Training needs from the perspective of the organisation or store as a whole can be identified from the business plan and strategy. This should set out planned store expansions, areas of diversification (eg into digital photographic services) and so on. JIK should address the implications of strategies in a coherent human resources plan, which would have many spin-off benefits for the planning of recruitment, selection, development and so on.

Training needs analysis may be carried out on a store-by-store or individual-by-individual basis. Training needs may be identified by the following means.

(i) **Monitoring new products**, legislation and customer demands which may create new skill or knowledge gaps (for example, the introduction of digital cameras).

(ii) **Monitoring critical incidents** which affect a key area of the organisation's effectiveness, and which may require training: customer complaints have already been identified.

(iii) Employee **self-assessments** and attitude surveys: inviting staff to identify areas in which they feel their performance is suffering from skill or knowledge gaps. (Many of the staff readily admit ignorance of new products and are keen to learn, since this is their area of interest.)

(iv) **Comparing the current skills**, knowledge and competence of staff (as assessed by specific testing or our usual appraisal systems) with the skills, knowledge and competence requirements indicated by the human resource plan, job descriptions and – most importantly – customer feedback. The shortfall may be called the 'training gap'.

III METHODS OF TRAINING

Once specific training needs have been identified, and specific objectives formulated, relevant and cost-effective training methods and media can be selected and tailored to the learning styles of our staff. At this stage, some broad suggestions might be as follows.

(i) **On-the-job instruction and coaching** can be offered in the product/technical knowledge area by more senior staff, and those with knowledge or expertise in particular new products or processes.

(ii) **Off-the-job courses may be advisable** in the areas of customer service skills in order to give staff a new perspective and to avoid distractions. These courses could be held in-house and given by myself or the head office customer services manager: this would enable us to tailor the course to the needs identified by customer feedback, and the specific product ranges and culture of JIK. Selected individuals could be sent on external courses, and could then act as supervisors, coaches and mentors to other staff.

(iii) **Video-based training packages** on customer service are also available, and these might be a cost-effective general orientation, but more interactive methods (include role plays) will be needed to encourage the application of learning.

(iv) In the area of technical and product knowledge, we could use **resources provided by the manufacturers**: Nikon, Pentax and the others supply detailed brochures and instructional videos, and may be willing to offer the services of their own experts to brief staff, since it will enable them to on-sell their products better.

IV EVALUATING TRAINING METHODS

It is recognised that JIK would wish to monitor the direct and indirect costs of training and to ensure that anticipated benefits actually accrue. Training can be evaluated by the following means.

(i) **Monitor and appraise the work performance of the trainee** for general improvement and/or the achievement of specific training objectives.

(ii) **Monitor and appraise the work performance of the store** for the achievement of its training objectives, ensuring that any individual improvements are integrated into the work of the whole team. A follow-up customer survey may be a good way of measuring post-training improvements in customer satisfaction, and customer perceptions of improvement.

(iii) **Test post-training skills**, knowledge and competence for comparison with pre-training testing.

(iv) Monitor and appraise the **satisfaction of trainees,** through attitude surveys and training feedback forms.

(v) Monitor and appraise the on-going development of trainees: the impact of training on promotion/succession (creating promotable individuals), recruitment (making more skills available within the store) and so on.

(vi) **Analyse potential indicators** of the knock-on effects of training: lower staff turnover, fewer disciplinary complaints, improved employee morale and so on.

V **EMPLOYEE DEVELOPMENT**

'Development' involves more than education and training to fill knowledge and skill gaps. Employee development includes:

(i) The development of job-relevant knowledge, skills and competence (through education and training)

(ii) Career development: the planned progression of competent individuals through the organisation, both 'upwards' through promotion and management succession, and 'laterally' through the acquisition of wide-ranging experience;

(iii) Personal development: taking account of people's wider needs and aspirations.

Career development is valuable for the organisation because it enables a smooth flow of trusted and culture-fitted individuals into supervisory and managerial vacancies and strengthens the highly cost-effective internal labour market. It requires attention to:

(i) The types of experience employees can acquire. It might be helpful if our supervisors rotated between sections, for example, to get to know the customers of repairs and servicing, sales, processing and so on;

(ii) The individual's guides and role models in the organisation. On-the-job training can encourage mentoring, for example;

(iii) The level of opportunities and challenges offered to 'stretch' individuals' abilities. We could rotate supervisory duties, for example.

Even encouraging personal development can be valuable for the organisation. If our employees hone their own skills and win photographic awards, for example, it would be a wonderful advertisement for JIK's expertise.

33 Training methods

Text reference. All these training methods are defined in Chapter 10.

Top tips. If you have done your study and revision on the topic of training and development, these terms should all be familiar. The main challenge was to ensure that you have written 3 marks' worth of explanation for each method. Start by defining the term, and noting whether it is primarily an on-the-job or off-the-job method of training; then expand on what the method involves. If you struggle to find a third mark's worth of detail, you might say something about what the method is particularly useful for, or how it is distinguished from other methods: check our answer for a range of points that might be made.

The only real pitfall is to read (d) and (e) carefully: check that you have really written about job rotation and job instruction (not job enrichment, enlargement, analysis, description, evaluation and so on)!

Easy marks. The terms here are quite straightforward: you should be able to pick up at least the first mark for each part by defining them, plus extra marks for explanation (which for most of these, you could probably do by common sense).

Examiner's comments.

Part (a) caused considerable misunderstanding. Computer-based training refers to training using a computer, and not training on how to use a computer. Part (b) was badly answered and/or confused with part (c).

Marking scheme

		Marks
(a)	Explanation of computer based training	Up to 3 marks
		(Maximum for part (a) 3 marks)
(b)	Explanation of coaching	Up to 3 marks
		(Maximum for part (b) 3 marks)
(c)	Explanation of mentoring	Up to 3 marks
		(Maximum for part (c) 3 marks)
(d)	Explanation of job rotation	Up to 3 marks
		(Maximum for part (d) 3 marks)
(e)	Explanation of job instruction	Up to 3 marks
		(Maximum for part (e) 3 marks)
		(Total for question 15 marks)

(a) **Computer based training** is an off-the-job training method, involving interactive programmed learning using a personal computer with stand-alone CD-ROM or software. An example would be typing tuition software or BPP's i-Pass programme. Software may be designed to cover tutorial content, use self-administered objective testing and/or allow guided skill practice.

CBT allows self-managed learning at the user's own pace, and is a cost-effective approach to tuition and assessment (for certain types of skills) where learners are geographically dispersed (across multiple organisation sites, say). It is generally distinguished from **e-learning**, which is computer-based learning through a network of computers or the Internet.

(b) **Coaching** can be used as an on- or off-the-job training and personal development method. A trainee is put under the guidance of a more experienced employee, who helps him or her to identify learning needs and plan learning experiences/opportunities to meet them. The coach acts as facilitator, instructor, feedback-giver and adviser. Coaching is typically a short-term one-to-one (or one-to-group) relationship, aimed at improving immediate job performance.

(c) **Mentoring** is, like coaching, a form of developmental relationship, but it is typically longer-term and focused on wider issues of the trainee's personal and career development. Unlike coaching, the mentor is not usually a technical expert or the trainee's immediate superior: this allows for more open communication and a broader range of goal-setting and problem-solving. The mentor is a more experienced or senior person who acts as a teacher, counsellor, role model, supporter and encourager, through an ongoing series of meetings for discussion.

(d) **Job rotation**, in this context, is an on-the-job or experiential approach to training, which involves giving the trainee several jobs in succession, in order to gain experience of a wider range of activities and environments. This approach is commonly applied at a managerial level in the Civil Service, for example, but it may also be used in other settings, often in induction programmes. It is similar to other on-the-job approaches such as temporary promotions or work shadowing, which aim to develop people by widening their experiences and opportunities.

(e) **Job instruction** is a systematic on-the-job training technique, designed to formalise the traditional 'sitting with Nellie' approach in which a more experienced worker shows a trainee what to do, using the actual materials and equipment involved in the job. In job instruction, the goals and objectives of learning are more carefully planned. The trainer gives a full explanation and demonstration of the task, then the trainee attempts the task under close instruction and supervision. A feedback session is used to appraise and adjust the trainee's performance and set further improvement/learning goals.

34 Induction

Text reference. Induction, as a form of training, is covered in Chapter 10.

Top tips. This is an interesting question, because it invites you to consider whether there may be *disadvantages* to induction training! Note that the question addresses *formal* induction training, not an informal 'showing recruits around' session: bear this in mind when suggesting your course outline. Bear in mind too that induction is an on-going process, not just a one-day activity...

Easy marks. The easiest marks are available for advantages of induction – but don't neglect the disadvantages on that account!

(a) **Advantages and disadvantages of formal induction**

The purpose of induction training is to integrate new recruits as quickly and effectively as possible into the social structure, work methods and culture of the organisation, in order to support and enable them in beginning to perform their task functions.

Advantages of formal induction training

(i) It helps **recruits to find their bearings**, minimising the disorientation and stress of starting in an unfamiliar setting. This benefits the organisation by facilitating early performance and reducing the risk of early staff turnover.

(ii) It **equips new recruits with the information** they require to begin performing (or learning to perform) usefully as quickly as possible.

(iii) It **connects new recruits with the social and communication networks** that will enable co-ordinated work performance and on-going support.

(iv) It gives **new recruits an initial positive experience** of the organisation which may contribute to morale and commitment.

(v) It begins to **integrate recruits into the culture**, behavioural norms and values of the organisation, so that they become well adapted and committed members.

(vi) It begins an **on-going process of training** needs identification and development planning.

The **disadvantages** of such a programme, in itself, make a less compelling argument. Induction training delays the start of on-the-job performance and may therefore frustrate recruits who are eager to 'get stuck in', while incurring unnecessary costs. However, this is short-term thinking, ignoring well-researched benefits. It may be argued with more justice that *poorly conceived or conducted* induction training may have disadvantages in creating a negative impression of the organisation, wasting time and money, teaching recruits bad habits or simply being irrelevant to recruits' needs.

(b) **Format for a formal induction course**

Step 1 A **general welcome** and briefing on the geography, structure and culture of the organisation.

Step 2 An **introductory tour** of the work facility, both for an overview of the work process and to orient the recruit to relevant amenities.

Step 3 **Briefing by the personnel manager** on HR policies and procedures: conditions of employment, access to benefits, training opportunities and so on. Guidance may be given in completing initial employment paperwork.

Step 4 **Introduction to co-workers** and other key figures (mangers, health and safety officers, union representatives and so on): ideally, appointing a co-worker (by agreement) as coach or mentor to integrate and develop the recruit on an on-going basis.

Step 5 **Briefing on relevant company policies:** discipline and grievance procedures, health and safety rules and officers, equal opportunity rights and obligations and so on.

Step 6 **Meeting with HR and/or department managers** or mentors to plan, agree and implement initial coaching and training required to commence performance.

Step 7 Involve recruits in **participative exercises** and interactions with other staff, both on the job ('sitting with Nellie') and informally (social interaction).

Step 8 **Monitor recruits' initial progress** and commence an on-going cycle of feedback, review, problem-solving and development planning.

35 Personal development plan

Text reference. Personal development is covered in Chapter 10.

Top tips. This is a relatively unstructured question, and assumes knowledge of the particular three-step model of personal development planning preferred by the examiner (and covered in the BPP Study Text). If you were familiar with more complex models, you would have had to think how you could describe them in terms of three steps. If you weren't familiar with any models, you might still have got to the answer by using a basic three-step planning framework: (a) Where are we now? (b) Where do we want to get to? (c) How do we get there?

Easy marks. Most essentially, however, make sure (and use your introduction to prove) that you understand what a PDP is and what it is for!

Examiner's comments. The examiner has recently indicated that this topic will not feature in this examination (even though this was not a well-answered question).

Marking scheme

		Marks
Explanation of the three steps in preparation of a personal development plan		
Step 1: analyse the current position	5	
Step 2: set goals to cover performance of the existing job	5	
Step 3: draw up action plan	5	
		15

A personal development plan is a clear developmental action plan for an individual, which incorporates a wide set of developmental opportunities, including formal training. It is designed to integrate individual development goals with the current and future human resource requirements of the organisation.

As with any systematic planning activity, the development of a PDP can be expressed as a three-step model: analysis of the current position, expression of the desired or improved position (in the form of goals), and statement of tactical steps to move from the one to the other.

Step 1 (analysing the current position) may be carried out in a variety of ways.

(a) Data on *job requirements* may be available from job descriptions and person specifications, or may be collected through job analysis.

(b) Data on *employees' existing skills levels* may be available through selection and induction records, performance appraisals, competence tests and/or monitoring and appraisal by supervisors or mentors.

Since [according to the question] this scheme is aimed at new employees, a comparison of job requirements and employee skills should have been carried out during selection. However, a more forward-looking, developmental analysis may be added by using, for example: skills analysis (mapping areas of high and low performance and 'liking' of skill areas); personal SWOT analysis (mapping strengths, weaknesses, opportunities and threats for current job competence and future career development) and so on.

Step 2 (setting goals) may be aimed at defining:

(a) a desired or improved level/standard of performance in the existing job;

(b) the competences required to meet anticipated changes in the current role or environment;

(c) the competences or performance levels required for promotion or transfer elsewhere in the organisation, or for the development of specialist expertise.

All goals should be formulated as SMART objectives (specific, measurable, achievable, relevant and time-bounded) in order to support detailed action planning, monitoring and evaluation.

Step 3 (action planning) involves the drawing up of systematic tactical plans to achieve the stated goals, including:

(a) The objective

(b) Methods to be used to develop the identified skills (including training; learning experiences; opportunities to practise new behaviours; people, information and other resources required)

(c) Timescales for review of progress

(d) Methods of monitoring and reviewing progress and the achievement of the objective (testing, feedback from a mentor and so on).

36 Coaching and mentoring

Text reference. These issues are discussed in Chapter 10.

Top tips. Mentoring may involve an element of coaching – but this question requires you to distinguish clearly between them. Notice also the other topic key words: (a) the coaching *process* and (b) the *purposes* of mentoring. (Don't just describe both...) For part (c) you would gain extra credit for citing a named model (Hamblin, Kirkpatrick) – but we take a general view. (The question 'suggests' a 5-level policy evaluation – but does not *specify* it: we have covered all areas, by considering how the learning of an *individual* trainee might be measured.)

Examiner's comments. Training and development is fundamental to any organisation. The answer to part (b) required recognition of higher-level evaluation of training, but too many dwelt upon lower level issues such as improved bonuses or individual status.

Marking scheme

			Marks
(a)	Explanation of:		
	(i) Coaching	5	
	(ii) Mentoring	5	
			10
(b)	Explanation of the ways in which training might be evaluated for the organisation as well as the individual		5
			15

(a) (i) **Coaching** is a form of on-the-job training. It is one element of the traditional method of skill training in which the trainee is placed beside an experienced worker and learns by observing and imitating him or her, under close supervision and instruction. Coaching may be used flexibly in a wide range of training situations, and at any time during performance on an on-going basis, where a more experienced person offers demonstration, guidance, correction or teaching.

The process of coaching involves:

(1) **Demonstrating** how areas of the job are performed and guiding the trainee's imitation.

(2) **Helping** the trainee to identify problems and development needs and to learn from mistakes and

(3) **Encouraging** the trainee to assess his or her own progress and performance and to formulate further plans for improvement.

Essentially, coaching is a collaboration between the coach and the trainee, in which the coach's special role is encouragement and guidance as the trainee develops on the job.

(ii) **Mentoring** is another form of on-the-job development, focused more on personal and career development than on specific skill training.

A mentor is a guide, ideally both more experienced and more powerful in the organisation, whose concern is the trainee's long-term personal development. (S)he may occupy a role as the trainee's teacher/coach, counsellor, role model, organisational champion, encourager, constructive critic and so on, as appropriate to the situation over time.

The process of mentoring involves:

(1) Helping the trainee to **greater self-awareness**.

(2) Helping the trainee to formulate and clarify his or her work and non-work **needs and ambitions**.

(3) Helping the trainee to identify **opportunities for development** at work.

(4) Encouraging the trainee to **take responsibility** for his or her development, while offering support where required, and

(5) Collaborating with the trainee to **plan his or her own development**.

(b) **Evaluation of training**

(i) From the point of view of the **organisation**, training may be evaluated by:

(1) Measuring **what the trainees have learned** on the course, by means of a test or assessment of competence linked to training needs and objectives,

(2) Measuring **changes in job behaviour** following training: studying the subsequent behaviour of the trainees in their jobs, to assess how the training scheme has altered the way they do their work in line with training needs and objectives.

(3) Measuring the **correlation between training and other indicators** (error/wastage rates, accident rates, absenteeism, labour turnover, disciplinary actions), to assess how training may have impacted on areas such as quality and employee morale.

(4) Measuring the **correlation between training and the achievement of organisational goals** and objectives, to assess bottom-line effectiveness.

(5) Measuring all the above in relation to the **costs** of training.

(ii) From the point of view of the **individual**, training may be evaluated by:

(1) Measuring **what trainees have learned** on the course, by means of a test or assessment of competence linked to departmental training needs and objectives. (This is an element in individual trainee motivation and learning, as well as organisational effectiveness).

(2) Measuring what trainees have learned and the qualifications they have obtained against their **personal aspirations**, goals and **personal development plans**.

(3) Measuring trainee **reactions to and perceptions of training**: using feedback forms and attitude surveys, for example, to ask the trainees whether they thought the training programme was relevant to their work, effectively implemented, suitable for their learning style and generally worthwhile.

(4) Measuring individual **post-training attainment** and trainee **satisfaction** against the costs of training.

37 Learning theory

Text reference. Both models are covered in Chapter 10.

Top tips. This should have been a straightforward question, as long as you knew your Honey & Mumford (learning styles) and experiential learning cycle (Kolb and/or Honey & Mumford). You may have chosen to draw the learning cycle – but make sure you earn the marks by describing the four stages (as required by the question). Note that part (b) has two requirements: describe the styles *and* discuss their implications for training programmes.

Easy marks. These are such accessible theories, they are easy to remember – but check that you've remembered them accurately!

Examiner's comments. This was a popular and well-answered question!

Marking scheme

		Marks
(a)	Brief description of the four stages in the experimental learning cycle	4
(b)	Description of the learning styles and their implications for training programmes	11
		15

Answer plan

A simple answer plan (to help you to recall and include the details) might be;

(a) Kolb learning cycle

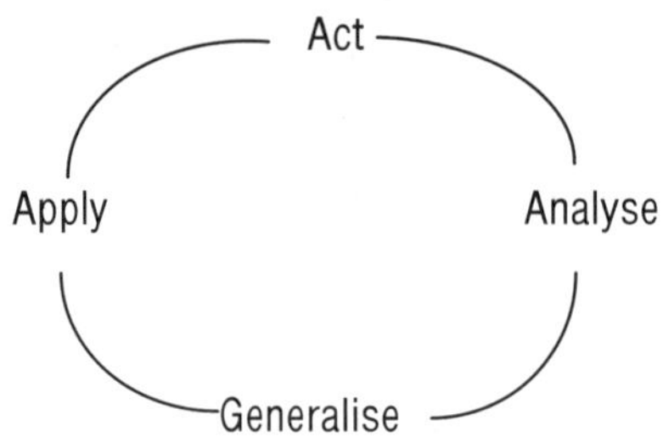

(b) *Honey & Mumford*

Theorist – Reflector – Activist – Pragmatist

(c) *Implications*

- Strengths & weaknesses
- Preference for types of trainer/activity
- Use of less preferred styles

(a) **Kolb** suggests that effective learning takes place in a cycle of four phases.

(i) The first stage (concrete experience) is to be fully involved in a new experience or activity.

(ii) The second stage (observation and reflection) is to review and reflect upon the experience and its results

(iii) The third stage (abstraction/generalisation) is to draw conclusions and formulate hypotheses about the experience, what happened and what could be done differently.

(iv) The fourth stage (application and testing) is to make use of the conclusions and hypotheses to plan to try out a new behaviour – thus generating a further concrete experience with which to perpetuate the cycle.

(b) **Honey and Mumford**

Peter Honey and Alan Mumford have drawn up a popular classification of four learning styles, based on the observation that people have certain psychological preferences in the way they learn best.

(i) **Theorists** seek to understand basic principles and to take an intellectual, 'hands-off' approach based on logical argument. They prefer training to be:

- Programmed and structured
- Designed to allow time for analysis
- Provided by teachers who share their preference for concepts and analysis

(ii) **Reflectors**

- Observe phenomena, think about them and then choose how to act
- Need to work at their own pace
- Find learning difficult if forced into a hurried programme
- Produce carefully thought-out conclusions after research and reflection
- Tend to be fairly slow, non-participative (unless to ask questions) and cautious

(iii) **Activists**

- Deal with practical, active problems and do not have patience with theory
- Require training based on hands-on experience
- Are excited by participation and pressure, such as new projects
- Are flexible and optimistic, but tend to rush at something without due preparation

(iv) **Pragmatists**

- Only like to study if they can see its direct link to practical problems
- Are good at learning new techniques in on-the-job training
- Aim to implement action plans and/or do the task better
- May discard good ideas which only require some development

Implications for training programmes

The implications of these styles for training programmes may be summarised as follows.

(i) Each style has strengths and weaknesses (as discussed above) in the way it learns: training approaches and methods can be adapted to build on the strengths and minimise the weaknesses of each style. For individual trainees, appropriate methods may be selected. For training groups, a balance of methods may ensure that no style is disadvantaged.

(ii) Reflectors and Theorists are suited to off-the-job training methods, while Activists and particularly Pragmatists are suited to on-the-job training methods. In either case, careful attention will have to be given to creating opportunities to *apply* knowledge in the workplace: Activists and Pragmatists may take risks applying learning too early – while Reflectors and Theorists may fail to apply what they have learned unless encouraged.

(iii) Honey and Mumford insist that style are merely 'preferences': we can all learn in different ways. They suggest that, in addition to exploiting the strengths of each style, training programmes should encourage people to learn using less preferred styles, in order to broaden their skill repertoire and enhance their flexibility.

38 Scenario: Appraisal

Text reference. All these aspects of appraisal are covered in Chapter 11.

Top tips. These are all fairly standard bookwork questions on appraisal – but remember to *apply* the theory to the specific challenges faced by Watkins Williams in the scenario. These are identified clearly in the third paragraph of the scenario. Start by underlining some key phrases as a guide to your application.

Easy marks. 'Underneath' the application, there are mostly mainstream topics here.

Examiner's comments. This was not a difficult question and was generally answered well. The scenario was constructed and presented in a manner which allowed candidates to display their understanding of the practical problems and challenges in actually operating the appraisal process, and its importance in the management of people in the profession. The appraisal process is an official activity which is well documented.

Most successful candidates identified the main components, the importance of the problems associated with appraisals and the appropriate documentation. One aspect of all the answers was the assumption that appraisals are only concerned with financial rewards. This of course is not the case. In most instances, appraisals simply form part of the organisation's standard approach to managing people.

Answers to part (a) required an understanding of the main principles upon which appraisal is based. Those who did not score well in this part of the question generally scored poorly overall.

Marking scheme

		Marks
(a)	Brief description of three main components of an appraisal system	3
(b)	Benefits for (i) employee and (ii) employer (up to 5 marks each)	10
(c)	Barriers to effective appraisal (1 mark each)	5
(d)	Description of the documentation (1 mark for each point)	8
(e)	Three approaches to appraisal interviews (3 marks each)	9
(f)	Explanation of follow up action	5
		40

(a) The process of appraisal is central to any system of **performance management**. It is very important that it is properly understood by the partners at Watkin Williams. Whilst performance management as a whole is forward looking, the process of appraisal is designed to **review performance** over the past period, with a view to identifying any deficiencies, and improving it in the future.

The general purpose of any appraisal system is to **improve the efficiency of the organisation** by ensuring that the individuals within it are performing to the best of their ability and developing their potential. There are three main components to understand.

(i) **Reward review**. Measuring the extent to which an employee is deserving of a bonus or pay increase as compared with his or her peers. This is what the Watkin Williams staff have focused on.

(ii) **Performance review**, for planning and following-up training and development programmes, ie identifying training needs, validating training methods and so on.

(iii) **Potential review**, as an aid to planning career development and succession, by attempting to predict the level and type of work the individual will be capable of in the future. This is a wider purpose of appraisals, and it is not necessarily well understood by the staff at Watkin Williams.

(b)

> **Examiner's comments**. In general, part (b) was answered well, but some answers confused the benefits of appraisal for the individual and for the organisation. Although there will be some overlap (improved motivation for example will benefit both), in general the benefits are different. Too few answers addressed the higher level application of appraisals, for example in human resource planning.

Employee	• **Objectives are established** in relation to the whole Watkin Williams organisation, thus allowing employees to feel more involved. • **Key results and timescales** are established • **Compares** past performance and future activities against standards • Basis for performance related **pay** schemes, and **training and development needs** (essential for an expanding organisation such as Watkin Williams)
Watkin Williams	• Suitable **promotion candidates** are identified • Areas of **improvement** can be seen • **Communication** is improved (very important for this company) • Basis for medium to long term **human resource planning**

(c)

> **Top tip**. If you remember Lockett's accessible framework, use it.
>
> **Examiner's comments**. The barriers to appraisal are well documented and researched. Some candidates failed the recognise them from the scenario, and answered part (c) only in general terms.

In theory, appraisal schemes may seem very fair to the individual and very worthwhile for the organisation, but in practice the **appraisal system often goes wrong**, as it has at Watkin Williams. The barriers to effective appraisal at the company are set out in the table below.

Appraisal barriers	Comments
Appraisal as confrontation	• There is likely to be a lack of agreement on performance levels, as Watkin Williams is expanding all the time • The feedback might be subjective, or badly delivered – in other words the partner is biased, allows personality differences to get in the way of actual performance etc. • Appraisals are based on yesterday's performance not on the whole year. • Disagreement is likely to arise about long-term prospects.
Appraisal as judgement	The appraisal is seen as a one-sided process in which the partner acts as judge, jury and counsel for the prosecution. The staff at Watkin Williams feel that the process is unfair because their appraisals are based to some extent upon the work performance of others.
Appraisal as chat	Some of the staff want their appraisal to be a friendly chat without purpose or outcome. Partners, embarrassed by the need to give feedback and set stretching targets, might reduce the appraisal to a few mumbled 'well dones!'. This only leads to more misunderstanding.
Appraisal as bureaucracy	There is a danger that its underlying purpose, improving individual and organisational performance, is forgotten.
Appraisal as unfinished business	Appraisal should be part of a continuing process of performance management at Watkin Williams.
Appraisal as annual event	Many targets set at annual appraisal meetings become irrelevant or out-of-date.

(d)

> **Examiner's comments**. A number of answers to part (d) showed a surprising lack of knowledge and did not identify the documentation required for the appraisal interview. The first and most obvious is the job description. Too many answers focused on the type of questions to be asked, the layout of the interview or interview techniques.

Assessments must be related to a **common standard**, in order for comparisons to be made between individuals: on the other hand, they should be related to **meaningful performance criteria**, which take account of the **critical variables in each different job**.

For this reason, the **job description** is a very important document to be used in preparing for the appraisal interview.

An **appraisal report** (or statement of performance) is written before the interview, and this may be supplemented by **other records of the employee's performance** (such as references from peers, former managers or even clients of Watkin Williams).

The employee's **file** from the human resources department may also contain relevant information.

Self-appraisals occur when individuals carry out their own self-evaluation as a major input into the appraisal process. Partner and appraisee might fill out a report each, and compare notes for discussion in the interview.

> **Top tips**. The phrase 'appraisal interview' should connect with Maier's framework. If you know it, use it.
>
> **Examiner's comments**. The three approaches to the appraisal interview are well-documented and many answers to part (e) earned good marks. However, too many answers described measurement and methods of appraisal. This indicated insufficient care in reading the question.

(e) According to Maier, there are three types of approach to appraisal interviews that could be considered by the Watkin Williams partners. Most appraisees prefer the third of the alternatives suggested, and this is likely to be the most appropriate method given the current atmosphere at Watkin Williams.

(i) **The tell and sell method**. The partner tells the subordinate how he/she has been assessed, and then tries to 'sell' (gain acceptance of) the evaluation and the improvement plan. This requires unusual human relations skills in order to convey constructive criticism in an acceptable manner, and to motivate the appraisee to alter his/her behaviour.

(ii) **The tell and listen method**. The partner tells the subordinate how he/she has been assessed, and then invites the appraisee to respond. The partner therefore no longer dominates the interview throughout, and there is greater opportunity for **counselling** as opposed to pure **direction**.

(1) The employee is **encouraged to participate** in the assessment and the working out of improvement targets and methods: it is accepted that participation in problem definition and goal setting increases the individual's commitment to changing his or her behaviour.

(2) This method does not assume that a change in the employee will be the sole key to improvement: the partner may receive helpful feedback about how job design, methods, environment or supervision might be improved.

(iii) **The problem-solving approach**. The partner abandons the role of critic altogether, and becomes a helper. The discussion is centred not on the assessment, but on the employee's **work problems**. The employee is encouraged to think solutions through, and to commit to the recognised need for personal improvement. This approach may also stimulate creative thinking on the part of employee and partner alike, to the benefit of the organisation's adaptability and methods.

(f)

> **Examiner's comments**. Part (f) was well-answered but far too many answers referred to financial rewards as being an automatic outcome of the appraisal. An interesting number of answers suggested that one action to follow the appraisal interview was to arrange the pay rise. This is neither automatic nor necessarily even part of many formal appraisal systems

Follow-up procedures to be taken at Watkin Williams after the appraisal has been completed. None of these procedures are likely to be taking place in the current situation.

The appraisal can also be used as an input to employees' **personal development plans**, if these are set up in the future at Watkin Williams.

(i) **Informing appraisees of the results** of the appraisal, if this has not been central to the review interview.

(ii) **Carrying out agreed actions** on training and promotion.

(iii) **Monitoring the appraisee's progress** and checking that he/she has carried out agreed actions or improvements.

(iv) Taking necessary steps to **help the appraisee to attain improvement objectives**, by guidance, providing feedback, upgrading equipment, altering work methods or whatever.

39 Trends in appraisal

Text reference. These issues are discussed in Chapter 11.

Top tips. If three 'new approaches to appraisal' do not immediately leap to mind, work through the criticisms cited in the introduction to the question. Performance management, for example, answers the 'backward-looking' and 'perfunctory' points. Various sources and directions of feedback (including upwards) remove the 'top down' power aspects. Results-oriented approaches (as opposed to 'personality assessments') address the relevance issues. Ensure that you include 5 marks' worth of content for each approach: this would be the basis of the *Marking guide*.

Easy marks. Once you've sorted out that performance management, multi-source and upward feedback (or whatever you select) are possible answers, it should be easy to describe them. (Even *two* approaches would secure you 10 marks.)

New approaches to appraisal

(a) **Performance management** (PM) is a new approach to appraisal, which includes continuous collaborative planning and control. Individuals and teams jointly set key accountabilities, objectives, measures and priorities for performance and performance improvement, and review and adjust performance on an on-going basis.

This approach answers the criticisms of appraisal.

(i) **PM is not primarily retrospective ('backward looking').** Performance management focuses on the following review period, and on progress towards continuous improvement goals: it is therefore more forward-looking, pro-active and stimulating in its orientation.

(ii) **PM is not 'perfunctory'** in the sense of merely being a once-a-year, bureaucratic requirement. Performance management is an on-going control system with in-built feedback and review timescales.

(iii) **PM is not** irrelevant to job performance, because primarily focused on the (personal) development and reward aspirations of the employee. Performance management is focused on adding value to the business through the integration of employee improvement and reward goals with the strategic objectives of the business.

(b) **Multi-source feedback** is a new approach which gathers appraisal information from different sources:

(i) The **appraisees** themselves. Self-appraisal helps individuals to see their goals in the light of organisation and unit objectives, and removes the element of judgement from appraisal.

(ii) The **appraisees' subordinates**. Upward appraisal offers meaningful feedback on leadership skills, empowers staff and encourages upward communication.

(iii) **Customers (internal or external).** Customer feedback likewise offers meaningful appraisal of customer service skills, and improves customer relations and loyalty.

(iv) **Multiple sources**. 360-degree appraisal gathers feedback from a range of stakeholders in an individual's performance: suppliers, customers, peers, subordinates and superiors.

This approach minimises the perception of appraisal as superiors passing judgement on subordinates – an application of 'top down' political or personal control. It is also more relevant to the job, since aspects of performance (such as leadership and customer care) are assessed by those directly affected by them.

(c) **Results-oriented criteria** reflect a new approach to appraisal, in which performance is measured against specific targets and standards of performance. This is a change from personality based appraisal systems which took as their criteria for assessment a range of personal qualities (loosely defined as 'personality traits') such as intelligence, reliability, initiative and so on.

Job– or results-oriented systems take as their criteria factors defined as being important for successful job performance: depending on the approach used these may be based on critical incidents, key results or competencies, as derived from job analysis, job descriptions, competency definitions or the plans, targets and standards set for the individual or unit.

Results-oriented approaches answer the criticism that appraisal is irrelevant to job performance, since the criteria for assessment are directly related to job performance and improvement.

40 The cost of accidents

Text reference. This topic is covered under health and safety, in Chapter 12.

Top tips. This is a fairly straightforward question in the health and safety area, as long as you bear in mind the full range of potential costs of accidents.

(a) **Potential costs to employers of accidents at work**

(i) Time lost by the injured employee

(ii) Time lost by other employees who choose to (or must) stop work as a result of the accident

(iii) Time lost by supervisors, managers, safety and maintenance staff through investigation, reporting, counselling, repair and other duties following an accident

(iv) A proportion of the cost of maintaining first aid materials and trained staff

(v) Lost output as a result of disruption to operations

(vi) Cost of replacement, repair or modification of equipment as a result of accidental damage or unsafe use

(vii) Costs associated with increased insurance premiums following claims

(viii) Reduced output from the injured employee on return to work

(ix) Reduced output as a result of poor employee morale, increased absenteeism, increased labour turnover among employees and so on, if they feel their work is unsafe and they are not being protected

(x) Costs of recruiting, training or redeploying replacements for injured workers

(b) **Steps to reduce the frequency and severity of accidents**

Step 1 Formulating a comprehensive, rigorous and relevant safety policy.

Step 2 Developing safety consciousness as part of the organisation culture: emphasising that safety is everyone's responsibility (not only that of safety officers or specialists) and that safety is a key value and priority of the business.

Step 3 Developing effective consultative participation between management, workers and trade unions so that safety rules are accepted and supported.

Step 4 Giving adequate instruction and training in safety rules and measures, especially for new or transferred workers and where methods have been changed.

Step 5 Minimising and managing known hazards such as materials handling, moving parts, hazardous substances and so on.

Step 6 Enforcing stringent maintenance standards for plant and fittings (such as safety guards and shut-offs).

Step 7 Monitoring general maintenance of the work environment to ensure that hazards (such as worn or slippery flooring) are controlled.

41 Health and safety

Text reference. These issues are discussed in Chapter 12.

Top tips. The topic and instruction key words are crucial to getting to grips with this question. For part (a) you need to briefly describe **three** hazards (don't waste time with more!) *and* **demonstrate why** these are hazards: in other words, show by examples or explanations *how* they pose a danger to people in the workplace. For part (b), address *general policies* to avoid risk: this is not the place to discuss detailed fire prevention, hygiene and other requirements. Focus on 'big picture' issues such as awareness, training, risk, identification and so on.

Easy marks. Workplace hazards should be a 'gift' of a question – if you *explain* the dangers, as required. There should be plenty of material for part (b) too, once you've focussed on policy issues...

Examiner's comments. Candidates in general provided good answers to part (a), although some gave trivial examples of workplace dangers. Answers to part (b) displayed a misunderstanding of the purpose of the question. Higher level policies, rather than minor specifics, were required.

Marking scheme

		Marks
(a)	Introduction and brief description of any three hazards	5
(b)	Description of policies (2-3 marks per point)	10
		15

(a) A **hazard** is something that is likely to cause injury, or a point of exposure to risk of accident, injury or illness. It is easy to assume that 'work hazards' apply mainly to building sites or factories, but there are also health and safety hazards that affect people like accountants working chiefly in more administrative, office based roles.

Office equipment is often electrical, or contains moving or heated parts, which could cause injury if misused. All equipment should be used in accordance with the operating instructions and any training that may be necessary.

Manual handling and lifting of heavy items can cause back injuries, which are common workplace accidents. Specifically trained personnel should always carry out any heavy lifting in the workplace. Other staff member, if they must lift heavy items, should make sure that they are aware of proper lifting techniques.

Computer workstations and VDUs are now basic tools for most administrative roles. Sitting at a computer for an extended period of time can cause physical discomfort and eye strain, among other problems.

(b) **Information**, **awareness** and **consultation** are important parts of an organisation's health and safety policy. Employers need to make sure that all systems and work practices are safe, the work environment itself is safe and healthy, and that all plant and equipment is maintained to the necessary standards.

Employees must be told clearly what the risks are, and how to minimize them, in order to be and feel safe at work. At the same time, employees themselves may be in the best position to put forward this information. This implies the need for a system of two-way **consultation**.

A system of preventative action in the workplace would have in place the following basic guidelines:

(i) **Assessment of key risks** via a process of consultation, resulting in the establishment of key safety standards, safety representatives and a written formal statement of safety measures

(ii) **Hazard minimization** via appropriate systems and procedures, equipment, safety rules and instructions, consultative participation and training

(iii) **Encouragement of safety consciousness** and responsibility on the part of all employees, not just the appointed safety officers

(iv) **On-going monitoring** of the safety procedures and record of the organization to make sure that policies continue to be relevant, understood and followed throughout the company. This will include regular equipment maintenance.

42 Scenario: Aspects of motivation

Text reference. All these topics are covered in Chapter 13.

Top tips. Use our question analysis to guide you through the requirements. Note particularly that the question becomes much more straightforward when you identify the underpinning theory being tested: Herzberg and bureaucracy.

Easy marks. Candidates so often write about Herzberg when they haven't been asked to, the opportunity to do so here should have given a good start!

Examiner's comments. The scenario for this question was designed in a deliberate manner to allow candidates to recognise and apply Herzberg's theory. Candidates needed to describe the two-factor theory, apply it to the scenario and then suggest ways in which the main problems described might be resolved. Some candidates wasted time by rewriting parts of the scenario in their answers, and too many made reference to Maslow when this clearly was not required.

Marking scheme

			Marks
(a)	Explanation of Herzberg's two factor theory and relevance to the scenario	5	
	Description of hygiene and motivator factors and relevance	10	
			15
(b)	Recognition and description of relevant role culture and bureaucracy		10
(c)	Advantages of training – relevance to individuals and organisation		15
			40

(a) A motivated individual will seek to acquire his chosen desired outcomes via his own behaviour. It follows from this that an organisation will do well if it can instil as goals for an employee those which will benefit the organisation (such as optimum productivity levels). It is all about getting the motivation of the employee to encourage co-operation in achieving the goals of the organisation, so if we understand what motivates individuals then organisational success will follow. 'Content' theories of motivation ask what motivates an individual.

Herzberg devised a two factor theory of motivation, determined by two basic need systems: the need to **avoid unpleasantness** and the need for **personal growth**. He identified factors which cause dissatisfaction at work – '**hygiene**' factors – and suggested that these could be controlled to satisfy the first type of need. Attention to these factors will prevent dissatisfaction, but they will not by themselves produce motivation.

Shortage of – or problems with – *hygiene* factors = poor morale

He also identified factors which cause satisfaction at work – '**motivator**' factors – and suggested that these alone satisfy the second type of need, and can positively motivate an individual to superior performance and effort. A shortage of these factors, as is the case at Swandiff Local Authority, will cause employees to focus attention on other factors which are not part of the job itself, such as to demand more pay or improved working conditions, to make comments like 'We've seen it all before', or to worry about job security or the quality of management.

Motivator factors are those factors directly concerned with the **satisfaction gained from the job itself**. They include:

- Status
- Advancement opportunities
- Responsibility
- Recognition
- Challenging work
- Achievement
- Growth in the job

Absence of *motivator* factors = poor morale

Motivators lead to satisfaction because of the need for personal growth. They do not appear to be too much in evidence at Swandiff Local Authority. Supervisors appear to gain very little intrinsic satisfaction from their work, and think of themselves as 'menial and unrecognised'.

Stemming from his fundamental division of motivator and hygiene factors, Herzberg encourages managers to **change the job itself** (nature of tasks, level of responsibility) rather than conditions of work, since the main motivators are in the satisfaction gained from the job itself.

(b)

Examiner's comments. Too many answers to this part of the question were confused. The scenario clearly set out the features of the prevailing culture and structure, and candidates were expected to see that it was inappropriate and had led to the problems being described.

One very influential metaphor for the structure of an organisation such as Swandiff Local Authority is that of the organisation as a 'machine'. The idea of **mechanistic organisation** (Burns and Stalker) sees organisations as a collection of many moving parts (people and processes) which act in defined, routine and expected ways.

This form of organisation is very **hierarchical** with a high degree of specialisation of labour. With a staff of 8,500 to control, such demarcation is inevitable at Swandiff. Employees in such organisations often work within **impersonal rules** and regulations to ensure that work practices are followed and performance is standardised and consistent. Innovation and imagination are not required.

Mechanistic organisations are also referred to as 'bureaucracies' and at their best these can be seen as stable, predictable, efficient and suitable for slow changing environments. Such an analysis corresponds to Handy's **role culture**, with its presumption of logic and rationality. However, such arrangements can be seen as dysfunctional for the following reasons:

Note the balance of *application* to Swandiff and *theory* using named writers where possible.

(i) **Slow decision making** would result from the rigidity and length of authority networks. The supervisors at Swandiff complain about their lack of capacity to make decisions for their departments

(ii) **Uniformity** inhibits the personal development of staff – seeing themselves as 'menial and unrecognised' without responsibility or role definition

(iii) **Lack of feedback**, especially upwards, creates frustration and mistrust between supervisors and management. At Swandiff it seems in any case that roles are not properly defined.

(iv) **Suppression of innovation** and a lack of adequate training for the supervisors means that, again, they feel undervalued.

(c)

Examiner's comments. Some candidates failed to use the issues raised and identified in parts (a) and (b) to answer this part of the question.

For the supervisors, the benefits of training would include the following.

(i) An enhanced **portfolio of skills**, to improve motivation and employability in the future
(ii) **Psychological** benefits through reassurance that (s)he is of value to Swandiff.
(iii) **Social** benefits from the development of more contacts
(iv) Increased **job satisfaction**, helping them to do their job better and seeing promotion prospects.

For Swandiff, proper training of the supervisors would support **staff retention**, both through increased opportunities for transfers and promotion and increased **commitment to the organisation**. Increased employee skills would enhance employee knowledge and so the value of the organisation's human assets.

Training programmes at Swandiff could be used to emphasise the **corporate culture** or re-communicate it to staff, by indicating key organisational values. In addition, training programmes could build much needed relationships between staff and managers in different areas of the business.

Note that you need to take a *realistic* view.

It should be borne in mind however that training cannot do everything and cannot automatically improve performance problems such as those faced by Swandiff that result from the following. These will need more far reaching and intensive management.

- Bad management
- Poor job design
- Poor work organisation
- Motivation (the supervisors may have lost the willingness to improve their job performance, even if they gain the ability)
- Poor recruitment

43 Theories of motivation

Text reference. Both of these aspects are covered in Chapter 13.

Top tips. This is an opportunity to show your understanding of some very basic theoretical models. In particular, distinguishing between paired terms (content/process and X/Y) which are often confused.

Easy marks. This is perhaps the easiest type of question. With attention to time management, hard to go wrong.

Examiner's comments. This was answered by almost all the candidates, who in general provided very good answers to what was a very straightforward question. Answers to part (a) were often too long, with candidates producing very long answers on the work of Maslow and very little on content theory. This again illustrates the problem of not reading the question.

Marking scheme

			Marks
(a)	Definition and understanding of content theory		5
(b)	(i)	Explanation and description of Theory X	5
	(ii)	Explanation and description of Theory Y	5
			15

(a) **Content theories of motivation**

Content theories ask the question: 'What are the things that motivate people'?

Content theories are based on the belief that human beings have an innate set of needs or desired outcomes, and that behaviour is driven and determined (motivated) by the desire to satisfy those needs or achieve those outcomes.

Maslow's 'hierarchy of needs' and Herzberg's 'two factor theory' are both content theories.

(i) **Maslow** specified seven innate needs in a hierarchy of relative pre-potency, whereby each level of need is dominant until satisfied, at which point the next level of need becomes the motivating factor. This theory was not specifically designed to be applied to work motivation, but it is limited in its ability to explain complex motivations, delayed gratification and the variety of behaviours.

(ii) **Herzberg**'s theory is based on a simpler need framework: the need to avoid unpleasantness (which is satisfied by 'hygiene factors') and the need for personal growth (which is satisfied by 'motivator factors' in the job).

Content theories are distinguished from *process* theories which focus on the decision-making process by which people choose which outcomes to pursue and how.

(b) **Theory X and Theory Y**

Douglas McGregor suggested that the style of management considered appropriate by a manager (or organisation culture) will depend on a set of assumptions about people's orientation and motivation to work. Theory X and Y represent two extreme sets of assumptions: they do not represent actual 'types' of worker. Most people will fall somewhere on the continuum between the two extremes.

(i) **Theory X** is based on the belief that:

- The average human being dislikes work, and will avoid it if possible
- People must be coerced, controlled, directed and/or threatened with sanctions in order to get them to make an adequate effort
- People fear responsibility and change
- People are motivated by basic needs for reward and comfort

A manager who operates on the basis of Theory X will feel (s)he has to direct and control workers with specific instructions, close supervision, rigid task structures and carrot and stick incentives.

(ii) **Theory Y** is based on the belief that:

- The average human being does not inherently dislike work: according to the conditions it may be a source of satisfaction or of deprivation
- People are motivated by the desire for personal growth and achievement
- People are capable of exercising self-direction and self-control
- People will actively seek challenge and responsibility, if they are committed to the task

A manager who operates on the basis of Theory Y will try to integrate subordinates' needs for development and self-expression with the organisation's objectives, so that both can be achieved together. (S)he will tend to use a democratic or consultative styles in order to obtain subordinates' involvement and commitment to the task, and will tend to encourage them to take on more responsibility and more challenging work.

44 Hygiene and motivator factors

Text reference. This topic is covered in Chapter 13 (look for Herzberg).

Top tips. The word 'motivated' in the stem should focus your attention, and 'hygiene' and 'motivator' factors should clearly refer to Herzberg's two-factor theory of motivation. This is a simpler question on this topic than some – but that also means that you need to ensure you have written 8 and 7 marks' worth of explanation for each factor!

Easy marks. This is one of the simpler questions set so far under the syllabus.

Examiner's comments. Part (a) was not difficult, requiring an explanation of hygiene factors, and in many cases good marks were earned. However, too many answers displayed a fundamental misunderstanding, or were based on guesswork and confused, suggesting (surprisingly) that hygiene factors were about personal hygiene or clean and sterile work conditions!

Part (b) was again a straightforward question, requiring a description of motivators. It was only from the wording of the question that references to motivator and hygiene factors required knowledge of the work of Herzberg. In many cases good marks were earned, however there were again some confused answers. Some suggested that motivators were individuals, some described general motivation, not the work of Herzberg while some described the work of Maslow.

Marking scheme

		Marks
(a)	Description of hygiene factors	8
(b)	Description of motivator factors	7
		15

(a) Herzberg devised a two factor theory of motivation, determined by two basic need systems: the **need to avoid unpleasantness** and the **need for personal growth**. He identified factors which cause dissatisfaction at work – 'hygiene' factors – and suggested that these could be controlled to satisfy the first type of need.

He also identified factors which cause satisfaction at work – 'motivator' factors – and suggested that these alone satisfy the second type of need, and can positively motivate an individual to superior performance and effort.

A lack of motivators at work will encourage employees to concentrate too much on visible hygiene factors, such as to demand more pay.

Hygiene factors lead to job dissatisfaction because of the need to avoid unpleasantness.

They are basically factors related to conditions at work which can be modified.

- Company policy
- Salary
- Quality of management
- Interpersonal relations
- Working conditions
- Job security

Attention to these factors will prevent dissatisfaction but they will not by themselves produce motivation.

Hygiene factors are loosely connected with the needs at the bottom of Maslow's hierarchy of innate needs, such as physiological and security needs.

(b) **Motivator factors** are those factors directly concerned with the satisfaction gained from the job itself. They include:

- Status
- Advancement opportunities
- Responsibility
- Recognition
- Challenging work
- Achievement
- Growth in the job

Motivators lead to satisfaction because of the need for personal growth, and can therefore be linked to the higher levels of Maslow's hierarchy.

Stemming from his fundamental division of motivator and hygiene factors, Herzberg encouraged managers to change the job itself (nature of tasks, level of responsibility) rather than conditions of work, since the main motivators are in the satisfaction gained from the job itself.

The two types of factor will vary between organisations and individuals. A factor such as increased responsibility may be a motivator for one person but be actively avoided by another.

45 Maslow

Text reference. Maslow's hierarchy of needs, and its relevance, is discussed in Chapter 13.

Top tips. First of all, recognise that if you write about any need/motivation theory other than Maslow here, you won't get any marks! In order to get good marks in part (a) you really need to *explain* the theory, rather than just identify the five innate needs: don't be afraid to state the 'obvious', by explaining what the hierarchy means. Even if you're struggling to find a full 10 marks' worth of points, *don't* be tempted to write about the difficulties of applying the hierarchy: you need that material for part (b), and you don't get marks for duplicated points.

Easy marks. Maslow's hierarchy of needs is a really mainstream topic, so you should have been well on the way to the first 5-7 marks, for basic information such as the drive to satisfy needs, the five innate needs and the concept of 'relative pre-potency' (hierarchy). Part (b) is more challenging, but there are plenty of points to choose from to earn the 5 marks available.

Marking scheme

		Marks
(a)	Explanation of Maslow's theory (Two marks per step)	Up to 10 marks **(Maximum for part (a) 10 marks)**
(b)	Application of the theory	Up to 5 marks **(Maximum for part (b) 5 marks)**
		(Total for question 15 marks)

(a) **Maslow's hierarchy of needs theory**

Abraham Maslow explained motivation as the drive to satisfy human needs: like other 'content' theories of motivation, his model suggests that human beings have a set of needs or desired outcomes that they act to satisfy.

Maslow described seven innate needs:

- Physiological needs: the most basic needs for oxygen, food, water and sleep
- Safety needs: for security, order, predictability and freedom from threat
- Love/social needs: for relationship, affection and belonging
- Esteem needs: for independence, recognition, status and respect from others
- Self-actualisation needs: for growth, development and the fulfilment of personal potential
- Freedom of enquiry and expression needs: for social conditions allowing free speech and encouraging justice, fairness and honesty

Knowledge and understanding needs (to gain knowledge of the environment, to learn and explore)

While these last two are overarching needs, Maslow considered that the first five could be arranged in a 'hierarchy of relative pre-potency'.

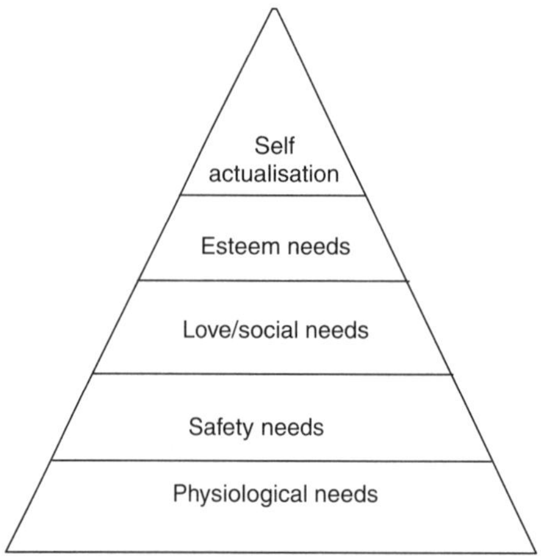

Each level of need is dominant until it has been satisfied: only then does the next (higher) level of need become a motivating factor. A need which has been satisfied no longer motivates an individual's behaviour. So, for example, a person who is starving will be driven to obtain food (even if it means a risk to his safety, say). Once his hunger is satisfied, it will no longer be a priority, and his actions will be motivated by the next highest unsatisfied need.

The hierarchy is not intended to be clear-cut: different individuals may have different priorities, and may act on them in different ways.

The highest level of need on the hierarchy, self-actualisation, can rarely – if ever – be satisfied.

(b) **Applying Maslow's theory to staff motivation**

Maslow did not intend his model to be applied specifically to workplace motivation. There is, for example, no explicit discussion of the role of pay – although money is potentially a 'stand in' for (or means of obtaining) a number of need satisfactions.

It does have a simple intuitive appeal, however, and may be used by managers to understand:

- What people seek to get from their work, and what rewards can be offered to motivate them. So, for example, neo-human relations theorists built on Maslow's work to explore how team-working might satisfy social needs; and how job design and development programmes could offer satisfaction of esteem and self-actualisation needs.

- What basic needs must be met in order to move people towards the higher motivations that will impact on their job performance. The hierarchy explains, for example, why inadequate pay and unsafe working conditions undermine motivation – even in high-status or challenging jobs.

The hierarchy does have limitations, however. Empirical verification of the theory has been hard to come by, especially in contexts outside the UK/US cultures in which Maslow's observations were made. The model is a simplification of complex human values and behaviours, and cannot be used reliably to explain or predict individual behaviour at work, or response to rewards.

46 Equity theory

Text reference. These aspects are covered in Chapter 13.

Top tips. This ought to have been a straightforward question, but you needed: (a) to have got clear the difference between 'content' and 'process' theories of motivation (common exam pitfall); and (b) to have learned equity theory in detail. (Note for the purposes of question selection: if you were unable to answer part (b) with any confidence, you could not answer part (c) either...)

Easy marks. Part (a) should offer easy marks, but if you hadn't learned equity theory in detail, you would have struggled (or more likely, not chosen to tackle this question).

Examiner's comments. Candidates who confused 'process' and 'content' theories went on to compound their mistake by talking (completely irrelevantly) about Maslow. (The examiner stated with some exasperation: 'Maslow is not the only theory of motivation!') Some candidates discussed 'equity' in terms of financial reward: wrongly, because it is (clearly, in this context) a psychological model of how motivation works.

Marking scheme

		Marks
(a)	Description of process theory	5
(b)	Description of equity theory	5
(c)	Description of negative equity	5
		15

(a) **Process theory**

Process theories of motivation ask the question: 'how are people motivated?' or 'how can they be motivated (by others, such as a superior at work)?' They focus on the processes through which:

(i) Outcomes become desirable to an individual

(ii) Individuals select particular behaviours in order to pursue desirable outcomes

(iii) Individuals calculate whether it is worth implementing and maintaining those behaviours in order to achieve those outcomes.

Examples of process theories include: Victor Vroom's expectancy theory, Charles Handy's motivational calculus and JS Adams' equity theory

(b) **Equity theory**

Equity theory (usually associated with the work of JS Adams) is a **process theory** of motivation which focuses on people's sense of whether they have been fairly treated in comparison with the way others have been treated.

It is based on exchange theory, which suggests that people expect certain **outcomes** or rewards in exchange for their **inputs** or contributions. If they perceive that the ratio of their outcomes to inputs is unequal to that of other people, they experience a sense of **inequity** – whether positive (they feel they have been treated 'unfairly' well) or negative (they feel they have been treated 'unfairly' badly). If someone feels they are not getting paid enough for their work, compared to others, for example, they will have a sense of negative inequity.

(c) A sense of inequity causes unpleasant tension, or dissonance, which motivates people to attempt to remove or reduce the perceived inequity. Various ways of doing so include:

- Changing the inputs (eg reducing their hours or quality of work)
- Changing the outcomes (eg demanding better pay)
- Cognitive distortion (eg believing they aren't really working as hard as they are)
- Withdrawal (eg absenteeism or resignation)
- Influencing others to do any of the above (eg getting co-workers to put in extra hours)
- Changing the comparison (eg comparing themselves with a different set of people)

47 The job as a motivator

Text reference. Job design is discussed in Section 5 of Chapter 13.

Top tips. The question itself notes that there is often confusion between these terms (different job re-designs recommended by Herzberg to improve satisfaction) – so if you weren't absolutely clear which was which, this was probably a question to avoid. 'Enlargement' is 'making *bigger*': think of it as a horizontal extension. 'Enrichment' is 'making *better*': think of it as a vertical extension. 'Rotation' is just 'going round and round'...

Easy marks. If you knew your terms, there was no barrier to your getting full marks here: the question itself is quite straightforward.

Examiner's comments. This was not a difficult question, but there was some confusion as to the differences between the different terms. For example, job enrichment is about providing greater responsibility for the job holder, not to do with bonuses or extra payments.

Marking scheme

	Marks
Definition and explanation of each given term (5 marks each)	15

(a) **Job enrichment**

Job enrichment is planned, deliberate action to build greater responsibility, breadth and challenge of work into a job. It is also referred to **vertical extension**. Job enrichment is similar to empowerment, although the emphasis of job enrichment is on the individual rather than on the team.

A job may be enriched by:

(i) Giving the job holder **decision-making capabilities of a higher order**. What is mundane detail at a high level can represent significant job interest at a lower level.

(ii) Giving the **employee greater freedom** to decide how the job should be done.

(iii) Encouraging employees **to participate** in the planning decisions of their superiors.

(iv) Giving the employee regular **feedback**.

(b) **Job enlargement**

Job enlargement is the attempt to widen jobs by increasing the number of operations in which a job holder is involved.

By reducing the number of repetitions of the same work, the dullness of the job should also be reduced. Job enlargement is therefore a **horizontal extension** of an individual's work.

Enlarged jobs can provide a **challenge and incentive**. For example, a trusted employee might be given added responsibilities, for example:

- **Checking the quality of output**
- **On the job training** of new recruits

Enlarged jobs might also be regarded as having **higher status** within the department, and as stepping stones towards promotion.

(c) **Job rotation**

Job rotation might take two forms.

(i) An employee might be **transferred to another job** after a period of, say, two to four years in an existing job, in order to introduce new interest and challenge, and to bring a fresh person to the job.

(ii) **Job rotation might be regarded as a form of training**. Trainees might be expected to learn a bit about a number of different jobs, by spending six months or one year in each job before being moved on. The employee is regarded as a trainee.

48 Rewards

Text reference. The terminology is explained clearly in Chapter 13.

Top tips. An incredibly easy question, as long as you knew the terminology. But remember you were asked to describe *extrinsic* rewards. If you listed 'recognition' or 'fulfilment' in the list, this would have been incorrect. Make sure you can get 'intrinsic' and 'extrinsic' the right way round every time!

Easy marks. The confusion of terms, such as 'intrinsic' and 'extrinsic', is a common exam pitfall. Once you have got past it (by learning and revising your terms accurately), these should all be easy marks. Note, however, that you have to earn your marks for part (c) by *describing* six extrinsic rewards: listing them will not be sufficient.

Examiner's comments. Candidates who gave opposite definitions for extrinsic/intrinsic were unable to score well.

Marking scheme

		Marks
(a)	Explanation of 'intrinsic' rewards	3
(b)	Explanation of 'extrinsic' rewards	3
(c)	Description of any six extrinsic rewards (1½ marks per reward to max of 9)	9
		15

(a) **Intrinsic rewards**

Intrinsic rewards are those which arise from the performance of the work itself. They are therefore psychological rather than material and relate to the concept of job satisfaction. Intrinsic rewards include the satisfaction that comes from completing a piece of work, the status that certain jobs convey, the feeling of achievement that comes from doing a difficult job well. Intrinsic rewards tend to be associated with autonomy in the planning and execution of work.

(b) **Extrinsic rewards**

Extrinsic rewards are those which are separate from, or external to, the job itself. They also tend to be dependent on the decisions of others, who control the desired outcomes or resources offered in exchange for work performance: in other words, they are also external to the control of the workers themselves. Pay, benefits and working conditions are all examples of extrinsic rewards.

(c) **Six extrinsic rewards**

Extrinsic rewards include:

(i) Basic pay, often in the form of wages or salaries, with the option of bonuses or incentives (such as overtime rates). As one of Herzberg's 'hygiene' factors, it minimises dissatisfaction rather than fostering positive motivation, but it is also an important indicator of value and equity.

(ii) Performance-related pay of various kinds, whether related to output or results achieved. It is based on the assumption of 'Rational-economic Man' (Schein) who is motivated by economic incentives, but in practice incentives are balanced against the deprivations required to earn them (Goldthorpe, Lockwood et al).

(iii) Financial benefits. Some benefits (eg for sickness, maternity and pensions) are governed by law and tradition, but employers may add more generous provisions, such as enhanced pension contributions, subsidised loans or insurances and so on.

(iv) Non-cash incentives. The organisation may offer a range of benefits (sometimes on a 'cafeteria' system, where employees may choose the benefits most relevant to them on a performance-based 'points' system): including access to private medical facilities or health services; additional holiday entitlements; use of fleet vehicles and so on.

(v) Family-friendly and work-life balance policies and facilities: crèche facilities, child-care assistance, flexible working, term-time contracts and so on may be provided as part of the total reward package.

(vi) Working conditions. The concept of total reward recognises that anything that enhances the quality of working life may be regarded as part of the reward 'package' for employees: a safe and pleasing working environment, the perceived status of employment and a people-focused organisational culture may be regarded as extrinsic rewards.

49 Scenario: Leadership styles

Text reference. Leadership style theories are covered in Chapter 14.

Top tips. (Since this is a compulsory question, it provides a useful warning on the importance of detailed revision!) If you weren't very familiar with Tannenbaum and Schmidt's model (part (a)), you could still gain marks by discussing the continuum or range of leadership styles – which might prompt your memory as to the broad categories of style shared by various style models. Adair's 'action-centred' model (part (c)), has been examined in detail recently, and should give you some basic marks. You really needed to get these basic points down on paper, in order to progress to the more challenging application aspects: even where the theoretical model doesn't apply particularly well to the scenario (as in part (d)), you have to refer to it – rather than to other models which you may know better.

Easy marks. There aren't too many easy marks here, if you haven't revised the full range of leadership theories (or read the examiner's pre-exam *Student Accountant* article on the topic!).

Examiner's comments. The scenario was constructed deliberately to allow candidates to display understanding of different leadership styles. It was pleasing that few candidates wasted time writing out parts of the scenario, or using report/memo format when not asked to do so.

Marking scheme

				Marks
(a)	(i)	Identification and description of the four broad leadership styles described by Tannenbaum and Schmidt (Three marks per style up to 12 marks)	12	
	(ii)	Brief description of the four factors (One mark each up to 4 marks)	4	
				16
(b)		The Tannenbaum & Schmidt leadership style which best describes		
	(i)	Dean Thomas	4	
	(ii)	Lee Allen	4	
				8
(c)		Explanation of action-centred leadership and justification of Lee Allen's approach		8
(d)		Description of Fiedler's two approaches and appreciation of Emma Jenkins' position		8
				40

(a) **Tannenbaum & Schmidt's continuum of management styles**

There are various classifications of leadership style. Although the labels and definitions of styles vary, style models broadly address a continuum of behaviours from wholly task-focused, directive leadership behaviours (representing high leader control) at one extreme, and wholly people-focused, supportive/relational behaviours (representing high subordinate discretion) on the other.

This was the specific model asked for : it *must* be addressed!

Tannenbaum and Schmidt proposed a continuum of behaviours which reflected the balance of control exercised in a situation by the leader and the team. Their four broad styles (clusters of behaviour) are defined as:

1 **Telling**

Corresponding to the Ashridge model's 'tells' style (or Lewin, Lippitt and White's 'autocratic' style), this style reflects a balance of power wholly in favour of the leader. It involves highly directive behaviours: the leader makes decisions and announces them, expecting them to be obeyed.

2 **Selling**

Corresponding to the Ashridge model's 'sells' style, this style reflects a balance of power substantially in favour of the leader, but with the attempt to motivate subordinates by communicating decisions more persuasively. The leader explains ideas, invites questions/comments and justifies decisions – without necessarily allowing feedback to influence them.

3 **Consulting**

Corresponding to the Ashridge model's 'consults' style, this style reflects a more even balance of control. While retaining final authority, the leader presents problems and draft plans, confers with subordinates and takes their views into account in formulating final decisions.

4 **Coaching**

Corresponding to the Ashridge model's 'joins' style (or Lewin, Lippitt and White's 'democratic' style), this style reflects a genuine sharing of control, with substantial employee discretion. The leader typically defines limits and goals, and then both allows and empowers subordinates to make decisions and manage their work accordingly.

The header reminds us exactly what we have been asked to discuss

Four factors in the choice of appropriate management style

The decision as to which management style will be most appropriate (according to Tannenbaum and Schmidt, and other contingency theorists), depends on:

1. **The leader**: his or her personality and preferred style of operating (since there is a limit to behavioural flexibility)
2. **The subordinates:** their individual and collective preferences for a particular style of leadership; their abilities, experience, motivation and attitudes (which contribute to what Hersey & Blanchard describe as their 'maturity' or 'readiness' to be less directively led)
3. **The situation:** the immediate context of leadership, including the nature of the task, plans and time-scales, the organisation's HR policies and the leader's position in the organisation structure
4. **The environment:** the wider context of the organisation structure, technology, culture and so on – as well as the external environment (including trade union influence, labour surpluses or shortages and so on).

Fairly clear from the scenario

(b) **Dean Thomas' management style**

Dean Thomas, from the data given, is a highly **democratic, non-directive, relational team leader**: an extreme form of what Tannenbaum & Schmidt call a 'coaching' style, bordering on what Lewin, Lippitt and White call 'laissez-fare' (almost abdicating the leadership role altogether). **This can be seen** in several of his leadership behaviours, notably:

Note use of scenario evidence

- His enjoyment of team communication and relationships (at the expense of achieving targets, for which he is responsible)
- His allowing the team to 'pick and choose' tasks and make their own decisions without intervention from him
- His non-contribution to the discussion of problems (carried out wholly within the team).

Lee Allen's management style

Lee Allen, from the data given, is more flexible (or less consistent) in his management style, depending on the circumstances.

Where performance is not an issue, he complies with the prevailing corporate style (a 'coaching' or democratic style) – as befits his highly experienced team.

You may have gone just for a 'telling' style: we have spotted a more subtle contingency approach.

However, where task performance appears (to him) to be falling short of (negotiated) targets, he reverts to his **naturally-preferred style, which is a more 'telling' style**. This is, arguably, appropriate if performance is at risk of falling short, especially if this is key factor in the leadership situation (emphasis on team performance, Lee's personal accountability for results etc).

However, looking at the wider environment (the team's expectations, based on WWM's relaxed culture), it may be that Lee's autocratic (and inconsistent) style is actively contributing to the team's poor morale and absenteeism – which may eventually erode its performance.

Identify the author of the named model/ theory if possible

(c) **Action-centred leadership**

Action-centred (situational or functional) leadership is a model devised by **John Adair** for management training and development.

It is part of the contingency school of thought, because it sees the leadership process in a context made up of three interrelated variables: task needs, the individual needs of group members and the needs of the group as a whole. These needs must be examined in the light of the whole situation, which dictates the relative priority that must be given to each of the three sets of needs.

Answering the second part of the requirement

Effective leadership is a process of identifying and acting on that priority: performing a range of leadership activities (such as task definition, planning, briefing, controlling and so on) as applied to a cluster of roles relevant to each set of needs.

Lee Allen's approach may be described as 'action-centred', in that he appears to decide, within the context of the whole situation, which set of needs has the higher priority at a given time – and employs a cluster of behaviours appropriate to that role at that time. So, for example, if performance appears to be slipping, he gives a lower priority to Adair's 'group maintenance' roles (encouraging, peace-keeping, clarifying and standard-seeking) and 'individual maintenance' roles (goal-setting, feedback, recognition, counselling and training). Instead, he focuses on the leader's 'task' roles: initiating, diagnosing, evaluating and decision-making.

However, it should be noted that information-seeking and opinion-seeking are also part of the leader's 'task' role, according to Adair: Lee may be neglecting the leadership activity of 'motivating' in these areas.

We explain the theory first ...

(d) **Fiedler's contingency theory of leadership**

F E Fiedler was a leading advocate of **contingency theory**. He studied the impact of leadership style on work group effectiveness and identified two types of leader:

- 'Psychologically distant managers' (PDMs) maintain distance from their subordinates by formalising roles, relationships and communication. They judge subordinates on the basis of performance and are mainly task-oriented.
- 'Psychologically close managements' (PCMs) are closer to their subordinates and more concerned to maintain good human relationships at work than to ensure that tasks are carried out efficiently.

Then apply it to the scenario as requested

It is possible to identify **Dean Thomas as a PCM, and Lee Allen as a PDM**.

Fiedler's model goes on to discuss how the effectiveness of the work group depends on the fit between the leader's style and the favourableness of the group situation. However, this is not directly relevant to Emma's request for a transfer.

Emma's desire to move to Dean Thomas' team is likely to be based, more loosely, on a simple psychological preference for the more psychologically close style of operating. This is turn may be based on expectations raised by company policy, culture and past experience: having enjoyed (and come to expect) input into decision-making, Emily is frustrated and dissatisfied by its absence in Lee's team – and sees that she is more likely to have it in Dean's.

50 Leadership skills and actions

Text reference. Both these aspects of leadership are covered in Chapter 14.

Top tips. You may have chosen to answer (a) using a named theory (such as Avolio's Four Is) but we show you could take a more general approach. (Remember, you only need 3 skills x 2 marks). Parts (b) and (c) depended on you recognising John Adair's model, and addressing its general principles and specific focus (task, group, individuals). It really isn't worth 'guessing' or 'bluffing' for 9 marks: if you didn't know the model, you would have done better to leave this option alone.

Easy marks. If you didn't know action-centred leadership, you could have got the first six marks under your belt – but probably better to seek a question with at least half the marks on areas you're more confident about...

Examiner's comments. This was not a popular question, and some answers indicated guesswork. Candidates who knew the topic scored well.

Marking scheme

		Marks
(a)	Brief outline of three skills of a leader (2 marks each)	6
(b)	Brief explanation of action-centred leadership (1 mark each point)	3
(c)	Description of the three major goals (2 marks each)	6
		15

(a) **Leadership** requires, above all, **strong communication skills**.

(i) **Creating a sense of direction** – usually borne out of dissatisfaction with the status quo. Out of this challenge a vision for something different is created.

(ii) **Communicating the vision** – which must meet the realised or unconscious needs of other people. The leader must work to give it credibility, and have the ability to inspire confidence and trust.

(iii) **Energising, inspiring and motivating** – in order to stimulate others to translate the vision into achievement. The leader must of course have a clear understanding of the task in hand.

(b) **Action-centred leadership**

This is concerned with what leaders actually do, rather than their particular style, and is therefore regarded as a functional approach to leadership. John Adair's action-centred leadership model sees the leadership process in a context made up of three interrelated variables.

(i) **Task** needs
(ii) The **individual** needs of group members, and
(iii) The needs of the **group** as a whole

The leader needs to balance the relative importance of these.

(c) The particular circumstances of each 'leadership' situation will dictate the relative priority that must be given to each of the three sets of goals identified in part (b). Effective leadership comes from identifying and acting on that priority. The actions required for each variable are set out in the diagram below.

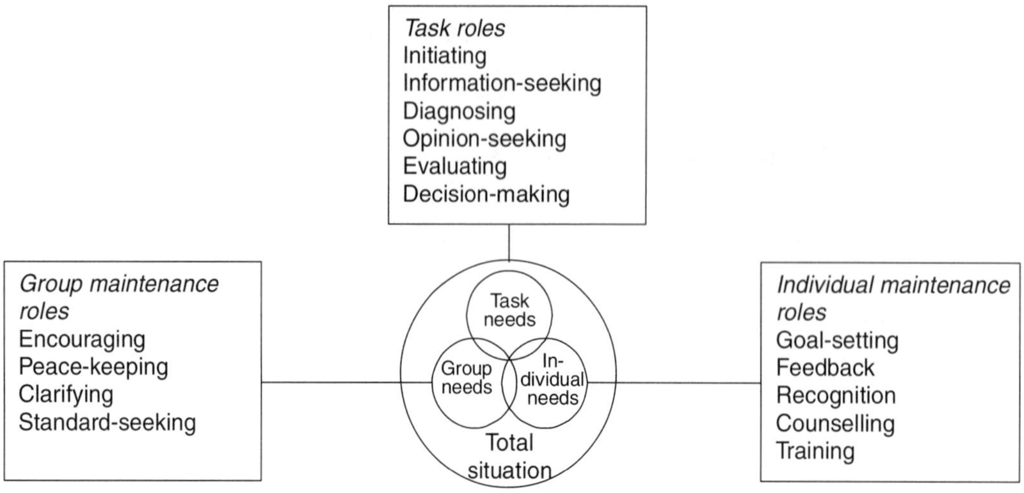

(Adair)

51 Leadership style

Text reference. The underlying theory is clearly covered in Chapter 14.

Top tips. This is an unstructured question, which means that you will need to impose your own structure on it. The instruction key words 'critically discuss' suggest an approach: you need to present arguments for and against the assertions and assumptions made by the quoted statement. First, analyse what assertions and assumptions it is making. We suggest there are actually three: (a) that managers can choose leadership styles; (b) that a leadership style can ever be 'entirely appropriate' to a given situation and that (c) this is an important skill for managers. This gives a coherent structure (and target mark allocation of 5 marks each) for our answer.

Answer plan

1 What is leadership style?

- Different behaviours suitable in different situations (Fiedler)

2 'A leader can choose a style to fit the situation.'

- Contingency or 'best fit' approach (Handy)

  BUT

- Leader may not have flexibility
- Loss of consistency for subordinates

3 A leader can choose an 'entirely appropriate' style

  BUT

- Situation too complex (eg contingency) to take into account
- 'Best fit' compromise rather than 'best way'

4 'Style choice is important skill'

- Key to effective management (eg Fiedler)

(a) **A leadership style can be chosen to fit the situation**

Early theorists concentrated on the 'traits' that successful leaders were said to 'possess'. However, the 'great man' theory failed to describe or facilitate the dynamics of the leadership situation.

It came to be recognised that a 'style' of leadership – a strategic pattern of attitudes and behaviours – could be adopted, and that different styles appeared to be effective in different contexts, according to such variables as the relationship between the leader and the group, the nature of the task and the power of the leader in relation to the group (Fiedler).

It therefore seemed desirable for a would-be leader to select and adopt a style for 'best fit' (Handy) with the situation, as suggested in the quote.

However, there are limitations to such a 'pure' contingency view.

(i) Not all would-be leaders will have the behavioural flexibility to change style convincingly to suit the situation, or to adopt a style which is not 'natural' to them.

(ii) Consistency is important to subordinates, and they may regard a constantly changing 'contingency' approach to leadership style with insecurity or mistrust.

(b) **It is possible to choose a leadership style which is 'entirely appropriate' to any given situation**

Various **contingency theories** of leadership suggest a complex mix of **variables** in the leadership context, including (in John Adair's model) the **task needs**, **group needs** and **individual needs** of the group members and leader, as well as the 'total situation' which dictates the relative priority to be given to each set of needs.

At best, effective leadership consists of creating a balance **or 'best fit' between the different (and often conflicting) demands of all these factors**. Arguably, no style can be considered 'entirely appropriate' to all factors in a situation: from whose perspective is the 'appropriateness' to be judged?

It is important to be realistic in one's expectations of managers and of theoretical tools such as the concept of leadership style.

(c) **Choosing an appropriate style is one of the most important skills of an effective manager**

Style theorists agree that choosing an appropriate style is the key to effective management. Fiedler, for example, concluded that 'group performance will be contingent upon the appropriate matching of leadership styles and the degree of favourableness of the group situation for the leader.'

52 Blake and Mouton

Text reference. Blake and Mouton are covered in Chapter 14, as a leadership model.

Top tips. This is a fairly straightforward, and helpfully structured question on a mainstream topic. If you'd attempted question 50, it would be quite familiar. Just pay careful attention to the specific key words: (a) 'what it measures'; (b) 'the five extreme scores'; and (c) 'usefulness'...

Easy marks. This question should pose no difficulties if you are well prepared.

Examiner's comments. This was a popular question. Parts (a) and (b) were well answered, but part (c) suggested that insufficient care was taken in reading the question: some candidates simply repeated part (b) material.

Marking scheme

		Marks
(a)	Description of the management grid	5
(b)	Examples of scores (1 mark per score)	5
(c)	Discussion of the usefulness of the grid	5
		15

(a) **Blake** and **Mouton** carried out research (The Ohio State Leadership Studies) into managerial behaviour and observed two basic dimensions of leadership: **concern for production** (or task performance) and **concern for people.**

Along each of these two dimensions, managers could be located at any point on a **continuum** from very low to very high concern.

Blake and Mouton observed that the two concerns did not seem to correlate, positively or negatively: a high concern in one dimension, for example, did not seem to imply a high or low concern in the other dimension. Individual managers could therefore reflect various permutations of task/people concern.

Blake and Mouton modelled these permutations as a grid. One axis represented concern for people, and the other concern for production. Blake and Mouton allotted nine points on each axis, from 1 (low) to 9 (high).

The managerial grid was intended as an **appraisal and management development tool.** It recognises that a balance is required between concern for task and concern for people, and that a high degree of both is possible (and highly effective) at the same time.

(b) The extreme scores identified by Blake and Mouton are these.

(i) 1.1 **impoverished:** the manager is lazy, showing little interest in either staff or work.

(ii) 1.9 **country club:** the manager is attentive to staff needs and has developed satisfying relationships. However, there is little attention paid to achieving results.

(iii) 9.1 **task management:** almost total concentration on achieving results. People's needs are virtually ignored.

(iv) 5.5 **middle of the road** or the **dampened pendulum:** adequate performance through balancing the necessity to get work done, while maintaining the morale of people at a satisfactory level.

(v) 9.9 **team**: high performance manager who achieves high work accomplishment through 'leading' committed people, who identify themselves with the organisational aims.

(c) The grid offers a number of useful insights for the identification of management **training and development** needs. It shows in an easily assimilated form where the behaviour and assumptions of a manager may exhibit a lack of balance between the dimensions and/or a low degree of concern. It may also be used in team member selection, so that a 1.9 team leader is balance by a 9.1 co-leader, for example.

However, the grid is a **simplified** model, and as such has **practical limitations.**

(i) It assumes that 9.9 is the desirable model for effective leadership. In some managerial contexts, this may not be so. Concern for people, for example, would not be necessary in a context of comprehensive automation: compliance is all that would be required.

(ii) It is open to oversimplification. Scores can appear polarised, with judgements attached about individual managers' suitability or performance. The grid is intended as a simplified 'snapshot' of a manager's preferred style, not a comprehensive description of his or her performance.

(iii) Organisational context and culture, technology and other factors influence the manager's style of leadership, not just the two dimensions described by the grid.

(iv) Any managerial theory is useful only in so far as it is useable in practice by managers: if the grid is used only to inform managers that they 'must acquire greater concern for people', it may result in uncertainty and inconsistent behaviour.

53 Theory Z

Text reference. Ouchi's work is covered in Chapter 14.

Top tips. Theory Z is a less well-known area than Theory X and Y – but there is no excuse for confusing them! You should have recognised Ouchi's model incorporating Japanese management techniques, which may have suggested at least one point worth making in part (b).

Examiner's comments. Some candidates committed the commonplace error of thinking that Theory Z fitted with (or was part of) Theory X and Y. Others completely ignored the specific question requirements and described other management ideas such as bureaucracy. Even if you are hard-pressed in an exam, it is not worth doing this: you just don't earn any marks.

Marking scheme

		Marks
(a)	Description of Theory Z (1 mark per characteristic)	10
(b)	Discussion on Theory Z	5
		15

(a) **Theory Z**

WG Ouchi *(Theory Z: How American Business Can Meet the Japanese Challenge)* compared the cultural values of American (Theory A) and Japanese (Theory J) management, and formulated an 'ideal' organisational model – which he called Theory Z – incorporating elements of both. In particular, it was considered that Japanese principles such as consensus decision-making and mutual loyalty in the employment relationship should be adopted to improve Western productivity and labour relations.

Ouchi described the Theory Z organisation as having:

(i) Long-term employment, with slow-progressing managerial career paths (as in the Japanese system, but with greater specialisation of skills)

(ii) Broad concern for employee welfare inside and outside work (not just work performance, as in the American system): commitment to the 'organisation family'

(iii) Implicit informal controls alongside explicit, formal measures

(iv) Collective consensus decision-making processes (Japanese), but with individual retention of ultimate responsibility (American)

Marks & Spencer in the UK has been cited as an organisation operating on principles akin to Theory Z.

(b) **Applicability of Theory Z**

Theory Z was welcomed in its time as helping western management answer the challenge posed by Japanese industrial success: it was, therefore, specifically designed to allow for transfer of values and practices from one culture to another, in a suitably modified form.

Some of its insights have been successfully incorporated by some western organisations – using concepts such as quality circles, self-managed team-working and single status agreements – but not as eagerly or enduringly as Japanese manufacturing systems and work organisation techniques. It is less easy to transfer underlying cultural values to foreign contexts than methods and techniques.

It is also necessary to take a contingency approach to managerial techniques in general. As suggested by Handy's loose-tight continuum (among other contingency models), some organisational situations suit tight 'command-and-control' managerial approaches – while others suit more people-centred approaches (such as Theory Z). The suitability of *any* management style or model will depend on factors such as organisational environment, structure, objectives and culture; the nature of the task and technology; the skills and expectations of the personnel; and the skills of the individual managers.

54 Scenario: Interpersonal skills

Text reference. All these issues are discussed in Chapter 15.

Top tips. This is a challenging question, as it requires a detailed knowledge of a particular psychological theory (assertive behaviour) and an unusually high degree of application to the scenario (clearly indicated by specific references to David Lowe and Simon Price). However, there are straightforward marks to be gained, as the underlying requirements of the questions include key topics like the importance of effective interpersonal skills. Make sure you can define and distinguish clearly between passive, aggressive and assertive behaviour.

Examiner's comments. This question was poorly answered. Far too many candidates either repeated the contents of the case without analysis of the problem – or 'wandered round the topic' with irrelevant material. Lack of interpersonal skills was basic to the problems presented in the case study, so there should have been no lack of material.

Marking scheme

			Marks
(a)	Definition and description of inappropriateness of aggressive behaviour	6	
	Definition and description of appropriateness of assertive behaviour	7	13
(b)	Explanation of passive behaviour and application to case study		6
(c)	Explanation of importance of interpersonal skills		6
(d)	Discussion on David Lowe's need for good interpersonal skills in the specific three areas requested (up to 5 marks for each)		15
			40

(a) **The inappropriateness of aggressive behaviour**

Aggressive behaviour is a 'fight' reaction to frustration, conflict or threat, usually in the form of verbal or physical attack. According to Back & Back it implies standing up for your rights in such a way that you violate the rights of others, and expressing your own needs, wants and opinions in inappropriate ways. In this situation, for example, an aggressive response might be to say loudly: 'You're always loading work on me – and I'm sick of it. If you want the cashbook done tonight – do it yourself!'

It would clearly be inappropriate for Simon Price to act in such a manner, because:

(i) David Lowe is his superior: it would be unprofessional and counter-productive – and may lay Simon open to disciplinary action.

(ii) Aggressive behaviour is generally counter-productive. It may have the effect of Simon immediately getting his way and 'letting off steam' – but in the long term, it leads to broken working relationships, resentment and hostility (which are already a problem in the department).

(iii) Aggressive behaviour often leads to escalation of conflict – and this is particularly likely to be the case since David Lowe seems to be an aggressive communicator.

(iv) Another of the counter-productive effects of aggressive behaviour is guilt feelings on the part of the aggressor – and Simon would be particularly prone to this, being naturally an unassuming and quiet individual.

Appropriateness of assertive behaviour

Assertive behaviour is a considered response to frustration, conflict or threat which seeks to satisfy the needs and wants of all parties involved in the situation. According to Back & Back, such behaviour involves: standing up for your own rights in such a way that you do not violate another person's rights; and expressing your needs, wants, opinions, feelings and beliefs in direct, honest and appropriate ways. In this situation, for example, an assertive response might be to say calmly: 'I appreciate that you'd like the cashbook done immediately. However, I'd really prefer to complete the sales invoicing work this evening.'

It would be more appropriate for Simon to behave in this manner, because:

(i) It acknowledges that David has the right to ask him to change tasks – just as he has the right to express his feelings about it.

(ii) It defuses the potential for conflict, by showing David that his request has been heard and taken into account, and by not blaming or accusing David: instead, Simon merely states his own feelings in the matter, honestly and calmly.

(iii) It protects both David's and Simon's self-respect. Simon does not have to justify himself or 'fix' the situation by offering alternative solutions: it is up to David to generate other options.

(iv) It maintains the working relationship between David and Simon. There may be an opportunity, later, to be equally assertive in tackling the underlying problem of David's poor management style.

(b) **Diagnosing Simon's passive behaviour**

Passive (or non-assertive) behaviour is a 'flight' reaction to frustration, conflict or threat. It usually takes the form of giving in to others' demands. According to Back & Back, non-assertion implies failing to stand up for your rights, and failing to express your needs, wants, opinions and feelings in clear, honest and self-respecting ways.

Simon's behaviour has clearly been passive up to this point.

(i) He is characterised by others as 'unassuming' and 'quiet' – which means that he is generally diffident or self-effacing about his feelings, despite that fact that his workload has increased dramatically and that he shares the general dissatisfaction with David Lowe.

(ii) Simon has 'tried explaining' the problem to David – but has clearly failed: despite the fact that David is regarded as having poor interpersonal skills, the onus is on Simon to explain the problem more clearly and firmly.

(iii) Despite the fact that he is feeling tired and miserable and has just been ill, he has tried to carry a double workload – apparently without complaint.

(c) **Why does David need effective interpersonal skills**

Interpersonal skill are skills in dealing one-to-one with other people in relationships and transactions. They include: skills in rapport– and relationship-building; skills in verbal and non-verbal communication; skills in persuasion and influence; and skills in relationship maintenance and problem solving (conflict resolution, assertiveness, counselling and so on).

David needs such skills in order to:

(i) Understand and manage the roles, relationships, attitudes and perceptions operating in the work situation

(ii) Communicate clearly and effectively

(iii) Achieve his short– and long-term aims from interpersonal encounters (which includes allowing the other parties to emerge satisfied too)

In another sense, David needs such skills because he clearly lacks them at the moment – and the negative effects can be seen in his department.

(i) He is unpopular and not respected by his staff, explicitly because of his 'poor interpersonal skills'

(ii) Effective working relationships are breaking down because of his failure to listen and lack of sensitivity: this can clearly be seen in his failure to empathise with David as he has tried to express the problem.

(iii) Staff absenteeism is widespread because of poor morale, at least partly caused by his poor managerial style.

(d) **Motivation**

David's current interpersonal skills are actively de-motivating his team. Interpersonal skills are required in motivation because:

(i) Leadership is an interpersonal process: skills are required to inspire/persuade staff for committed performance.

(ii) Effective interpersonal relations at work satisfy employees' social needs, and can enhance job satisfaction, morale and loyalty.

(iii) Good-quality, open information on performance goals, standards and attainments supports the motivation calculus (Handy).

(iv) Interpersonal praise, recognition and concern provide positive reinforcement for desired behaviours/performance.

Negotiation

David is not currently a skilled negotiator where his staff are concern: he appears to 'pursue his own agenda' with no attempt at 'win-win' solutions. Interpersonal skills are important in negotiation because:

(i) They are required to maintain working relationships despite different interests (and the use of power to secure outcomes)

(ii) Negotiating skills (eg interpreting, using and countering influencing strategies) are required to gain acceptable long-term outcomes

(iii) Interpersonal influence can be used to replace command-and-control styles of direction in the employment relationship, harnessing commitment rather than compliance

Team-building

David is currently disintegrating his team, rather than building it. Interpersonal skills are important in team-building because:

(i) Successful team formation and building depends on skills in building trust, encouraging communication and forming relationships

(ii) In order to maintain co-operative working, skills are needed in the control of conflict and the management of differences

(iii) Interpersonal skills are required to manage group processes and dynamics (communication styles, compromise, negotiation, decision-making)

(iv) Skills in motivation and communication facilitate the group's task performance, which is also important in team cohesion and morale.

55 Aggressive or assertive?

Text reference. Assertive and aggressive behaviours are discussed under the topic of interpersonal skills in Chapter 15.

Top tips. If you have studied and revised the topic, you should be able to distinguish clearly between aggressive and assertive behaviour, so the most important key words here are 'explain *and give examples'* (ie more than one example). As part of your explanation, you might explain what aggressive/assertive behaviour is: you might also explain why it occurs – an opportunity to discuss the attitudes/beliefs underlying the behaviours. In terms of examples, don't worry about inventing complex scenarios and conversations: you can include simple examples of verbal/non-verbal behaviour.

Easy marks. You should be able to get the first 4-6 marks with concise definition and explanation of the terms aggressive and assertive (getting the distinction right, and the terms the right way round). There should also be at least one mark available for each example you can cite, so you should be able to gather marks quite quickly.

Examiner's comments.

A relatively popular but poorly answered question. The question was designed to test candidates ability to explain the differences between aggressive and assertive behaviour.

Marking scheme

		Marks
(a)	Explanation and examples of aggressive behaviour	Up to 8 marks
		(Maximum for part (a) 8 marks)
(b)	Explanation and examples of assertive behaviour	Up to 7 marks
		(Maximum for part (b) 7 marks)
		(Total for question 15 marks)

(a) **Aggressive behaviour**

Aggressive behaviour has its origins in the primitive 'fight' reaction to conflict, frustration or threat. It is based on the underlying assumption that the aggressor's rights are more important than those of others, so that the main aim of aggressive behaviour is to 'win' or dominate – if necessary at the expense of other people.

Typical aggressive behaviours include:

- Standing up for your rights in such a way that you violate the rights of others
- Ignoring or dismissing the needs, wants, feelings or viewpoints of others
- Expressing your own needs, wants and opinions in inappropriate ways.

At the 'micro' level, this may show itself in verbal and non-verbal behaviours such as: physically intimidating posture or gestures (clenched fists, pointing, standing over people); loud, emphatic vocal tone; interrupting others or shouting them down; intimidating intensity of eye contact and so on.

As an example in context, if a team member says to a manager that she is unable to attend a meeting, an aggressive response by the manager might be to stand over her, front heavily, point his pen right at her face and say in a loud, cold tone of voice: 'That wasn't a request, it was an order. Do you understand me?'

The immediate result of aggressive behaviours may be to release frustration and get one's way, but the longer-term result is often guilty feelings, broken relationships and loss of co-operation. This is why professional organisations stress the importance of managing aggression and cultivating a more constructive alternative: assertive behaviour.

(b) **Assertive behaviour** has its origins *not* in the primitive 'fight' or 'flight' reaction to conflict, frustration and threat, but in a more rational 'flow' response. It is based on the underlying assumption that the person's rights are important – but so are the rights of other people. The main aim of assertive behaviour is therefore not to win or dominate (aggressive) or to avoid conflict and please others at all costs (passive) but to communicate clearly and honestly and to maintain relationship, in order to get the needs of both parties met as far as possible.

Typical assertive behaviours include:

- Standing up for your own rights in such a way that you do not violate another person's rights
- Expressing your needs, wants, opinions, feelings and beliefs in direct, honest and appropriate ways.

At a 'micro' level, this may show itself in verbal and non-verbal behaviours such as: using non-emotive language; using 'I' statements to separate opinions from facts; maintaining open, confident but calm body language; and using repetition (without added volume) to ensure that you are heard.

As an example in context, if a team member says to a manager that she is unable to attend a meeting which is important for her to attend, an assertive response by the manager might be to meet her eye, maintain an open/positive posture and facial expression, and calmly state: 'I would really like you to attend, as there are important matters to discuss that affect us all. How can we make it possible for you to be there?'

The benefit of assertive behaviour in a professional setting is that you get your needs met, while maintaining positive working relationships, and often finding mutually satisfying solutions to problems.

56 Communication barriers

Text reference. This topic is discussed in Chapter 15.

Top tips. It is worth explaining what you understand by 'good communication' – but you *still* need to earn five marks for part (a) by explaining why it's important!

Easy marks. This is another straightforward question on a topic area that is very often tested.

Examiner's comments. Worryingly, far too many answers displayed a vague knowledge of what communication is, why it's important and the barriers to it that exist. Again candidates appeared not to have read the question – too many answers discussed downward and horizontal communication patterns, or what communication is (in part (a)), or methods of communication (in part (b)), *not* what the question required.

Marking scheme

		Marks
(a)	Explanation of the importance of good communication	5
(b)	Description of five major barriers (2 marks per barrier, 1 for identification, 1 for description)	10
		15

(a) **Good communication** may be defined as communication which is:

(i) **Effective**. It achieves the communicator's purpose in communicating, such as the message being received and understood, and eliciting the desired response

(ii) **Efficient**. It achieves its purpose without unnecessary waste of time, money and other resources. Everyone in the organisation knows what is expected of them.

Good communication is vitally important, particularly in a business organisation, because the achievement of organisational objectives depends on:

- The exchange of information for planning, decision-making and control
- The giving of orders and instructions for operations and transactions
- The establishing and maintenance of interpersonal relationships
- The transmission of information about products and services
- The exchange of information for problem-solving and innovation

If communication is inefficient, there will be a waste of resources (for example, money on unnecessarily long telephone exchanges, employee time on clarifying and correcting misunderstandings) and poor control and co-ordination, for which the organisation is accountable to its stakeholders.

(b) **Major barriers to good communication** *(note only five required for the answer)*

(i) **Poor basic communication skills** on the part of sender (distorted message, inappropriate choice of medium) or receiver (inattentive listening or reading)

(ii) **Failure to give or seek feedback**. Feedback – the response which confirms or questions receipt of a message – is essential to effective communication

(iii) **Misinterpretation or ignorance** of non-verbal communication. Non-verbal messages may confirm or contradict verbal ones, and are often a source of misinterpretation

(iv) **Differences in language**. People may not understand each other's national language, or technical jargon, or the particular set of symbols with which they are familiar

(v) **Personal differences, or 'social noise'**. Age, gender, education, social background, ethnic origin or functional specialism and priorities may encourage differing interpretation of words and events, and therefore misunderstanding

(vi) **Conflict**, which may create unwillingness to communicate helpfully. Withholding or distorting information may be used as a weapon in interpersonal conflict

(vii) Inappropriate amount or accuracy of **information**. Information may be insufficient or excessive for the use for which it is intended

(viii) **Active or implied discouragement** of communication. An organisation, for example, may ignore or respond negatively to input or the exchange of information

(ix) **Lack of trust in the source**. If the source of the message is unknown, or regarded with suspicion for some reason, it may be rejected

(x) **Context and perception**. People hear what they want and expect to hear: a message that is ill-timed, or apparently unrelated to the recipient's needs, will not be attentively received

57 Communication flows

Text reference. Flows and patterns are covered in Chapter 15.

Top tips. This is a tricky question, because of the specificity of its key words. In part (a) you are asked to explain *purposes*: what are these channels used for? In part (b) you have to select *three* of the patterns and explain what they are *and* how effective they are. (We have covered all four in our answer, for your revision.)

Easy marks. If you read the question carefully, part (a) should offer you good marks. Part (b) is either something you've covered or it isn't. This is actually a fairly obscure piece of laboratory research on written communication within groups... You could scrape some marks by working out obvious patterns (try drawing the shapes) such as the Circle and Y, if you needed to.

Examiner's comments. This question tested candidates' understanding of simple communication methods and the appropriateness of particular communication systems. Part (a) attracted strong answers, while in part (b) there was some evidence of guesswork, and far too many candidates described all four patterns when only three were asked for. Candidates must read the question carefully.

Marking scheme

		Marks
(a)	Description of the 3 communication flows (3 marks each)	9
(b)	Brief description of each pattern (2 marks each)	6
		15

(a) (i) **Downward communication** is very common, and is the most easily recognised. Its purpose is in giving out direct instructions, briefings, rules and policies and the announcement of plans, from superior to subordinate.

(ii) **Upward communication** is rarer, but at the same time is very important for the organisation. It takes the form of reporting back, feedback and suggestions. Managers need to encourage upward communication to take advantage of employees' experience and know-how, and to be able to understand their problems and needs in order to manage better.

(iii) **Lateral or horizontal communication** occurs between people of the same rank, in the same section or department, or different ones, for the purpose of task coordination through mechanisms such as meetings or brainstorming sessions. Ideas can be shared and problems solved. Horizontal communication between peer groups is usually easier and more direct than vertical communication, being less inhibited or controlled by considerations of rank. It can be either **formal** or **informal**.

(b) (i) In **the Circle**, each member of a group only communicates with the person directly next to them. This gives no scope for free sharing of ideas or coordination and also takes a very long time for all ideas to be heard. Participants in such patterns are unlikely to feel any satisfaction with the process.

(ii) In the **'Y'**, each member can only participate and contribute via the central figure, who collates all responses from his or her controlling position. Again, this inhibits the free flow of ideas and discussion is likely to be dominated by the central figure.

(iii) In **the Wheel**, similar to the Y, members can only communicate through the central mediating figure. This configuration solves problems more quickly as there is a greater number of participants. Its success depends on the ability of the central figure to coordinate the various responses.

(iv) The **all Channel** allows communication in all directions. While this has the advantage of encouraging participation and contribution from all quarters, and is best for solving complex problems which require such a level of contribution, it can disintegrate under pressure because of its relative lack of structure.

58 Scenario: Managing conflict

Text reference. All these aspects are covered in Chapter 16.

Top tips. The questions set should have given you a fairly clear hint as to what the scenario was meant to portray. Once you realised this was a conflict question, there should be plenty of ammunition for part (a): there are classic conflict issues of intra-team competition, personality clashes and competition for limited status symbols and resources. You might note that conflict can exist without 'overt' displays of hostility such as argument, and that loss of communication is an indicator of possible underlying conflict. In part (c), you will need to address each of the causes you identified in part (a): you may choose to take a comprehensive 'ecology'-based approach, or to discuss a specific win-win conflict resolution process. (We have used elements of both, for your revision.)

Answer plan

(a) What is happening?

Reasons why:

- Competition
- Politics
- Personal style

(b) Tactics
Conflicting parties use of tactics
Management response tactics

(c) Managing conflict
Ecological strategies
Regulation strategies
Motivation issues : possibility of 'win win'

(d) Value of conflict
Constructive (relate to GBH)

(a) **Analysis of the situation in the GBH Accounts Department**

It appears that there is underlying conflict within the department. The fact that this is not emerging as overt argument is not an indication to the contrary, since conflict can be very subtle and submerged. The withdrawal of co-operation manifested in decreased communication and emerging inefficiencies is sufficient to investigate the possibility of conflict further.

The current situation in the accounts department presents a number of **classic causes** of conflict.

(i) **The introduction of the 'Employee of the Month' competition has certainly provided potential for conflict,** particularly since no such attempt to compare individual performance has previously been used. This may have created a perception that management is carrying out some kind of selection process for promotion or (once insecurities grow out of proportion) even redundancy.

Deutsch reported a classic experiment in which students were given puzzles to work at in two different styles of group: 'co-operative' groups were told that the grade each individual got at the end of the course would depend on the performance of the group; 'competitive' groups were told that each student would receive a grade according to his own contributions. The co-operative groups, compared with the competitive ones, had greater productivity, better quality of output and discussion, better co-ordination and work sharing and better relationships.

(ii) The **directly competitive element discussed above has been reinforced by the more 'political' competition between department members for prime office space.** In any department, there will be some competition for scarce resources (including space, window area and so on): **office space** is particularly powerful in political game-playing, however, because **it symbolises the status and worth of the individual in the organisation.** Some of the insecurities of the Employee of the Month rivalry – and what it may be used to prove – may be exaggerating the importance of the office re-allocation.

(iii) **The reportedly abrasive personal style of the new supervisor is likely, in this highly-charged climate, to create interpersonal conflict and perhaps further insecurity about the way the department is being changed**. Personality clashes are in themselves a source of irritation and hostility, and can cause resistance in the team which would help to explain the reduction of communication: withholding information is an application of negative power.

The above is, of course, partly speculation on the basis of the evidence available. It would certainly be worth having an informal discussion with individual members of the team to get a sense of their perception of the situation in the department to confirm or deny the conflict hypothesis.

(b) **Tactics used in the conflict situation**

Common tactics used by conflicting parties

(i) **Withholding** information from one another, since 'knowledge is power'.

(ii) **Distorting information**. This will enable the individual presenting the information to manipulate the recipients and perhaps manoeuvre them into difficulties.

(iii) **Empire building**. A group (especially a specialist group, as in accounting) which considers its influence to be neglected might seek to impose rules, procedures or restrictions on other groups, in order to increase their power.

(iv) **Informal organisation**. Individuals and groups seek to by-pass formal channels of communication and decision-making by establishing informal contacts and coalitions with people in positions of influence.

(v) **Fault-finding** with the work of others: trying to prove rivals wrong, or to damage their position of influence or trust.

Tactics used by management in response to conflict

(i) **Denial/withdrawal**: 'sweeping it under the carpet'. If the conflict is trivial, ignoring it until it 'blows over' may be sufficient, but underlying causes can blow conflict up to unmanageable proportions.

(ii) **Suppression**: 'smoothing over', to preserve working relationships. Some cracks, however, cannot be papered over.

(iii) **Dominance**: the application of power or influence to settle the issue. The disadvantage of this is in setting up winners and losers.

(iv) **Compromise**: bargaining, negotiating, conciliating. To some extent this will be inevitable, but it can polarise positions (in order to allow for eventual compromise) and can be seen as a weak solution to a problem.

(v) **Integration/collaboration**: subordinating the needs of individuals to the requirements of the task. Individuals must accept the need to modify their views for the sake of the task, and group effort must be seen to be superior to individual effort.

(vi) **Encourage co-operative behaviours**: setting goals for all teams/departments, establishing joint problem-solving teams and so on.

(c) **Managing the conflict in the GBH Accounts Department**

There are a number of approaches to the conflict (if such it is found to be on investigation).

'Ecological' strategies are aimed at creating conditions which facilitate co-operation and positive interpersonal relations. For example:

(i) Reinforcing the 'team' nature of the department, and its shared objectives, through direct communication, supervisory style and team-based recognitions and rewards (over and above the 'Employee of the Month scheme).

(ii) Encouraging more (and more open) communication in all directions: more regular departmental meetings, informal contacts, management by walking around and so on.

(iii) Minimising political gameplaying. We may, for example, consider allocating offices by ballot, or taking the seriousness out of the 'Employee of the Month' competition so it becomes good-humoured.

Handy also discussed '**regulation'** strategies for controlling conflict where it is likely to arise. One such strategy, which could be applied in our case, is the provision of conflict **resolution counselling**, and (if necessary) arbitration of disputes. We may start with some informal counselling of the new supervisor and those who have a grievance because of his style.)

Conflict can most constructively be managed with a belief in the possibility of a 'win-win' solution, in which nobody 'loses': even if such a solution is ultimately impracticable, the effort to find it (by motivated communication and co-operative problem-solving) may in itself resolve the conflict in a creative way. It is recommended to have a meeting (facilitated according to 'win-win' guidelines) on the issue of office space. It may be that different people actually want or fear different outcomes: needing more natural light, say, or proximity to equipment, or fearing that 'missing out' on an office means losing status in the department.

Once these motivations are out in the open, it may be possible to find alternative solutions to each of the expressed needs or fears.

(d) **Constructive conflict**

Conflict can be highly positive, in any context, where its effect is to:

- Introduce different solutions to problems
- Define power relationships and limits more clearly
- Encourage creativity by testing ideas
- Improve the quality of decisions by challenging them
- Focus attention on individual contributions
- Bring emotions out into the open where they can be resolved

In the current situation at GBH, the conflicts may have some of these positive effects.

(i) **They have highlighted the fact that staff are not motivated by the new supervisor's abrasive style.** This can now be dealt with by counselling the supervisor, although it may be that the team's resistance is sufficient feedback to motivate him to change his style, once it becomes clear that it is not effective in creating a motivated or performing team.

(ii) **The Employee of the Month competition has stimulated some genuine extra performance,** dispute the negative consequences for co-operative team-working. It may be that, if individual effort is recognised and reinforced, and people feel less threatened by comparison, competitiveness will subside into more constructive competition.

(iii) **The conflict for priority in office space has highlighted some genuine issues of concern about current office facilities which can now be addressed.** It has also highlighted some personal insecurities about status and recognition in the department, symbolised by prime office locations: these issues of motivation and morale need to be dealt with at a deeper level so that staff feel secure and appreciated without political point-scoring.

(iv) The practice of conflict has brought out some interpersonal differences within the team which, having been identified, can be constructively managed to improve our appreciation of diversity and teamworking skills.

59 Conflict

Text reference. Chapter 16 covers all these topics.

Top tips. This is a straightforward question on some key topics – as long as you noted the instruction and topic keywords: '*Define...* conflict' (part (a)); ' *causes*' (part (b)); and '*characteristics... observed in the workplace*' (part (c)). Time and structure your answer according to the mark allocations.

Easy marks. Definitions, causes, symptoms (or characteristics): as long as you can sort out the one from the other (a question reading issue), the answers should be easy.

Examiner's comments. Some candidates focused on inter-personal causes and characteristics of conflict, neglecting wider organisational causes and symptoms. There was also some confusion between 'causes' and 'characteristics': absenteeism, for example, is primarily a characteristic of conflict – not a cause.

Marking scheme

		Marks
(a)	Definition of conflict	3
(b)	Causes of conflict (up to 1 mark each)	7
(c)	Characteristics of conflict (up to 1 mark each)	5
		15

BPP LEARNING MEDIA

(a) **Definition of conflict**

Conflict is, fundamentally, a state of opposition between two or more forces, ideas/positions or interests – and/or the people who represent them.

There are, however, different interpretations of organisational conflict. From a unitary perspective, conflict is defined as a dysfunctional state, caused by misperceptions, poor communication or poor management. From a pluralist perspective, conflict is defined as a natural process by which the organisational system preserves its equilibrium in the face of competition for limited power and resources.

(b) **Causes of conflict**

The following may be identified as typical causes of conflict in organisations.

(i) Differences in the objectives of different groups or individuals, especially where shared 'super-ordinate' goals are not emphasised, and individuals and groups are held accountable for achievement of their own goals – often in competition with each other.

(ii) Scarcity of resources, information and power, for which individuals and groups must compete. The pluralist viewpoint regards this as inevitable in all organisations.

(iii) Interdependence of individuals and/or departments which have to work together: this may cause frustration because of different expectations and perceptions of each others' contributions; different work cultures, time scales, and levels of effectiveness and so on.

(iv) Disputes about the boundaries of authority. The technostructure (Mintzberg) may attempt to encroach on the roles or territory of line managers. One department might start 'empire building' and try to take over the authority of others. This is often exacerbated where role and authority definitions are unclear.

(v) Interpersonal differences, as regards goals, attitudes, perceptions, status and so on. Interpersonal conflict often arises from lack of communication, lack of trust, prejudice and competition. It is exacerbated by poor interpersonal skills, eg aggressive behaviour or poor negotiation skills.

(c) **Characteristics of conflict in the workplace**

The characteristics or 'symptoms' of conflict in the workplace may be briefly outlined as follows.

(i) Poor communication in all directions, including withheld communication, deliberate sabotaging of information or distorting of meanings, and increasingly inflexible attitudes

(ii) Interpersonal friction, including arguments, hostility, aggressive or passive-aggressive behaviour, negative stereotyping, harassment and so on

(iii) Inter-group rivalries and jealousies, expressed as disputes, withholding of information or resources, 'us and them' thinking and other political games (Mintzberg)

(iv) Low individual and team morale, arising from poor relationships, deteriorating performance and loss of 'esprit de corps': this may show up in other indicators, such as absenteeism and high labour turnover

(v) Widespread use of arbitration, appeals to higher authority, grievance and disciplinary actions and so on. At the collective level, this may erupt into industrial action of various kinds.

60 Conflict good and bad

Text reference. This issue is discussed in Chapter 16.

Top tips. Make sure you are clear in your mind that 'constructive' (think 'building') is positive or helpful; 'destructive' (think 'destroying') is negative or unhelpful.

Easy marks. This question covers two key, mainstream areas in conflict theory. If you have done the revision, all these marks should be relatively easy. You could get basic marks for parts (b) and (c) through common sense and a well-structured answer – although 'extra' marks are available for citing relevant theories to back up your points. Part (a) may present the only real challenge, if you hadn't covered this topic – but, even then, it should be possible to think logically about it: what positive outcomes might come from a work-focused argument in a team meeting, say, or from rivalry between two teams?

Examiner's comments. Candidates who planned their answers (rather than duplicating material across sections), and read the keywords carefully (rather than discussing conflict in general) scored well.

Marking scheme

		Marks
(a)	Explanation of constructive conflict	5
(b)	Explanation of destructive conflict	5
(c)	Brief description of any five causes of conflict (1 mark per cause to max of 5)	5
		15

(a) **Constructive conflict**

The 'evolutionary' view of conflict suggests that conflict is a helpful way of maintaining the status quo in organisations while stimulating evolutionary change.

Conflict is constructive when its effect is to:

(i) Introduce different solutions to problems (by permitting differences to emerge)

(ii) Define power relationships more clearly (by displaying each party's influence in relation to the other)

(iii) Encourage creativity and the testing of ideas (by challenging assumptions, dominant theories and cosy consensus, or 'group think')

(iv) Focus attention on individual contributions (rather than submerging individual viewpoints in the group, which can lead to risky decision-making and neglected potential)

(v) Bring emotions out into the open (particularly, releasing hostile feelings that might otherwise be repressed).

(b) **Destructive conflict**

The 'happy family' view argues that conflict is dysfunctional, disrupting the smooth and harmonious functioning of the organisation. Charles Handy notes that difference, competition and argument (which are positive) can become dysfunctional if they degenerate into conflict.

Conflict is destructive when its effect is to:

(i) Distract attention from task performance, focusing employees' energy on the conflict, political game-playing or group maintenance (peace making)

(ii) Polarise views: stifling communication, escalating the conflict further – and creating the risk of poor decision-making

(iii) Disintegrate teams, preventing co-operation and communication between members

(iv) Stimulate emotional, win-lose conflicts (interpersonal hostility) rather than rational problem-solving

(v) Encourage defensive or 'spoiling' behaviours which have a wider effect on team and organisational performance.

(c) **Five causes of conflict**

The following may be identified as typical causes of conflict in organisations.

(i) Differences in the objectives of different groups or individuals within the organisation. These are often made worse where individual and sub-unit goals are not clearly articulated or integrated with each other.

(ii) Scarcity of resources, information and power, for which individuals and groups must compete. This is at the root of 'political' conflicts, inter-group competition and feelings of inequity or unfairness.

(iii) Interdependence of units which have to work together. This may cause frustration because of different cultures, time scales, ways of working or levels of effectiveness.

(iv) Disputes about the boundaries of authority. These may occur where roles and responsibilities are not clear, or where individuals or units seek to add to their power and influence (eg by 'empire building').

(v) Personal differences. In diverse organisations, there will inevitably be conflicts in regard to goals, attitudes and feelings – 'personality clashes'.

61 Scenario: Discipline and grievance

Text reference. The full range of disciplinary and grievance issues is covered in Chapter 16.

Top tips. The key to this question is distinguishing clearly between 'discipline' and grievance. (Note that a breach of *disciplinary* procedure may *lead* to a grievance...) The examiner has given extra help by italicising the distinction between grievance *procedure* (part (c)) and interview (part (d)). A good understanding of discipline is required for part (b), to identify where the procedures were breached by David Morgan. Having tackled part (a), however, this should be relatively clear.

Easy marks. The bulk of the marks are available for the fairly straightforward bookwork. Don't be tempted to leave part (b) aside because of its application requirements, the sequence of questions is helpful in clarifying the issues!

Examiner's comments. The question was designed to test candidate's knowledge of an important aspect of management in the professions, that of fairness, equity and discipline. It was, in general, very poorly-answered. The scenario was constructed and presented in a particular and deliberate way to allow candidates an opportunity to examine a disciplinary issue and determine the correct and fair way of dealing with it.

Many successful candidates approached the question in the way required: identifying and describing the six stages of a formal disciplinary procedure, correctly interpreting the issues raised in the scenario, and describing the correct grievance and interview procedure stages. However, it was surprising that far too many candidates seemed not to have read the question carefully enough.

Marking scheme

		Marks
(a)	Description of the six steps in the procedure (2 marks each)	12
(b)	Explanation of grievance	9
(c)	Description of the formal procedure (2 marks per stage)	10
(d)	Description of the three stages of the grievance interview (3 marks each)	9
		40

(a) The disciplinary procedure is a progressive, six stage process. The steps are usually thought of as consecutive, reflecting a progressive response. However, it may be appropriate to miss out one of the earlier stages when there have been serious infringements, although this does not appear to be the case with Oliver's timekeeping. The six steps are set out below.

1 **Informal talk** – this may be enough to resolve the issue, if the infringement is a minor one

2 **Oral warning** – this should include the reason behind issuing it, notice that it constitutes the first step of the disciplinary procedure, and details of the right of appeal. A note of the warning should be kept on file but disregarded after a specified period.

3 (a) **Written warning** – a first written warning is appropriate in more serious cases. It should inform the worker of the improvement required and state that a final written warning may be considered if there is no satisfactory improvement. A first written warning may also be appropriate if there has not been satisfactory improvement after an oral warning has been issued.

(b) **Final written warning** – If an earlier warning is still current and there is no satisfactory improvement, a final written warning may be appropriate. Also, sufficiently serious infringements may lead directly to the issue of a final written warning. A final written warning should give details of the offence, state that failure to improve may lead to dismissal or a lesser sanction and explain the appeals procedure.

Note that, depending on the offence, it is not necessary to progress through all of these levels of warning. One could go straight to the final written warning. This is thus a very flexible system, capable of dealing with disciplinary problems in a measured and proportionate way. It is, however, always necessary to investigate the allegations, and to give the worker opportunity to reply to them. This has not happened in Oliver's case.

The next stages move on to the imposition of sanctions.

4 **Suspension** – This course of action would be next in order if the employee has committed repeated offences and previous steps were of no avail. Disciplinary lay-offs usually extend over several days or weeks. Some employees may not be very impressed with oral or written warnings, but they will find a disciplinary lay-off without pay a rude awakening. This penalty is only available if it is provided for in the contract of employment.

5 **Demotion** – This course of action is likely to bring about dissatisfaction and discouragement, since losing pay and status over an extended period of time is a form of constant punishment. This dissatisfaction of the demoted employee may easily spread to co-workers, so most enterprises avoid downgrading as a disciplinary measure like suspension without pay, this sanction may only be imposed if it is provided for in the contract of employment.

6 **Discharge** – This is a drastic form of disciplinary action, and should be reserved for the most serious offences. For the organisation, it involves waste of a labour resource, the expense of training a new employee, and disruption caused by changing the make-up of the work team. There also may be damage to the morale of the group. It appears from the scenario that Oliver has been treated in a very severe manner, especially as it has not been applied to his peers, and Hoopers and Henderson needs to have a proper procedure in place that does not become influenced by personality clashes.

(b) Oliver is entitled to feel that he has a legitimate grievance against his manager. He has settled in to the job well, and was even recommended for his position by one of the partners, but is worried that some rules and regulations are not clearly laid out. He has been reprimanded for poor timekeeping, which in itself would appear to be reasonable if his colleagues (who are guilty of being at least as late as Oliver on occasion, and sometimes even more so) had also been given a warning. That the rules on timekeeping are not clear is an important omission that needs to be addressed, but one gets the feeling from this scenario that David Morgan would have found other reasons for reprimanding Oliver.

The fact that Oliver's colleagues have not been dealt with in the same way suggests that the basis for Oliver's treatment rests more upon his 'icy' relationship with his manager than the timekeeping itself. Oliver's manager, David Morgan, has done nothing to try and improve relations between them and has dealt with Oliver's relatively minor transgressions extremely heavily. This is a clash of personalities that is getting in the way of fair and effective human resource management.

David Morgan has not followed the stages of a formal disciplinary procedure properly. It is not clear from the outline given in the scenario, but it appears that at the oral warning stage, Oliver was not told about his right to appeal or the stages of the process that might follow if his timekeeping did not improve.

When he was given his written warning, Oliver should have been informed of the improvement required and it should have been made clear that a final written warning could be considered if there was no satisfactory improvement, and that such a warning could lead to disciplinary sanctions if there was no improvement.

Instead of this, David Morgan then jumped straight from a written warning to dismissal, bypassing the final written warning and less severe methods of sanction such as suspension or demotion (assuming that these would be appropriate in such a case). As indicated in the answer to part (a) this is a drastic form of disciplinary action, and should be reserved for the most serious offences.

It is also important to note that Oliver was never given the opportunity to reply to the charges. This is a very important part of the process to ensure fairness of treatment.

(c) **Formal grievance procedure**

An individual with a grievance such as Oliver's should be able to pursue it and ask to have the problem resolved. Some grievances should be capable of solution informally by the individual's manager, but given the relationship between Oliver and David Morgan this is unlikely to be the case in this scenario. However, if an informal solution is not possible, there should be a formal grievance procedure at Hoopers and Henderson, set out in writing and made available to all staff. These procedures should do the following things.

(i) State what **grades of employee** are entitled to pursue a particular type of grievance.

(ii) State the **rights of the employee** for each type of grievance. For example, an employee who is not invited to attend a promotion/selection panel might claim that he has been unfairly passed over.

(iii) State what the **procedures for pursuing a grievance** should be. In this particular case:

Step 1 Oliver should discuss the grievance with a staff/union representative (or a colleague). If his case seems a good one, he should take the grievance to David Morgan's boss.

Step 2 The first interview will be between David Morgan's boss and Oliver, who has the right to be accompanied by a colleague or representative.

Step 3 If this does not resolve the matter, or Oliver is otherwise dissatisfied with the first interview, the case should be referred to an even higher authority.

Step 4 Cases referred to a higher manager should also be reported to the personnel department. Line management might decide at some stage to ask for the assistance/advice of a personnel manager in resolving the problem.

(iv) **Distinguish between individual grievances and collective grievances.** Collective grievances might occur when a work group as a whole considers that it is being badly treated. This does not seem to have occurred here – none of Oliver's colleagues have been singled out for reprimands for their timekeeping even though they have been as late (or later) than Oliver.

(v) Allow for the **involvement of a representative** if appropriate. A person pursuing a grievance may wish for a colleague to be in attendance.

(vi) **State time limits** for initiating certain grievance procedures and subsequent stages of them.

(vii) **Require written records** of all meetings concerned with the case to be made and distributed to all the participants.

(d) **Grievance interviews**

Oliver wants a positive result from the grievance interview, which the management of Hoopers and Henderson may or may not be able to give. Prior to the interview, management should have some idea of the complaint and its possible source. The meeting itself can then proceed through three phases.

Step 1 Exploration. What is the problem: the background, the facts, the causes (manifest and hidden)? At this stage, the manager should simply try to gather as much information as possible, without attempting to suggest solutions or interpretations. The situation must be seen to be open. This may be difficult if the grievance is caused by a clash of personalities, as is the situation here. The person dealing with it must be seen to be fair.

Step 2 Consideration. There are three tasks.

(i) Check the facts
(ii) Analyse the causes – the complaint may be only a symptom
(iii) Evaluate options for responding to the complaint and the implication of any response made.

Step 3 Reply. The manager, having reached and reviewed his conclusions, reconvenes the meeting to convey (and justify, if required) his decision, hear counter-arguments and appeals. The outcome (agreed or disagreed) should be recorded in writing.

This procedure is very important. Certain grievances can have very serious repercussions for a company if not dealt with appropriately. Legal action for unfair dismissal could be costly and damaging.

62 Discipline

Text reference. Discipline is discussed in Chapter 16.

Top tips. An easy question if you had done your revision. The only tricky point may have been restricting your answer to part (a) to a brief (3 mark) *definition* (while showing awareness of the positive aspects of discipline) – and saving *description* of the process (6 steps for 12 marks) for part (b). Again, analysis of the instruction keywords and mark allocations offers clear guidance.

Easy marks. 12 marks for a description of progressive discipline stages – even in correct order – should be regarded as a 'gift'.

Examiner's comments. Far too many candidates provided a very simple definition of discipline based on punishment alone. In part (b), answers were expected to highlight a formally structured, transparent disciplinary procedure – *not* rambling personal anecdotes or general comments. Too many answers omitted steps in the disciplinary process or placed steps in the incorrect order.

Marking scheme

		Marks
(a)	Definitions (1 mark each)	3
(b)	Description, in the correct order, of the six steps involved in a formal disciplinary procedure (up to 2 marks per step – 1 for the correct position in the order and 1 for the description)	12
		15

(a) **Discipline**

Discipline can be considered as a condition in an enterprise in which there is **orderliness**, in which individuals and teams behave responsibly in accordance with the values and goals of the organisation and accepted norms. It is not merely about the use or threat of punishment for infringements of organisational rules and standards.

'**Negative**' discipline is based on the threat of sanctions. Even so, it is not primarily designed to be punitive (punishing an offence), but to encourage people to **choose to behave in the desired way**, as a **deterrent** (warning people not to behave in undesirable ways) or **reformative** (encouraging offenders not to re-offend).

'**Positive**' discipline refers to measures which **ensure compliance**: for example, safety guards on machinery. In a general sense, however, discipline is positive in so far as it reflects the willing co-operation of individuals in the shared goals and values of the enterprise.

(b) **Formal disciplinary procedure**

In the UK, ACAS Guidelines highlight the need for a formal, systematic, fair and transparent approach to applying disciplinary action, in the event of a breach of organisational rules and standards of behaviour. Such a framework protects employees from unfair treatment – and employers from damaging allegations of discrimination and (in extreme cases) unfair dismissal. A six-step framework of **progressive discipline** would be as follows.

(i) **Informal talk**

If the infringement is not serious, an informal counselling approach may be taken by the supervisor, aimed at highlighting organisational rules and expectations, and collaborative problem-solving to support improvement.

(ii) **Oral warning**

A formal oral warning or reprimand should include clear explanation of the nature of the infringement, the relevant rules and expectations, and the consequences of any repetition or failure to improve.

(iii) **Written (official) warning**

A written warning informs employees formally of the nature of the complaint against them, any penalties imposed, requirements for improvement and further consequences of repeated infringement. It also informs them of their rights: eg to appeal the decision. The written warning becomes part of the employment record, and may be used in evidence for further proceedings.

(iv) **Suspension**

Suspension, or temporary lay-off without pay, is one form of sanction which can be imposed for serious or repeated infringements. It should be of strictly limited duration, as provided for in the contract of employment.

(v) **Demotion**

Demotion (and related penalties, such as loss of benefits or downgraded salary) are a more serious form of sanction. This is likely to have a demotivating effect – and may even be construed as 'constructive' dismissal: it should be used only as a measure of last resort, and with careful attention to evidence and progressive warnings.

(vi) **Dismissal**

Disciplinary dismissal is reserved for serious misconduct, and all proceedings should be carefully documented: in the UK, and many other countries, employment protection law prohibits 'unfair' or unjustified dismissal.

63 Grievance interview

Text reference. Grievance is covered in Chapter 16.

Top tips. This should be straightforward as long as you noted the introduction to the question and correctly distinguished 'grievance' from 'discipline' and as long as you paid attention to the topic keywords 'grievance *interview*' (in part (a)) and 'matters that should be stated' and 'policy' (part (b)).

(a) **Grievance interview**

The subordinate wants a positive result from the grievance interview, which the manager may or may not be able to give. Prior to the interview, the manager should have some idea of the complaint and its possible source. The meeting itself can then proceed through three main phases.

(i) **Exploration**. The manager should try to gather as much information as possible on the problem: its background, the facts, the causes (manifest and hidden). At this stage, the manager should not attempt to offer interpretations or solutions: the subordinate must feel thoroughly heard and understood, and the outcome must be seen not to be pre-judged.

(ii) **Consideration**. The manager has three essential tasks.

- Check the facts.
- Analyse the causes – the problem of which the complaint may be only a symptom.
- Evaluate options for responding to the complaint and the implications of any response made.

It may be that information can be given to clear up a misunderstanding, or the employee will – having aired his or her feelings – withdraw the formal complaint. However, the meeting may have to be adjourned (say, for 48 hours) while the manager gets extra information, considers both sides and evaluates other response options.

(iii) **Reply**. The manager, having reached and reviewed his conclusions, reconvenes the meeting to convey (and justify, if required) his decision, hear counter-arguments and appeals. The outcome (agreed or disagreed) should be recorded in writing.

Follow-up action will need to be carried through as agreed and minuted in the interview. Further interviews – for conflict resolution or counselling – may be included in this action.

(b) **Matters that should be stated in a formal grievance policy**

(i) What grades of employee are entitled to pursue a particular type of grievance

(ii) Employees' rights in each type of grievance

(iii) What the procedures for pursuing a grievance should be, including: whom to approach in the first instance. Who will conduct investigations and interviews; in what circumstances appeals can be made and to whom

(iv) The rights of the employee to be accompanied by a colleague, trade union or staff association representative

(v) Time limits for initiating certain grievance procedures and subsequent stages of them

(vi) The requirement for written records of all meetings to be made and distributed to concerned parties.

64 Counselling

Text reference. Counselling is covered as a communication process, in Chapter 15.

Top tips. Bear in mind that 'counselling' is a specific process of supporting and advising employees where they have problems or under-used potential. (The term is unlikely to be used in the exams in the more general sense of 'giving advice or instructions'.) Address each of the requirements accurately: (a) definition; (b) skills; and (c) advantages (for the *organisation*).

Easy marks. This question *looks* easy, but you couldn't get far on common sense alone. If you were well prepared, it would be quite straightforward.

Examiner's comments. The accountancy profession relies on individuals. This question was designed to test candidates' understanding of those occasions when the professional accountant as a manager has to understand and deal with the personal problems of others, in the role of counsellor. Part (a) attracted good answers, but some candidates described counselling as a routine, work-related issue and confused it with appraisals and motivation rather than supporting and advising. Part (b) was answered well, but in part (c) many candidates suggested that the advantages of counselling were restricted to motivational areas.

Marking scheme

		Marks
(a)	Explanation of the term 'counselling'	2
(b)	Explanation of the skills required for the counsellor's role (1 mark per skill)	7
(c)	Brief description of three advantages of counselling for the organisation (2 marks each)	6
		15

(a) **Counselling** occurs when one person agrees to offer time and support in order to help another to help him or herself. That person is helped to explore thoughts, feelings and behaviour with the aim of reaching a clearer understanding and maybe a plan of action for the future. In the organisational context, it is likely to relate to giving career development advice, or the coaching of staff.

(b) A manager who undertakes a counselling role will need strong interpersonal skills, despite the fact that the counsellor tends to take a rather passive role in order to encourage the participant to solve the problem him/herself. Particular skills will include:

(i) Helping the employee to see the problem and suggest solutions for him or herself, when it will often be the case that the employee expects the manager to solve it

(ii) Avoiding the temptation to put his or her own interpretation of the facts, as this may 'lead' the employee

(iii) Allowing plenty of time for the discussion so that every relevant area or event is discussed, even if they are in the past, or even if the discussion becomes repetitive: this will require patience

(iv) Encouraging the employee to talk about many issues, even those that they may be reluctant to discuss, because of fears for their status or their job

(v) Using open questions to help the employee to probe issues and statements more deeply

(vi) Clarifying decisions reached, without taking sides or putting his or her own interpretation on the discussion

(vii) Using active listening, without becoming distracted or interrupting the employee – the greater the perceived level of listening, the more likely that the employee will accept comments and contributions

(viii) Resisting the temptation to discuss other problems that may be on the manager's mind

(c) Effective counselling is very much in the interest of the organisation. It can help to achieve several objectives:

(i) **Prevent underperformance**, reduce labour turnover and absenteeism and increase employee commitment

(ii) Provide a **confidential service** that will encourage employee feedback regarding problems that it may in fact be in the organisation's interest to resolve, for the benefit of all employees

(iii) Demonstrate the organisation's **commitment** to and concern for its employees, which will be reflected in its **human resources policy** and will help to make it an attractive employer when recruiting

(iv) Give employees the **confidence and encouragement** necessary to take responsibility for personal and career development

Mock Exams

ACCA

Paper 1.3

Managing People

Mock Examination 1

<table>
<tr><td colspan="2">Question Paper</td></tr>
<tr><td>Time allowed</td><td>3 hours</td></tr>
<tr><td colspan="2">This paper is divided into two sections</td></tr>
<tr><td>Section A</td><td>This question is compulsory and MUST be attempted</td></tr>
<tr><td>Section B</td><td>FOUR questions ONLY to be attempted</td></tr>
</table>

DO NOT OPEN THIS PAPER UNTIL YOU ARE READY TO START UNDER EXAMINATION CONDITIONS

SECTION A – This ONE question is compulsory and MUST be attempted

Question 1

Sunshine Sweets is a manufacturer of additive free, organic children's candies. With the rise in demand for additive free children's products, Sunshine Sweets has expanded its production capacity to almost double what it was two years ago and trebled the number of employees. Until recently the board of directors, made up of the two founders Emma Watkind and Jenna Pain, took charge of day to day business. Both have now allowed management more freedom than before.

Despite success in the market, as the company has grown some problems have begun to arise. Phil Short, the factory manager has been with the company since the beginning and since the expansion in the number of employees, finds controlling and communicating with such a large workforce difficult. He has resorted to pinning notices and memos of all kinds to notice boards, circulating his own reports to colleagues who should not be receiving them and refusing to organize meetings.

The newly appointed production manager Mark Mason is an engineer and deputy to Phil. He has found that he has little idea of what's going on in the factory and is finding communication channels are non existent between the management team, supervisors and directors. The financial controller, Debbie Purple is equally frustrated and finds communicating with anyone in the production area of the factory to be almost impossible.

In addition, the workforce, despite being well paid and trained, is fragmented and not working together. The rapid expansion of the company has led to poor internal communication. As a consequence workers are suffering from absenteeism, low morale and confusion brought about by endless rumours about the future of the company. This is because the line supervisors are also unaware of what is going on and consequently are unable to communicate management's plans and objectives to the workforce, or to make management aware of the concerns of the workforce.

Required

You are a consultant brought in by the directors to advise on the current problems. They believe the current problems stem from poor and mis-directed communication and think that establishing committees will improve communication. You have been asked to:

(a) Explain the need for good communication within any organisation. **(5 marks)**

(b) Identify five barriers to communication that might exist in Sunshine Sweets. **(5 marks)**

(c) Explain how the barriers identified in (b) can be overcome and identify the alternative methods of communication available to the management. **(10 marks)**

(d) Explain to the management of Sunshine Sweets the importance of communication, the form it takes and the directions in which it might flow in an organisation. **(10 marks)**

(e) Advise on the suitability of committees as methods of communication, outlining their usefulness and shortcomings. **(10 marks)**

(Total = 40 marks)

SECTION B – FOUR questions ONLY to be attempted

Question 2

Centralisation and decentralisation refer to how authority is distributed in an organisation.

Required

(a) Describe the main advantages and disadvantages of centralisation. **(10 marks)**
(b) What factors influence the extent of decentralisation in an organisation? **(5 marks)**

(Total = 15 marks)

Question 3

Your organisation advertises itself as an 'equal opportunities employer' in recruitment literature, but it appears to you that it does only the bare minimum to comply with the law.

Required

(a) Outline a five-step plan to make the claim a reality. **(10 marks)**

(b) List five specific measures to encourage job and/or training applications by different groups who are otherwise disadvantaged in employment. **(5 marks)**

(Total = 15 marks)

Question 4

Training programmes play an important part in improving employee skills and organisational performance.

Required

(a) Briefly explain the advantages of training for the organisation. **(5 marks)**

(b) Briefly explain the advantages of training for the individual. **(4 marks)**

(c) Briefly explain what is meant by the following different types of training:

(i) Computer based **(2 marks)**
(ii) Job rotation **(2 marks)**
(iii) Work shadowing. **(2 marks)**

(Total = 15 marks)

Question 5

Understanding motivation theory is an important part of managing people.

Required

(a) Explain what is meant by the 'content theories' of motivation. **(3 marks)**
(b) Briefly describe Maslow's hierarchy of needs theory. **(5 marks)**
(c) Discuss the limitations of Maslow's theory to managing people. **(7 marks)**

(Total = 15 marks)

Question 6

The accounts manager does not understand what is meant by discipline within the employment context. You have been asked to explain.

Required

(a) What do you understand is meant by the term 'discipline' in the employment context? **(3 marks)**

(b) Explain what is meant by the terms:

(i) Positive discipline **(2 marks)**
(ii) Negative discipline. **(2 marks)**

(c) Provide four examples of situations where disciplinary action may be required. **(8 marks)**

(Total = 15 marks)

Answers

DO NOT TURN THIS PAGE UNTIL YOU HAVE COMPLETED THE MOCK EXAM

PLAN OF ATTACK

As stated in the 'Passing 1.3' section at the front of this Kit, the keys to passing this paper are:

- **Demonstrating preparation**. You can't rely on 'common sense'. The questions are often factual, and you are expected to be able to cite, explain and apply supporting theories (some of them specifically named in the question) and background knowledge.
- **Time management.** Section A should take 72 minutes *maximum*, and each of the four Section B questions should take 27 minutes.
- **Demonstrating thought**. You need to show that you haven't thrown points together at random. Plan your answers so that they have a coherent structure which reflects the requirements of the question. Use section headings to highlight the structure for the examiner.

First item on your agenda must be to **read the rubric**. You must do Section A (Question 1), and you have to choose four out of the five questions in Section B. So your only **choices** are:

- The **order** in which you will tackle the questions
- Which **one** of the Section B questions you will **not** attempt.

Looking through *this particular paper*, you will note that Section A covers various issues in communication and Section B offers a variety of questions covering other syllabus areas: management and team development (centralisation [question 2]); recruitment and selection, [question 3]; training and development (advantages/ disadvantages [question 4]); motivation and leadership (Maslow [question 5]; and effective communication practices (discipline [question 6]).

Should you do Section A first?

The Examiner's Comments for this paper have repeatedly noted that students who left the compulsory question until last appeared, due to poor time management, to have 'rushed' their answers – missing out on vital marks. If, having underlined the **topic and instruction keywords** of all the questions on the paper, you feel relatively comfortable with Question 1, it would be a good idea to attempt it early in the exam: get it out of the way! If you feel less confident, you may prefer to start with your **strongest question** from Section B, to boost your confidence and recall.

In this paper, Question 1 has some straightforward parts that you might feel confident about: the need for communication, barriers and how they can be overcome, methods, direction of flows. Your only hesitation may come from point (e) – worth 10 marks out of the 40 available – if you hadn't revised committees in detail. You might therefore decide to tackle Question 1 first.

Tackling Section A

Remember to spend no more than **72 minutes** in total on Section A. Allowing 5 minutes to read the scenario through carefully, parts (b), (c) and (d) should take you 16-17 minutes each and parts (a) and (b) about 8 minutes each. Tackle the parts in order, but analyse them all carefully first, to ensure that you don't use points in an earlier part that you'll then have to duplicate for a later part. (A brief answer plan helps to solve this problem, among other benefits.)

Choosing Section B questions

The Section B questions are all fairly straightforward, requiring mostly factual descriptions/ explanation, but also some evaluation and thinking about implications. Your 'least favourite' or 'weakest' Section B question will therefore depend mostly on your revision: which topics you have covered and recall most strongly. You may, for example, simply not recall equal opportunity policies in sufficient detail to be confident in tackling question 3, in which case, that's the one to leave out.

If you find more than one such question, remember to underline the **topic/instruction keywords** of all the questions.

(a) They may well jog your memory of the topic (which is partly what they are there for).

(b) They will enable you to assess how many marks you are confident of getting for each question, bearing in mind the **marks available** for different question parts. (In question 6, for example, you may not be confident about the difference between positive and negative discipline. Look at the mark allocations: you potentially still have at least 11 marks out of the possible 15 under your belt.)

Tackling Section B

Tackle your stronger questions first – but **don't** be tempted to take longer on them than the 27 minutes allocated for each. You can't get *more* than 15 marks for a question, however long you spend polishing your answer – and if you finish one question short, because you run out of time (or don't like your fourth question), you automatically *lose* 15 marks!

Even if you are struggling with your fourth question, leave yourself time to give it some thought and do an answer plan, which may jog your memory. At the very least, an answer plan will give the examiner some indication of your having thought the topic through.

Question 1

Text reference. All these aspects are covered in Chapter 15.

Top tips. This is quite a dense little scenario. When you read it through for a second time, underline key phrases addressing communication issues: this should help you focus on the essentials. Note, for example, that there has been swift expansion: control and co-ordination are issues. Phil Short is hooked on excessive written communication between different levels *or* functions. Make sure you can find these elements in the scenario: and note their relevance to the questions! (Use them to show your application of theory to the scenario.)

Easy marks. 'Underneath' the application, these are mainstream questions on communication. Work through then systematically, to avoid overlaps.

Examiner's comments. In general, this question was answered well, but there were some problems. Too many candidates wasted time rewriting parts of the scenario in their answers, and others produced detailed accounts of communication patterns without any reference to the scenario itself. Writing all that you know about a topic, in the hope of earning some marks, without looking at the issues involved in the scenario is never a good strategy. Candidates must read the question thoroughly. The answer to part (a) required an appreciation of the general importance of communication in the organisation at the higher levels.

Marking scheme

			Marks
(a)	Factors of importance in ensuring good communication		5
(b)	Identification of five barriers		5
(c)	Identification and explanation (1 mark per barrier identified)	5	
	Identification of alternative communication methods	5	
			10
(d)	Explanation of communication channels		10
(e)	Usefulness of committees		10
			40

(a) Accountants provide information to others, and so clear and concise communication as a core management activity is vital. When a company undergoes swift expansion, as has occurred at Sunshine Sweets, communication channels can become strained because there are suddenly too many people who need to be kept 'in the loop'. 'Good communication' may be defined as communication which is:

(i) **Effective**: that is, achieves the communicator's purpose in communicating, such as the message being received and understood, and eliciting the desired response. Every member of Sunshine Sweets needs to know what is expected of them. Good communication will ensure that individuals and departments are well coordinated, even though the workforce has grown so much.

(ii) **Efficient**: that is, achieves its purpose without unnecessary waste of time, money and other resources. Information needs to be received by the appropriate people.

Good communication is vitally important because the achievement of Sunshine Sweets' organisational objectives depends on the exchange of information for planning, decision-making and control and the giving of orders and instructions for operations and transactions. Rumours thrive in an atmosphere of uncertainty. The establishing and maintenance of interpersonal relationships, which are important to morale and motivation, rely upon the open transmission of information about the organisation's products/services. Open exchange of information and ideas for problem-solving and innovation will also ensure that the workforce, from factory staff to senior management, is no longer fragmented.

If communication is inefficient, there will be a waste of resources (for example, employee time spent in clarifying and correcting misunderstandings) and poor control and co-ordination.

(b)

> **Examiner's comments**. It was surprising how many candidates misunderstood the concept of communication barriers, confusing it with general environmental 'noise'.

Major barriers to good communication in Sunshine Sweets

(i) Poor basic communication skills on the part of Phil Short. He has chosen an inappropriate medium (the noticeboards) which not everyone will necessarily see, and is making little effort to circulate information beyond his own direct area of responsibility.

(ii) Personal differences, or 'social noise'. Age, gender, education, social background, ethnic origin or functional specialism and priorities may encourage differing interpretation of words and events, and therefore misunderstanding. It is possible that Phil Short feels threatened by Mark Mason and Debbie Purple and so the relationship has become strained.

(iii) Conflict may create unwillingness to communicate helpfully. Withholding or distorting information may be used as a weapon in interpersonal conflict. The line supervisors and factory staff seem to be suffering from a lack of information, which is giving rise to rumours and innuendo.

(iv) Inappropriate amount or accuracy of information. Information may be insufficient or excessive for the use for which it is intended. Phil Short's reports may be full of useful information, but he is circulating them to the wrong audience.

(v) Active or implied discouragement of communication. The supervisors at Sunshine Sweets feel stuck because of the lack of information coming from above. As a result, management is left unaware of what is happening 'below'. It is up to the more senior management to address these concerns and put a more effective communication system in place.

(c)

> **Examiner's comments**. This was answered quite well, although some candidates failed to take the opportunity to describe more modern methods of communication within the organisation.

Overcoming communication barriers

The barriers to good communication can be overcome, broadly, by addressing their underlying causes. A flexible approach will be the key, because there is no universal formula for every situation in which barriers to communication exist, particularly in organisations such as Sunshine Sweets, which of necessity draw together diverse functions, personalities and priorities.

(i) **Training** and guidance can be given in communication and dialogue skills, including **choice of medium and method** and the encouragement of feedback and dialogue.

(ii) People can be made aware of the potential for misunderstanding arising from **differences in perception**, and taught (by various forms of awareness training and the example of managers and mentors) to take others' viewpoints and information needs into account. This may include cutting out the use of technical jargon.

(iii) **Conflict and organisational politics** can be managed so that no basic unwillingness to communicate exists between individuals and groups. Measures may range from interpersonal grievance handling to the adjustment of the whole corporate culture to encourage free transfer of information, and perhaps cutting down the number of links in the communication chain.

(iv) **Technology, systems and procedures** can be adapted to facilitate communication: making it more effective (regular meeting schedules), faster (electronic methods, such as e-mail), more consistent (standard instructions for the production and distribution of reports).

(v) Communication must be **encouraged, facilitated and rewarded** as a key component of the culture at Sunshine Sweets. Status barriers (particularly to upward communication) and functional barriers (to horizontal communication) can be minimised by encouraging teamworking, project management and other facilitative structures.

(d)

> **Examiner's comments**. This part of the question was answered well, with many candidates recognising the importance of communication and correctly describing the three basic information flows within the organisation and their purpose. However, some answers concentrated too much on different communication patterns.

Information is the lifeblood of organisations. It is essential to interpersonal relationships and organisational coordination and activity.

Communication – the transfer or exchange of information – is therefore a vital and complex organisational process which must be planned for and executed properly.. Effective communication is the supply of the right information in the right form to the right person at the right time. It can take several forms.

(i) **Vertical: downwards**

Communication that goes **down** the chain of command may serve these purposes.

(1) **Instructions and plans.** A team leader might require a team member to do something – the team is, in a way, at the manager's disposal. Such instructions need not be direct orders. They might take the form of a work schedule allocating different members of the team to do different tasks, or **standard** ways of doing things.

(2) **Information**. Downwards vertical communication may contain information. An example of this is a **team briefing**, whereby the team leader gives information about some important development in the business. Information is thus 'cascaded down'. Of course, many types of information do not have to be communicated in this way, and can instead use the corporate intra-net for example.

(3) **Performance review and feedback**. Downwards vertical communication is often part of the overall company appraisal scheme, but this is often combined with upwards communication.

(4) **Authorisation**. At certain levels, the involvement of someone 'higher up' is needed.

(ii) **Vertical – upwards**

(1) **Managers need information** about the performance of the business or operations. Sometimes it suits people to tell their managers what they think the managers want to hear – the culture must encourage open communication. Many managers prefer 'reporting by exception'.

(2) **Requests for information**. People lower down may need information from those higher up.

(3) **Requests for decisions**. People may need decisions to be taken which are outside the scope of their authority, or which require the co-operation of other departments or the authorisation of a senior manager.

(iii) **Horizontal or lateral communication** occurs between people of the same rank, in the same section or department, or in different sections or departments. Horizontal communication between 'peer groups' is usually easier and more direct then vertical communication, being less inhibited by considerations of rank or position.

(1) **Formally:** to co-ordinate the work of several people, and perhaps departments, who have to co-operate to carry out a certain operation.

(2) **Informally:** to furnish emotional and social support to an individual.

Lateral communication is often quicker than vertical communication and means that senior managers do not get overwhelmed with detail on a day to day basis.

(e)

Examiner's comments. This part of the question was answered well, although there was some confusion as to the construction, activities and appropriateness of committees as an instrument of communication.

Committees

A committee is a group of people who meet for a particular purpose, often on a permanent basis. When properly structured, they are extremely useful, and very familiar. It is very important to note, however, that they need to be structured and controlled properly. Assuming that they are, the uses of committees are these.

(i) **Making decisions**, if the consent and or expertise of many people are needed. These decisions can still be disseminated throughout the organisation, vertically and laterally.

(ii) **Delaying decisions** (and requesting more information), again, vertically or laterally.

(iii) The **relaying of decisions** and instructions (eg **briefings**). Minutes of the meetings should be taken and circulated, with any **action points** arising out of the meetings notified to the members responsible for doing the work.

(iv) The **dissemination of information** and the collection of feedback.

(v) **Problem solving**, by consultation with people in different departments or fields (eg a task force or working party). This can involve **brainstorming**: free exchanges with a view to generating new approaches and ideas.

(vii) **Co-ordination** of the efforts of a large number of people representing department or interest groups.

(viii) Formal **recommendations** that others follow a course of action.

(ix) **Representation** of a number of people from divergent disciplines or departments. The members of the committee must have the necessary skills and experience to do the committee's work.

(x) Where the committee is expected to **liaise** with functional departments, the members must also have sufficient **status and influence** with those departments.

Question 2

Text reference. This is discussed in Chapter 1.

Top tips. The introduction to the question indicates the sense in which the terms centralisation and decentralisation are being used. Make sure you know which is which (centralisation = less delegation, decentralisation = more delegation) and note that part (a) refers only to one term and part (b) to the other: don't duplicate your material in both parts. Part (b) is perhaps the more challenging question. You need to grasp exactly what it is asking: what factors determine whether there is *more* or *less* decentralisation in an organisation.

Easy marks. The advantages and disadvantages of centralisation should be basic – and will earn you the bulk of the marks. (For this paper, it may be helpful to think of 'advantages/disadvantages', lists of factors, stages in a procedure, and so on, as potential easy exam marks: they make good 15-mark questions!).

(a) **Advantages and disadvantages of centralisation**

A centralised organisation is one in which authority is concentrated at what Mintzberg called the strategic apex: lower levels of the hierarchy have little decision-making authority and merely carry out instructions or set procedures.

Advantages

(i) **Decisions are made at one point**, and so may be made more quickly (particularly important in crisis) and with better control and consistency.

(ii) **Senior managers** in an organisation can take **a wider view** of the objectives, problems and consequences of decisions for the whole organisation: they see 'the big picture'.

(iii) Senior management can **balance the needs and interests of different units** and stakeholders of the organisation, where there might otherwise be political competition and conflict.

(iv) The quality of decisions should (theoretically) be higher due to senior managers' skills, experience and access to wider sources of information.

(v) There may be a **reduction in the cost of management overheads.**

Disadvantages

(i) Senior managers may be **overloaded** in terms of workload and the stress of responsibility.

(ii) Lower **levels of management may be demotivated** by the absence of opportunities to exercise authority or develop their roles.

(iii) The organisation may **fail to develop managerial successors** and skills in entrepreneurship, initiative and innovation which are crucial in a fast-changing market environment.

(iv) **Head office managers may lack local and front-line knowledge** to respond to customer requirements and the realities of working conditions.

(v) **Slow decision making.** Decisions required by changing operational and customer demands are slowed down by the need to refer them upwards.

(b) **Factors influencing the extent of decentralisation**

Geographical dispersion and remoteness from the centre encourages a degree of autonomy, although information technology can reduce the effects of physical distance for co-ordination.

An organisation with a **variety of activities**, markets and/or product ranges may benefit from decentralisation, as varying specialist skills and knowledge will be required to manage different processes.

Competition and rapid environmental change will necessitate **decentralisation**, in order to speed up the organisation's response to customer demands and technological and market developments.

The **management style** and organisational culture will either support delegation/decentralisation or discourage it (in a 'power' culture, for example).

The **capabilities of the organisation's managers** will support or hinder decentralisation, according to whether they are able to deal with devolved responsibility, able to delegate effectively and so on.

Question 3

Text reference. Equal opportunity issues are covered in Chapter 9.

Top tips. Note that part (a) asks for a planning/implementation process – 'a five-step plan' – not a set of recommendations for specific positive action initiatives (which is the subject of part (b)). In other words, how would an organisation go about putting meaningful equal opportunities policies in place?

Easy marks. Once you've settled in your mind what the question is asking, you'll either be aware of steps that can be taken – or not. (A good guide to the choice of optional questions!)

(a) **Five-step plan to implement equal opportunities**

The following stages are necessary in order to create both the cultural support and policy framework for equal opportunities.

Step 1 **Secure support from the top of the organisation** for the formulation and implementation of practical policies. If necessary, senior accountabilities for equal opportunities may have to be created: for example, by appointing an Equal Opportunities Manager.

Step 2 **Set up a working party**, drawn from (for example) management, trade unions or staff associations, minority groups represented in the workforce, the HR function and staff representatives. This group's brief will be to produce a draft Policy and Code of Practice which will be approved at senior level.

Step 3 **Formulate action plans and allocate resources** (including staff) to implement and monitor the policy, publicise it to staff and other stakeholders, arrange training and counselling and so on.

Step 4 **Implement monitoring and review systems.** The numbers of women, ethnic minority and disabled staff, for example, can easily be monitored:

- On entering (or applying to enter) the organisation during recruitment
- On leaving the organisation
- On applying for transfers, promotions, training programmes and so on.

Step 5 **Plan and implement positive action initiatives** (discussed further below): taking active steps to encourage people from disadvantaged groups to apply for jobs and training and to compete for opportunities. (Note that this is not defined as 'positive discrimination'.)

(b) **Specific positive action measures**

(i) Using **ethnic languages** in job advertisements to facilitate applications from people of non-English-speaking background.

(ii) **Offering flexible hours**, part-time working, term-time or annual hours contracts (allowing for school holidays) to help women to combine careers with family responsibilities, with comparable terms to standard-contract workers. (Other measures friendly to women include workplace childcare facilities, training for women returners, career-break schemes and so on).

(iii) **Alteration of premises** and equipment to accommodate wheelchair users, blind/partially-sighted and deaf workers.

(iv) The **harmonisation of HR policies** and benefits for employees of a particular marital status and/or sexual orientation. For example, extension of 'spouse' benefits to same-sex partners, as at British Airways.

(v) **Fast-tracking school-leavers** as well as graduates, and posting managerial vacancies internally, giving more opportunities for groups currently at lower levels of the organisational or educational ladder.

Question 4

Text reference. Both topics are covered in Chapter 10.

Top tips. Note the similarities of some of these question requirements with those in questions 32 and 33 – and how much less you have to go on in any essay question than in a scenario! You may be more familiar with 'job rotation' in the context of job design and Herzberg: don't worry – it is the same technique.

Easy marks. With careful attention to topic key words, this should be straightforward.

Examiner's comments. Parts (a) and (b) were answered well with candidates providing good answers and showing awareness of the usefulness of training to the two different groups. Although there are common benefits of training for the individual and the organisation, they do differ. Too many answers repeated the same benefits in both parts. In part (c) a surprising number of candidates failed to recognise that computer-based training refers to its use as a training instrument, not training in how to use a computer.

Marking scheme

		Marks
(a)	Brief explanation of the advantages for the organisation	5
(b)	Brief explanation of the advantages for the individual	4
(c)	Brief explanation of each type of training (2 marks each)	6
		15

(a) **Advantages of training for the organisation**

(i) It fosters the **skills** the organisation needs. Training also ensures that people have the variety of skills needed – **multi-skilling** (and flexibility) is only possible if people are properly trained.

(ii) It eventually leads to **lower costs** and increased productivity, thereby improving performance.

(iii) It can contribute towards fewer accidents, and better **health and safety**. EU health and safety directives require a certain level of training. Employees can take employers to court if accidents occur or if unhealthy work practices persist.

(iii) There is **less need for detailed supervision**. If people are trained they can get on with the job, and managers can concentrate on other things. Training is an aspect of **empowerment**.

(iv) Training and development attracts **new recruits** and ensures that the organisation has a supply of suitable managerial and technical staff to take over when people retire.

(v) Training helps organisations **manage change** by letting people know why the change is happening and giving them the skills to cope with it.

(vi) Training programmes can be used to **build the corporate culture** or to direct it in certain ways, by indicating that certain values are espoused.

(vii) Training programmes can **build relationships** between staff and managers in different areas of the business.

(viii) Training programmes can increase **motivation** and **commitment** to the organisation's goals.

(b) **Advantages for the employee**

For the individual employee, the benefits of training and development are more clear-cut, and few refuse it if it is offered.

(i) **Enhances portfolio of skills**. Even if not specifically related to the current job, training can be useful in other contexts, and the employee becomes more attractive to employers and more promotable.

(ii) **Psychological benefits**. The trainee might feel reassured that he/she is of continuing value to the organisation.

(iii) **Social benefit**. People's social needs can be met by training courses – they can also develop networks of contacts.

(iv) **The job**. Training can help people do their job better, thereby increasing job satisfaction.

(c) (i) **Computer-based training** is interactive, hands-on training which involves self-learning via a PC, often without direct supervision. The typing program, Mavis Beacon, is a good example. It is also referred to as Computer Assisted Learning (CAL)

(ii) **Job rotation**. The trainee is given several jobs in succession, to gain experience of a wide range of activities. Even experienced managers may rotate their jobs, to gain wider experience; this philosophy of job education is commonly applied in the Civil Service, where an employee may expect to move on to another job after a few years.

(iii) **Work shadowing** might be used to encourage a junior manager with good potential. He or she may be appointed as 'assistant to' the managing director or another executive director to learn the skills involved. In this way, the individual gains experience of how the organisation is managed 'at the top'.

Question 5

Top tips. This illustrates a classic revision programme for any management theory: make sure you can (i) define and distinguish the terminology (eg don't confuse 'process' and 'content'); (ii) outline the theory; and (iii) critically evaluate its strong and weak points.

Easy marks. Parts (a) and (b) should be easy – but note that *more* marks are available for the more complex requirement to *criticise* the theory, in part (c).

Examiner's comments. The examiner noted that confusion between 'content' and 'process' theories (part (a)) could only come from guesswork: candidates who had studied the topic scored well. Too many candidates simply failed to describe or discuss the limitations explicitly asked for in part (c).

Marking scheme

			Marks
(a)	Explanation of content theories		3
(b)	Identification and description of needs theory:		
	Physiological	1	
	Safety	1	
	Social	1	
	Esteem	1	
	Self-actualisation	1	
			5
(c)	Identification and explanation of weaknesses	5	
	Recognition of dependence on organisational situation	2	
			7
			15

(a) **Content theories of motivation**

Content theories of motivation ask the question: '*What* are the things that motivate people?' They are based on the belief that:

- Human beings have an innate (and therefore universal) set of needs or desired outcomes
- Behaviour is driven and determined (motivated) by the desire to satisfy those needs or achieve those outcomes, and
- Satisfaction can be offered through the intrinsic and extrinsic rewards of work

David McClelland's needs classification and Herzberg's two-factor theory (in addition to Maslow's hierarchy of needs) are major examples.

(b) **Maslow's hierarchy of needs**

Abraham Maslow suggested that individuals have certain **innate needs**:

(i) **Physiological** needs: basic bodily needs for food, sleep, shelter
(ii) **Safety** needs: for security, order, predictability and freedom from threat
(iii) **Love/social** needs: for relationships, affection and belonging
(iv) **Esteem** needs: for independence, recognition, status and respect from others
(v) **Self-actualisation** needs: for personal growth and the fulfilment of one's potential

Maslow further suggested that these needs can be arranged in a 'hierarchy of relative pre-potency', depicted (as follows) in a triangle.

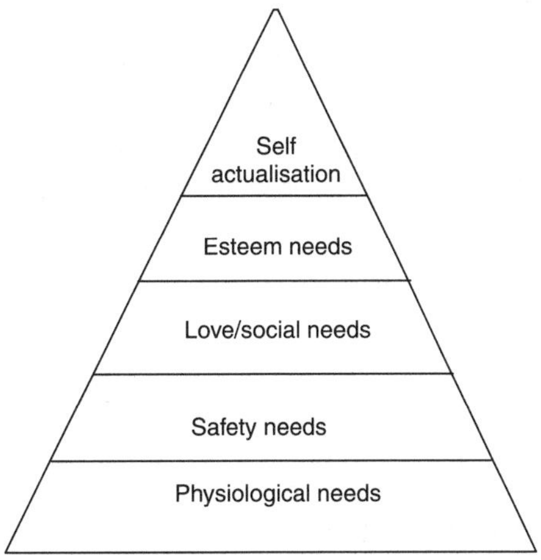

The hierarchy suggests that each level of need is dominant until satisfied: it then ceases to be a motivator and the next highest level of need becomes the primary motivating factor. Maslow recognised that the need for self-actualisation can rarely be satisfied. The neo-human relations school of management theorists focused on the 'higher order' social, esteem and self-actualisation needs in aiming to increase job satisfaction and worker motivation.

(c) **Limitations of Maslow's model**

Maslow's theory is easy to grasp and has a certain intuitive appeal, but it is not very useful in practice for a manager wishing to motivate a team. (To be fair, Maslow did not specifically intend his theory to be used in such a context.)

(i) It is difficult to **identify where an individual is** in the hierarchy: any given behaviour may be motivated by a number of different needs.

(ii) It is difficult to **predict behaviour** on the basis of where the individual is in the hierarchy: (s)he may satisfy a given need in any number of ways.

(iii) It is difficult to **design incentive and reward systems** on the basis of the hierarchy: the place of pay and the nature of self-actualisation are particularly ambiguous.

In addition, the theory has certain internal weaknesses.

(i) It ignores phenomena such as deferred gratification and altruism, which overturn the 'hierarchy of relative pre-potency'.

(ii) It has been difficult to verify empirically.

(iii) It has been found to be limited to a Western (US) cultural model: in many Asian cultures, for example, social needs have been found to be a key value overriding individual self-actualisation.

Like any theory, Maslow's hierarchy should be used to raise awareness, rather than to determine 'one size fits all' measures in the work place. A **contingency approach** – recognising the diversity of individuals, cultures and corporate frameworks – should be taken in practice.

Question 6

Text reference. Chapter 16 covers disciplinary action in detail.

Top tips. Remember not to use 'positive' and 'negative' discipline in part (a) – as you'll need them for part (b).

Easy marks. Parts (a) and (b) are straightforward theory – and part (c) allows you to use your practical awareness and experience. Close to full marks should be possible here.

Examiner's comments. This was a popular question which attracted good marks. Most answers to part (a) correctly described what is meant by discipline and adherence to workplace rules. Some answers wrongly assumed that discipline is always about punishment. Most could correctly describe 'positive' and 'negative' discipline in part (b), and there were some excellent examples of disciplinary situations given for part (c).

Marking scheme

		Marks
(a)	Description of 'discipline'	3
(b)	Positive and negative discipline (2 marks each)	4
(c)	Examples of disciplinary situations (2 marks each)	8
		15

(a) **Discipline** can be described as a situation where the members of the enterprise behave sensibly, and conduct themselves according to the **standards of acceptable behaviour** as related to the goals and rules of the organisation. Even before they start to work, most mature people accept the idea that following instructions and fair rules of conduct are normal responsibilities that are part of any job.

(b) Another definition of 'positive' and 'negative' discipline makes the distinction between methods of maintaining sensible conduct and orderliness which are technically co-operative, and those based on warnings, threats and punishments.

(i) **Positive** (or constructive) discipline relates to procedures, systems and equipment in the work place which have been designed specifically so that the **employee has no option** but to act in the desired manner to complete a task safely and successfully. A machine may, for example, shut off automatically if its safety guard is not in place.

(ii) **Negative** discipline is the promise of **sanctions** designed to make people choose to behave in a desirable way. Disciplinary action may be **punitive** (punishing an offence), **deterrent** (warning people not to behave in a certain way) or **reformative** (calling attention to the nature of the offence, so that it will not happen again).

(c) **Types of disciplinary situations** (note only four required in the answer)

There are many types of disciplinary situations which require attention by the manager. Internally, the most frequently occurring are these.

- Excessive absenteeism
- Poor timekeeping
- Defective and/or inadequate work performance
- Poor attitudes which influence others or reflect on the image of the firm
- Breaking rules regarding rest periods and other time schedules
- Improper personal appearance
- Breaking safety rules
- Other violations of rules, regulations and procedures
- Open insubordination such as the refusal to carry out a work assignment.

Managers might be confronted with disciplinary problems stemming from employee behaviour 'off the job'. These may be an excessive drinking problem, the use of drugs or some form of narcotics, or involvement in some form of law breaking activity. In such circumstances, whenever an employee's off-the-job conduct has an impact upon performance on the job, the manager must be prepared to deal with such a problem within the scope of the disciplinary process.

ACCA

Paper 1.3

Managing People

Mock Examination 2

Question Paper		
Time allowed		**3 hours**
This paper is divided into two sections		
Section A	**This question is compulsory and MUST be attempted**	
Section B	**FOUR questions ONLY to be attempted**	

DO NOT OPEN THIS PAPER UNTIL YOU ARE READY TO START UNDER EXAMINATION CONDITIONS

SECTION A – This ONE question is compulsory and MUST be attempted

Question 1

Grosvenor Greyline is a travel consultancy, providing travel advice and bookings to business and personal clients. It was founded 5 years ago by John Grosvenor (Managing Director) and his brother James (HR director), and has now expanded from one London office to 8 regional offices in UK cities.

In the early days of the business, John and James used to recruit and select staff personally, but with the growth and geographic spread of the business, recruitment and selection have been devolved to the managers of the different offices.

Recently, however, a number of issues have arisen in regard to this area of HR management. James Grosvenor has had to deal with a number of disciplinary issues at regional offices, and has discovered that the staff concerned were temperamentally unsuited to their customer service roles. The costs of recruitment overall have been rising, and it appears that this is partly caused by high staff turnover, with many new staff leaving within a year of entering the firm.

James has realised that Grosvenor Greyline's existing recruitment policies and procedures are inadequate to guide office managers. He has recommended to the Managing Director, as a first step, a comprehensive audit of current practices. However, John has so far refused to authorise the expense of such an exercise. With new information technology and a booming market, he does not regard recruitment and selection as a priority area for the business: unsuitable staff 'can't cause much damage' and 'can easily be replaced', in his opinion.

More recently, however, another crisis has arisen. A 45-year-old woman of Indian origin, called Majuna, was interviewed for a job with the Bristol office, and was not selected. Majuna has made a written complaint to James Grosvenor, stating that, in her opinion, the job advertisement (placed exclusively in the youth section of local newspapers) was discriminatory to a person of her age, and that questions asked of her in the interview in regard to her child-rearing responsibilities were also discriminatory. When she asked the interviewer about the organisation's diversity policy, no such policy could be found. Attempting to investigate these complaints, James has found that the Bristol manager has no recollection of the interview or his specific reasons for rejecting Majuna's application.

Confronted with these events, John Grosvenor has admitted that perhaps Grosvenor Greyline needs to look at its recruitment and selection. 'Perhaps it's not something we should be doing ourselves, though', he has said. 'Can't we hand it all over to an external consultant and stick to what we do best?'

As James Grosvenor's assistant, you have been asked to clear up some of these areas.

Required

(a) Explain to John Grosvenor why recruitment and selection are important to an organisation and what their main aims are. **(6 marks)**

(b) Identify six factors that Grosvenor Greyline should to take into account when deciding on whether to outsource its recruitment and selection to external consultants? **(6 marks)**

(c) Evaluate Majuna's complaint that she has been discriminated against, and suggest how similar complaints could be avoided in future. **(7 marks)**

(d) Describe four methods by which James could evaluate the effectiveness of Grosvenor Greyline's recruitment and selection procedures. **(8 marks)**

(e) List seven performance indicators of effective recruitment and selection procedures. **(7 marks)**

(f) Make three specific recommendations to improve the effectiveness of recruitment and selection at Grosvenor Greyline. **(6 marks)**

(Total = 40 marks)

SECTION B – FOUR questions ONLY to be attempted

Question 2

It is often said that 'team building', or the encouraging of team cohesion, is the key to successful teamworking. You have been asked to set up a new temporary project group, and will have to address these issues.

Required

(a) Propose three measures for encouraging cohesion in your team. **(6 marks)**
(b) Outline the drawbacks to creating a very cohesive team. **(4 marks)**
(c) State what you understand 'successful' teamworking to mean. **(5 marks)**

(Total = 15 marks)

Question 3

Currently, your employer has no formal recruitment procedures, but now realises that formal procedures are required.

Required

Identify and explain the stages involved in planning for recruitment. **(15 marks)**

Question 4

Appraisal systems are increasingly being used to measure performance within organisations.

Required

(a) Describe the benefits of performance appraisal systems for:

(i) the organisation **(3 marks)**
(ii) the line manager **(3 marks)**
(iii) the individual **(3 marks)**

(b) Describe the following approaches to measurement used in performance appraisal systems:

(i) Classification
(ii) Factor comparison
(iii) Points rating **(6 marks)**

(Total = 15 marks)

Question 5

An important part of management is understanding the role of leadership.

Required

(a) Describe Blake and Mouton's Managerial Grid. **(5 marks)**
(b) Discuss the relevance to management of Blake and Mouton's Grid in understanding leadership styles. **(10 marks)**

(Total = 15 marks)

Question 6

A key part of an accountant's job is communicating information to others.

Required

(a) Explain the importance of good communication. **(5 marks)**

(b) List five possible barriers to good communication. **(5 marks)**

(c) Describe how these barriers to communication can be overcome. **(5 marks)**

(Total = 15 marks)

Answers

DO NOT TURN THIS PAGE UNTIL YOU HAVE COMPLETED THE MOCK EXAM

PLAN OF ATTACK

Managing People is a 'wordy' subject, without the clear 'right' and 'wrong' answers you can achieve in the other papers at this level. That doesn't mean that you can waffle your way to a pass in your sleep, but there are some easy marks to be had.

As stated in the 'Passing 1.3' section at the front of this Kit, the keys to passing this paper are:

- **Demonstrating preparation**. You can't rely on 'common sense'. The questions are often factual, and you are expected to be able to cite, explain and apply supporting theories (some of them specifically named in the question) and background knowledge.
- **Time management.** Section A should take 72 minutes *maximum*, and each of the four Section B questions should take 27 minutes.
- **Demonstrating thought**. You need to show that you haven't thrown points together at random. Plan your answers so that they have a coherent structure which reflects the requirements of the question. Use section headings to highlight the structure for the examiner.

First item on your agenda must be to **read the rubric**. You must do Section A (Question 1), and you have to choose four out of the five questions in Section B. So your only **choices** are:

- The **order** in which you will tackle the questions
- Which **one** of the Section B questions you will **not** attempt.

Looking through *this particular paper*, you will note that Section A covers various issues in recruitment, selection and equal opportunity, and Section B offers a variety of questions covering other syllabus areas: management and team development (team cohesion [question 10]), recruitment and selection (recruitment planning [question 3], training and development (appraisal [question 4]); motivation and leadership (Blake and Mouton [question 5]; and effective communication practices [question 6].

Should you do Section A first?

The Examiner's Comments for this paper have repeatedly noted that students who left the compulsory question until last appeared, due to poor time management, to have 'rushed' their answers – missing out on vital marks. If, having underlined the **topic and instruction keywords** of all the questions on the paper, you feel relatively comfortable with Question 1, it would be a good idea to attempt it early in the exam: get it out of the way!

In this paper, Question 1 has some straightforward parts that you might feel confident about: parts (b), (d) and (e), for example, are bookwork questions offering easy marks if you've covered this area. Don't be put off by the problem-solving and application required by parts (c) and (f): see if you can jot down some ideas. If you still aren't confident, tackle your best Section B question first, to boost your confidence.

Tackling Section A

Remember to spend no more than **72 minutes** in total on Section A. Allowing 5 minutes to read the scenario through carefully, the 6-mark parts should take you about 11 minutes each; and part (e) 12 minutes. This leaves you 13 minutes for part (c) and 14 minutes for part (f): a bit of extra time for the analytical/problem-solving requirements. Tackle the parts in order, building up to the more challenging part (f) by refreshing your memory of the topic through parts (a)-(e).

Choosing Section B questions

The Section B questions are all fairly straightforward, requiring mostly factual descriptions/ explanation, but also some evaluation and thinking about implications. Your 'least favourite' or 'weakest' Section B question will therefore depend mostly on your revision: which topics you have covered and recall most strongly. You may, for example, simply not recall job evaluation in sufficient detail to be confident in tackling question 4: in which case, that's the one to leave out.

If you find more than one such question, remember to underline the **topic/instruction keywords** of all the questions.

(a) They may well jog your memory of the topic (which is partly what they are there for).

(b) They will enable you to assess how many marks you are confident of getting for each question, bearing in mind the **marks available** for different question parts. (In question 5, for example, you may be delighted to see 'Blake and Mouton' – but then realise that the 10-mark part is quite challenging, leaving you confident only of 7-8 marks. By contrast, in question 4, you may not be confident about all the methods of job evaluation, but strong on appraisal. Look at the mark allocations: you potentially have 9-12 marks out of the possible 15 under your belt.)

Tackling Section B

Tackle your stronger questions first – but **don't** be tempted to take longer on them than the 27 minutes allocated for each. You can't get *more* than 15 marks for a question, however long you spend polishing your answer – and if you finish one question short, because you run out of time (or don't like your fourth question), you automatically *lose* 15 marks!

Even if you are struggling with your fourth question, leave yourself time to give it some thought and do an answer plan, which may jog your memory. At the very least, an answer plan will give the examiner some indication of your having thought the topic through.

Question 1

Text references. Material for this answer can be found in Chapters 7 (overview of recruitment and selection), 8 (evaluating recruitment and selection) and 9 (discrimination and diversity).

Top tips. Like any scenario question, the important thing is to focus on what theory is required by each question part, and how far it is related (or can be related) to the specific circumstances of the scenario.

In part (a), note the two separate requirements: importance, and aims. Unlike John, you need to show an appreciation of the importance of a systematic approach.

Part (c) requires you to refer directly to the scenario. Think through all the various legal (and ethical) provisions on equal opportunity in order to assess Majuna's claim: remember that discrimination can be indirect as well as direct. The second requirement gives you a broader opportunity to discuss equal opportunities measures: keep an eye on the time!

Part (d) refers specifically to methods of evaluation – not criteria, which you will need to save for part (e)!

Part (f) gives broad scope: our recommendations are only indicative, although they address some key areas raised by the scenario.

Attempt the parts in order: they have a logical flow which should help you to avoid answer duplications and confusions.

Easy marks. Parts (b), (d) and (e) are more or less straight bookwork, and should furnish a good base of marks. Parts (c) and (f) look more challenging, but the underlying theory is still basic: use it as a checklist until you hit on points that are most relevant to the scenario.

Marking scheme

			Marks
(a)	Importance of recruitment and selection	3	
	Main aims	3	
			6
(b)	Factors in decision to outsource (1 mark per factor)		6
(c)	Discussion for/against Majuna's discrimination	3	
	Anti-discrimination measures (1 mark per measure)	4	
			7
(d)	Four methods of evaluation (2 marks per method)		8
(e)	Seven performance indicators (1 mark per criterion)		7
(f)	Three recommendations (2 marks per recommendation)		6
			40

(a) **Importance of recruitment and selection**

Recruitment issues are central to business strategy, because:

- The business needs quality skills to succeed (particularly in a fast-changing and competitive sector like travel)
- Knowledge and skills are essential in the service sector: poor customer service staff *can* (contrary to John's opinion) cause damage to customer relations, lost business and lost competitive edge

- Ineffective recruitment and selection (as GG is now seeing) creates high turnover, with raised recruitment/training costs, damage to the firm's reputation as an employer and potential costs of discrimination claims.

Main aims of recruitment and selection

The main aims of recruitment and selection are:

- To supply the organisation with the skilled employees it requires to service its customers, maintain its competitive edge and (potentially) have the flexibility to grow its business in future
- To attract and select people who will 'fit' the culture and objectives of the organisation and the requirements of the job, minimising subsequent turnover and disciplinary problems
- To ensure that all potential applicants for jobs are treated fairly and with respect, and that the organisation reflects (and benefits from) the diversity of its labour pool.

(b) **Six factors to take into account in decision to use external consultants**

If GG wishes to engage recruitment consultants, it will need to consider which activities it will outsource and which it will retain for its head-office HR department or line managers. The outsourcing decision will depend on factors including:

(i) The level of expertise, specialist knowledge and contacts which the consultant can bring to the process (eg in compliance with equal opportunities legislation or interviewing/assessment skills)

(ii) The level of recruitment expertise available within the organisation (currently fairly low within GG)

(iii) The need for impartiality which can only be filled by an outsider (eg for undertaking the audit of GG's current practices)

(iv) Whether the use of the outside agent will be supported or resented by in-house staff: in GG's case, provided that consultants adequately understand the travel sector's needs, help is more likely to be welcomed, given the existing problems.

(v) Whether there is time available for the consultants to learn about the organisation and its requirements: in this case, the audit would be a good opportunity for them to learn, and there is no specific deadline.

(vi) The cost of using consultants, compared to the costs of conducting the process in-house.

(c) **Majuna's discrimination complaint**

Majuna may have grounds for complaint of indirect age discrimination, on the grounds that the job was advertised in such a way as to reduce the opportunity of older people to see it. It may be argued that people of any age can read the youth sections of newspapers – but the placement does imply a preference for younger employees.

Majuna may also have grounds for complaint of indirect sex discrimination under the Sex Discrimination Act, because of the questions asked of her in the interview – *unless* it could be shown that the same questions were asked of single, married, male and female applicants.

Racial or religious discrimination does not appear to be a cause of complaint in this case, but the absence of a diversity policy may be symptomatic of lack of thought on these issues.

Measures to prevent future complaints of discrimination

In order to improve the situation – as well as to avoid laying itself open to future complaints (and legal claims), GG should give systematic thought to equal opportunity measures.

(i) A working party (including line managers, staff representatives and external consultants) should be formed to produce a draft Equal Opportunity and Diversity Policy and Code of Practice, which will be approved by John and James for use throughout the firm.

(ii) Detailed procedures should be drawn up for job advertising, application forms, interviews and selection tests, in order to minimise the risk of discrimination.

(iii) Managers and staff involved in the process may need awareness and skills training.

(iv) Detailed record keeping should be established for all recruitment and selection processes, so that in the event of complaint, the details (eg of questions asked, as in Majuna's case) can be accessed.

(d) **Four methods of evaluating effectiveness**

(i) **Monitoring the composition of, and changes in, the workforce**

For example, the proportion of women or ethnic minorities in the workforce might indicate effective or ineffective practice in the light of equal opportunities policies. The labour retention (or turnover) rates among new recruits might indicate effective or ineffective management of the expectations of recruits, as currently at GG.

(ii) **Monitoring the job performance and development of successful recruits**

Expectations and predictions made on the basis of interviews and selection testing can be compared to actual job performance, to indicate where criteria are more or less relevant and predictive, or where assessment has been inaccurate.

(iii) **Using attitude surveys and feedback questionnaires**

GG or consultants can gather qualitative data in order to analyse successful and unsuccessful candidates' experience and perceptions of the recruitment and selection process. This may highlight areas of perceived unfairness, poor public relations, unnecessary stress and so on.

(iv) **Monitoring the effectiveness of recruitment policies**, campaigns, methods and media according to specific performance indicators (discussed below).

For example: the organisation may analyse the cost effectiveness of different recruitment advertising media, defined as the cost per applicant, or cost per applicant short-listed for interview.

(e) **Eight performance indicators**

(i) Number of candidates attracted

(ii) Number of suitable candidates attracted (eg number or proportion of candidates who proceeded to interview or short-list)

(iii) Number of women, ethnic minorities or disabled people attracted and selected, in relation to relevant policies and targets

(iv) Cost of recruitment and selection per suitable (short-listed) candidate or successful candidate

(v) Cost-effectiveness of each advertising medium or selection method used (for comparison)

(vi) Average time taken to process applications, or time taken for the whole process from job requisition to employment

(vii) Post-selection performance of successful candidates in terms of meeting performance or development targets

(viii) Number or proportion of recruits still employed after one year, two years

(f) **Three recommendations for improvement**

In addition to the equal opportunity/diversity policy measures discussed in part (c), GG may consider the following measures.

(i) Ensure that person specifications and other selection criteria are more closely related to the requirements of the organisation and job roles, both in terms of skills and disposition (as in Rodger's

Seven Point Plan, for example). These would minimise the current problem whereby recruited staff turn out to be temperamentally unsuited to their roles.

(ii) Ensure that adequate information about the organisation and job role is provided to applicants in the job advertising and interview process. This would help to minimise turnover within the first year of employment from recruits 'discovering' that they are not suited to the organisation. (Investigation should also be made into terms and conditions of work and other potential causes of poor retention.)

(iii) Establish systematic procedures and criteria for all recruitment and selection processes. These would be the basis for training and appraising recruiters/selectors, to ensure a minimum standard of effectiveness and compliance. They would also ensure that the basic aims of the process are met.

Question 2

Text reference. Cohesion is discussed in Chapter 4.

Top tips. The main pitfall here is the 'micro scenario' set up in the introduction to the question: this is a *new, temporary* project (cross-functional) group. This will present some specific challenges to encouraging cohesion (eg people don't know each other yet; people work in different departments)...

Easy marks. Once you've taken on board the element of application, the *theories* should be straightforward: team building; group think; team success.

(a) **Three measures for encouraging cohesion**

Cohesion should naturally increase once the team has progressed through its 'storming' phase (Tuckman). However, the following team-building measures may facilitate this process.

(i) **Reinforce the group's sense of identity**

Since we are a temporary project group, it will not be possible to build a collective history or long-term badges of identity. However, I propose that we adopt the meetings room allocated for our briefings as a Team Headquarters, so we can have our own space, marked by our charts, resources and so on. Introducing all members to the client will also reinforce team identity.

(ii) **Reinforce team solidarity (loyalty, trust, relationships)**

Again, we will not have a long history together, so it is essential to accelerate relationship-building by expressing solidarity; encouraging informal communication between team members (perhaps by out-of-work social contact); dealing with conflict swiftly and openly; and controlling competition by treating everyone fairly. If possible, we could also establish an element of competition with other project groups: perhaps offering a prize for the best client evaluation.

(iii) **Reinforcing commitment to shared team objectives**

The project depends on team member co-operation, so this should be easy to emphasise. I propose to set out team objectives clearly, and to allow the team to participate in setting tactics and targets; to seek and give regular feedback on progress and on the client's responses; to celebrate (and, with the partners' approval) reward all group achievements.

(b) **Drawbacks to ultra-cohesive teams**

Top tips. If you didn't immediately connect to 'group think' you could still work your way to most of these points. However, it helps to show that you have done some reading – and aren't just relying on common sense!

The dangers of teams becoming too attached to group maintenance activities, at the expense of task activities, are well researched. The phrase 'group think' was coined by Janis to describe a situation in which a group becomes completely absorbed with its own maintenance, members and priorities, and is blinkered to what is going on around it. The implications of this for task performance are as follows.

(i) The desire for consensus within the group, and hostility to outsiders, may **prevent consideration of alternatives**, constructive criticism or dissenting views. This can lead to **complacent and risky decision-making**.

(ii) The **sharing of responsibility** for decisions further leads to **riskier decision-making.**

(iii) Ultra-cohesive groups **focus a lot of their energies on member satisfaction**, potentially at the expense of task objectives.

(iv) Attachment to existing group processes and membership may **create hostility towards newcomers and changes** (such as the reforming of the group for the next project).

(v) **Group cohesion is often intensified by inter-group competition**, which can lead to a culture of competitiveness, hostility and political game-playing.

Attention will need to be given to focusing the group's energies on the project, welcoming feedback (including constructive criticism), and emphasising competition rather than competitiveness.

(c) **What do we mean by team success?**

(i) The meeting of **task objectives**, standards and targets: in other words, effective job performance on the project.

(ii) The **satisfaction of individual team members**, in the relationships, processes and performance of the team. This can be measured by expressed attitudes, as well as by signs such as low absenteeism, open communication and so on.

(iii) **Effective and efficient team functioning**: co-operation, the balanced exercising of roles, workload sharing, individual contribution, consensus decision-making, performance in the leader's absence and so on.

(iv) **Effective and efficient task functioning**: few interruptions to work flow, ideas generation and problem-solving, constructive feedback, client focus and so on.

(v) The **fulfilment of the team's role** within the organisation: projecting a positive image of the organisation, reflecting organisational values, commitment to organisational goals.

Question 3

Text reference. This topic is covered in Chapter 7.

Top tips. This question was phrased rather loosely: it isn't really about 'stages in *planning* for recruitment' so much as the stages *in a recruitment plan* – in other words, a systematic approach to recruitment. Once you realised this, the answer should be straightforward, providing its own structural outline (since the marks available give little structural guidance). You might validly have confined your answer (strictly) to recruitment: a process from job analysis and HR planning through to job advertisement and the sending out of application mechanisms. However, we have followed the examiner's guidance in taking a looser interpretation here, and covering recruitment and selection together.

Easy marks. Once your answer is planned, the elements should be straightforward. Note the similarity of this question to question 21 – but how *different* the answer here is, because of the 'looser' question requirements.

Examiner's comments. The examiner was looking for tasks within a systematic formal recruitment and selection procedure. Too many candidates introduced matters of detailed practice (such as placing interviewees at ease) or failed to describe an orderly sequence of steps.

Steps in a formal recruitment and selection procedure

The overall aim of a recruitment and selection procedure is to ensure that organisations can obtain the quantity and quality of employees required to fulfil their objectives. As the complexity of the business environment has increased, recruitment has become more integrated with long term human resource and business planning – not just 'filling vacancies' as they arise.

(a) **Human resource planning** to define the human resources required by the organisation to meet its objectives, and the source of labour (internal and external) that are available.

(b) **Identification of vacancies**, from the requirements of the human resource plan or via job requisition from a department that has a vacancy that the plan determines should be re-filled.

(c) **Description of the role or vacancy**. This may already exist, or be done via a job analysis or role definition exercise. Two outputs will be required for effective recruitment:

 (i) A **job description**: specifying the key tasks and responsibilities of the job and its relation to other tasks and units of the organisation. Alternatively, a role definition may be used.

 (ii) A **personnel specification** (or competence definition): reworking the job/role requirements in terms of the kind of person needed to perform the job. This is commonly expressed as attributes which are essential, desirable and contra-indicated, using a framework such as the Seven Point Plan (Rodger) or Five Point Pattern (Munro-Fraser). Alternatively, a competence definition may be used.

(d) Preparation and publication of **recruitment advertising**, with three key aims: to attract the attention and interest of potentially suitable candidates; to give a favourable (but accurate) description of the job and organisation; and to equip candidates to make an appropriate application (how and to whom to apply etc)

(e) Preparation of **application mechanisms**, such as applicant information packs (including role definitions and requirements) and application forms (printed or on-line).

(f) **Screening of applications**. For some jobs, hundreds of people may apply, so recruiters need structured ways of sifting the data and assessing applications against key criteria: using computer matching or recruitment consultants, say. Applications will be sorted and dealt with accordingly: 'possibles' may be short-listed for interview, 'marginals' placed in reserve and 'unsuitables' sent standard letters of refusal.

(g) **Interview**. Despite its lack of predictive validity, the interview is still the most common selection tool. It should be planned with three key aims in mind: identifying the best person for the job; managing expectations and encouraging self-selection in candidates; and treating all applicants fairly. Provision should be made for training interviewers and providing a clear (and equitable) framework for questioning, evaluating and comparing candidates.

(h) **Selection testing** and other methods, as appropriate, to confirm or follow-up judgements made during interview. Techniques include: intelligence, aptitude, proficiency and personality testing; biographic data surveys; and the gathering of references. The selection of techniques will depend on the nature of the attributes required and the costs of administration relative to the value of a 'best possible' recruitment decision.

(i) **Follow-up procedures**: provisional offers to successful candidates; negotiation of contract terms (if required); reviewing of unsuccessful candidates (if required, or to keep in reserve for future vacancies); notification of unsuccessful candidates; planning of recruit induction; and so on.

Question 4

Text reference. Both these topics are covered in Chapter 11.

Top tips. The instruction keyword in part (a) is 'benefits': don't waste time simply describing appraisal systems! The question 'stem' – with its reference to performance appraisal – may have been something of a red herring when it came to part (b): you should have identified the techniques cited as methods of *job evaluation*, the key point of which is that it measures the worth of the job and *not* the performance of the job holder. Stick to instructions – 'describe the following approaches' – and this should not have been a problem.

Examiner's comments. Appraisal is basic to human resource management, and it was disappointing that few candidates attempted this question and that answers (especially to part (b)) were very weak.

Marking scheme

				Marks
(a)	(i)	Describe usefulness for the organisation	3	
	(ii)	Describe usefulness for the line manager	3	
	(iii)	Describe usefulness for the individual	3	
				9
(b)	Description of:			
	(i)	Classification	2	
	(ii)	Factor comparison	2	
	(iii)	Points rating	2	
				6
				15

(a) **Benefits of performance appraisal systems**

Benefits to the organisation

(i) Systematic information for strategic human resource management, including recruitment, succession and development planning, to ensure that the right skills are available at the right time to meet the requirements of the corporate plan.

(ii) A consistent appraisal methodology and criteria across the organisation, supporting effective and fair reward/development decisions and programmes.

(iii) A framework of performance standards and criteria which aids in maintaining discipline and motivating employees: staff know what is expected of them, and the organisation is able to demonstrate commitment to performance improvement and employee development.

Benefits to the line manager

(i) A framework of guidelines by which staff performance can be objectively, consistently and (to a degree) impersonally measured – minimising the potential for interpersonal difficulties and demoralisation in negative feedback.

(ii) Systematic information about staff members' work problems, challenges, needs and aspirations: an aid to more effective management and development planning.

(iii) Increased opportunities for performance-focused communication, which may both improve interpersonal relations with staff and highlight potential improvements and innovations.

Benefits to the individual

(i) Increased opportunities for upward communication: offering suggestions, solving work problems, getting needs met and aspirations known.

(ii) Added impetus for systematic training and development planning, which may widen employee opportunities for growth in the job.

(iii) Systematic appraisal allows goals, standards and responsibilities to be clarified so that individuals know exactly what is expected of them.

(iv) 'Judgements' about the individual's performance (especially those on which rewards will be based) are more likely be objective and consistent than random impressions and feedback from managers.

(b) **Approaches to job evaluation**

Job evaluation is a systematic method of arriving at a wage or salary structure so that the rate of pay for a given job is fair in comparison to other jobs in the organisation.

(i) **Classification** is a method of job evaluation in which each job is considered as a whole (rather than in terms of job elements). The organisation defines what **salary grades** there ought to be (say, grades A, B, C, D and E). Jobs are then analysed according to their role in accomplishing the objectives of the organisation, and allocated to a given grade.

This method is simple and unscientific, and may be sufficient for the needs of a small organisation. However, the evaluations are recognised as being highly subjective. Such a non-analytical approach could not, for example, be used to justify salary decisions under Equal Pay legislation in the UK.

(ii) **Factor comparison** begins with the selection of a number of qualitative **factors** on which jobs will be evaluated (such as technical knowledge or physical skill). Key **benchmark jobs**, for which the rate of pay is considered to be fair, are analysed, determining a monetary value for each factor. Other (non-benchmark) jobs can then be analysed, adding up the pay rates allocated to each factor to derive a total **value for the job**.

This is an analytical method, sufficiently objective to be used to justify salary decisions under Equal Pay legislation.

(iii) **Points rating** begins with a list of qualities required by the jobs to be evaluated (such as skill, mental effort, responsibility for subordinates). A number of points is allocated to each factor, as a maximum score. Jobs are then analysed and point scores awarded to reflect the importance of each factor within a job. The total points scored for each job provides a basis for ranking jobs within the salary structure.

This is a flexible and objective method: probably the most popular form of formal job evaluation.

Question 5

Text reference. The Grid is covered in Chapter 14.

Top tips. Part (a) is straightforward – as long as you notice that it is only worth 5 marks! Resist the temptation to write everything you know about the Managerial Grid too early: you need 10 marks' worth of material for part (b). Note the instruction keywords of part (b): 'discuss' the 'relevance' of the Grid for managers seeking to understand leadership styles. You will need to show how it is relevant/useful, and how far: if in doubt, look for both these aspects in our suggested solution.

Easy marks. Part (a) should be easy, particularly if you use a (quick, neat) diagram. Part (b) requires more thought: use our helping hand if you need to.

Examiner's comments. Most candidates were able to offer a brief description of the Grid: fewer were able to offer the deeper explanation and application to leadership in the workplace required by part (b).

Marking scheme

			Marks
(a)	Description of Management Grid	2	
	Examples of 'scores'	3	5
(b)	Discussion of leadership	4	
	Discussion of relevance of Grid and examples of styles	6	10
			15

(a) **Blake and Mouton's Managerial Grid**

Robert Blake and Jane Mouton suggested that there are two basic dimensions of leadership: concern for production (or task performance) and concern for people. Along each of these two dimensions, managers can be located at any point on a continuum from very low to very high concern. Blake and Mouton modelled these permutations as 'the Managerial Grid'.

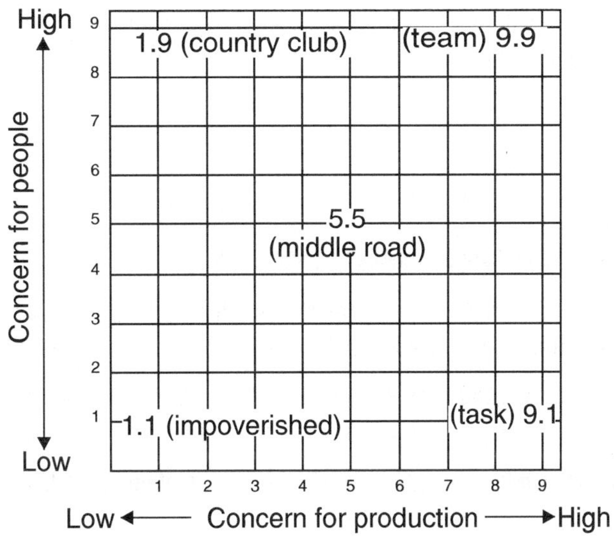

A questionnaire was designed to enable users to analyse and plot the 'positions' of individual respondents on the Grid. Descriptions of extreme positions were designed to highlight the nature and consequences of various leadership styles, with a view to managerial self-development.

(b) **Relevance of the Grid**

Leadership styles are patterns of leader behaviour, which can (according to style theories) be consciously adopted to achieve desired effects. Understanding leadership styles has, in itself, become increasingly relevant for managers.

(i) Old 'trait' theories of leadership have been discredited, and emphasis placed on leader behaviour.

(ii) Contingency approaches have emphasised the need for intentional behavioural flexibility to fit specific managerial contexts.

(iii) 'Leadership' has emerged as an influential interpersonal factor which is said to secure team member commitment (over and above mere compliance), facilitate change and innovation, and energise teams and organisations, (Kotter, among others). In competitive, fast-changing business environments, where people are a key resource, 'leadership' (as distinguished from management) is considered crucial to organisational survival and success.

The Managerial Grid is only one model of leadership style – and 'style' models are not the only approach to discussing leadership effectiveness: contingency and functional approaches (eg Adair) are also popular.

Nevertheless, among style theories, the Grid is accessible and popular – especially in its intended context of management appraisal and development. It recognises that a balance is required between concern for the task and concern for people, and that a high degree of both is possible (and highly effective) at the same time. It thus offers a number of useful insights for the identification of management development needs, showing in an easily assimilated form where the habitual behaviours and assumptions of a manager may exhibit a lack of balance and/or a low degree of concern in either dimension or both.

However, the Grid is a simplified model and as such has practical limitations.

(i) It assumes that 9.9 is the desirable model for effective leadership style. In some contexts, this may not necessarily be so. Where there is high unemployment or heavy automation, for example, concern for people may not be a high priority.

(ii) Organisational context and culture, technology and other 'givens' (Handy) influence the manager's style of leadership as well as the two dimensions covered by the Grid.

(iii) Any managerial theory is only useful in so far as it is useable in practice by managers. If the Grid is merely used to pressure managers to adopt a particular 'style' of leadership, against their context and inclinations, it may result in stress for the manager, and inconsistent leadership behaviours: the most stressful and least popular of all leadership 'styles' for subordinates (Likert and others).

Question 6

Text reference. Communication is discussed in detail in Chapter 15.

Top tips. This is a straightforward question on some key topics. They might equally well have been set as problems to diagnose and solve in a case study. See Mock Exam 1, question 1 – and note the difference in approach.

Remember to watch out for basic instruction key words – like *'five* barriers to good communication' (part (b)). Note that none of these question parts ask what good communication is: even part (a) is about why it is *important.*

Easy marks. You should have been able to get close to full marks here, if you read the question requirements accurately.

Examiner's comments. Although the question was popular and attracted good answers, some candidates did not read the question carefully enough.

Marking scheme

		Marks
(a)	Explain importance of good communication (1 mark per factor)	5
(b)	List five barriers to communication (1 mark per barrier)	5
(c)	Description of overcoming barriers (1 mark per factor)	5
		15

(a) **Importance of good communication**

'Good communication' may be defined as communication which is efficient and effective in achieving its purpose.

Good communication is vitally important, because the achievement of organisational objectives depends on these factors:

(i) Exchange of information for planning, decision-making and control between different units

(ii) Giving of orders and instructions for operations

(iii) Establishing and maintenance of working relationships, for co-ordination and employee morale

(iv) Exchange of information for problem-solving and improved customer care

(v) Communication of a positive image of the organisation and its services to customers and potential customers.

If communication is *ineffective*, none of the above will be achieved: instructions may not be carried out on time, or errors may be made; management may not be made aware of problems; customers may be given a poor impression of the service and reliability of the organisation; and so on.

If communication is *inefficient*, there will be a waste of resources (including staff time clarifying and correcting misunderstandings) and poor control and co-ordination, for which the organisation is accountable to its stakeholders.

(b) **Five major barriers to good communication**

(i) **Poor basic communication skills** on the part of senders (giving distorted messages, for example) or receivers (inattentive listening or inability to interpret non-verbal signals, for example), or both (failure to give or receive feedback say).

(ii) **Personal differences, or 'social noise'.** Differences in age, gender, education, ethnic origin and task culture will encourage different perceptions and interpretations of messages, with potential for misunderstanding. This may be exacerbated by the use of technical jargon or symbols – or indeed different languages.

(iii) **Conflict**, which may create unwillingness to communicate helpfully. Withholding or distorting information may reflect lack of respect, hostility or political game-playing.

(iv) **Active or implied discouragement of communication.** An organisation may, for example, ignore or respond negatively to input or the exchange of information, especially upward.

(v) **Poor communication channels, media and technology.** Staff who are physically separated from the organisational centre, especially if they are on the move, need to be linked to it by efficient and effective communication systems and tools (mobile phones, regular contact routines and so on).

(c) **Overcoming communication barriers**

In broad terms, the barriers to good communication can be overcome by addressing their underlying causes. A flexible contingency approach will be the key, because there is no universal formula for every situation – especially in organisations which by their nature draw together diverse functions, personalities and priorities.

(i) **Communication can be encouraged, facilitated and rewarded**. Status and functional barriers (particularly to upward and lateral communication) can be minimised by improving opportunities (such as planning committees) for formal and informal networking and feedback.

(ii) **Training and guidance** can be given in communication skills, including consideration of audience needs, listening, giving feedback and so on.

(iii) **People can be made aware of the potential for misunderstanding** arising from differences in perception and work culture, and taught to consider others' viewpoints.

(iv) **Technology, systems and procedures can be adapted** to facilitate communication: making it more effective (clearer mobile phone reception), faster (laptops for the e-mailing of instructions) and more consistent (regular reporting routines).

(v) **Conflict and organisational politics** can be managed so that no basic unwillingness to communicate exists between units. Measures may range from specific conflict resolution to adjusting culture to appreciate diversity and focus on customer service.

ACCA

Paper 1.3

Managing People

Mock Examination 3

(December 2006)

Question Paper		
Time allowed		3 hours
This paper is divided into two sections		
Section A	This question is compulsory and MUST be attempted	
Section B	FOUR questions ONLY to be attempted	

DO NOT OPEN THIS PAPER UNTIL YOU ARE READY TO START UNDER EXAMINATION CONDITIONS

SECTION A – This ONE question is compulsory and MUST be attempted

Question 1

Bailey's is a large toy manufacturer based in a traditional industrial region. Established in the 1970s, it has faced many changes in the market and survived. This has been due in part to employing a largely unskilled low paid staff, and maintaining its main advantage, that of low production costs based on low pay. Most of the production involves repetitive and boring work with little challenge and opportunity for innovation. Although many of the employees have been with the company for some time, there has been a high level of employee turnover.

However, an unhappy atmosphere has been apparent for some time. There has been a number of instances of arguments between the staff, friction between different departments, disturbance, low morale, poor production and general unrest, made worse recently by a decline in business which may lead to staff reduction and redundancy. Poor pay is leading to family problems that are affecting the commitment and motivation of the employees.

The business was recently sold to the new owner, Rebecca Stonewall. She is concerned that the negative atmosphere she has found will harm the prospects of the business and is determined to address the issues that have become apparent.

She has therefore decided that it is time to take account of opinions and views of the employees in an attempt both to identify the problems and to resolve them. She has appointed external counsellors since she thinks that a programme of individual counselling might be appropriate and is also of the opinion that some form of different or improved approach to motivation might be the answer to the problems at Bailey's.

Required

(a) Define the role that the external counsellor must fulfil at Bailey's. **(3 marks)**

(b) Describe the skills that a counsellor should possess. **(14 marks)**

(c) Briefly describe three advantages to Bailey's of counselling. **(3 marks)**

(d) Explain to the management of Bailey's why consideration should be given to resolving the problems through:

(i) job rotation **(5 marks)**
(ii) job enlargement **(5 marks)**
(iii) job enrichment **(5 marks)**

(e) Briefly provide five reasons to the management of Bailey's why financial rewards could be considered to improve motivation. **(5 marks)**

(Total = 40 marks)

SECTION B – FOUR questions ONLY to be attempted

Question 2

Traditionally, the only objective of a business was to make a profit. However, some writers have suggested that this idea is simplistic and that profitability is only one objective amongst many.

Required

State and explain Drucker's eight classifications of objectives. **(15 marks)**

Question 3

An organisation has decided to compare the benefits of promoting existing staff with those of appointing external candidates and to assess whether the use of external recruitment consultants is appropriate.

Required

(a) Describe the advantages of internal promotion. **(5 marks)**

(b) Describe the advantages of external recruitment. **(5 marks)**

(c) Briefly describe five factors to be taken into account when deciding whether to use recruitment consultants. **(5 marks)**

(Total = 15 marks)

Question 4

A properly conducted appraisal interview is fundamental in ensuring the success of an organisation's performance appraisal system.

Required

(a) Describe three approaches to conducting the appraisal interview. **(5 marks)**
(b) Describe five main barriers to an effective appraisal interview. **(10 marks)**

(Total = 15 marks)

Question 5

All managers need to understand the importance of motivation in the workplace.

Required

(a) Explain the 'content theory' of motivation. **(5 marks)**

(b) Explain what is meant by McGregor's

(i) Theory X **(5 marks)**
(ii) Theory Y **(5 marks)**

(Total = 15 marks)

Question 6

Communication is important for all organisations and requires an understanding of communication flows and channels.

Required

(a) Briefly explain the main purposes of the three main formal communication channels in an organisation:

(i) Downwards **(3 marks)**
(ii) Upwards **(3 marks)**
(iii) Lateral or horizontal **(3 marks)**

(b) Briefly explain the two types of informal communication known as the grapevine and rumour. **(6 marks)**

(Total = 15 marks)

Answers

DO NOT TURN THIS PAGE UNTIL YOU HAVE COMPLETED THE MOCK EXAM

PLAN OF ATTACK

Managing People is a wordy subject, without the clear 'right' and 'wrong' answers you can achieve in the other papers at this level. That doesn't mean that you can waffle your way to a pass in your sleep, but there are some easy marks to be had.

The keys to passing this paper are set out clearly in the *Passing Paper 1.3* section at the front of this Kit. If you need a refresher on general exam technique, you should start there.

First item on your agenda must be to **read the rubric.** You must do Section A (Question 1), and you have to choose four out of the five questions in Section B. So your only **choices** are:

- The **order** in which you will tackle the questions
- Which **one** of the Section B questions you will *not* attempt.

Looking through this paper, you will note that Section A covers various issues, and related theories, in the management of performance: specifically, counselling and motivation (job design and financial rewards). Section B offers a variety of questions covering each of the syllabus areas: management and team development (objectives [question 2]); recruitment and selection (internal/external recruitment [question 3]); training and development (appraisal interviews [question 4]); motivation and leadership (motivation theories [question 5]); and effective communication practices (formal and informal channels [question 6]).

Should you do Section A first?

The Examiner's Comments for this paper often note that students who leave the compulsory question until last appear, due to poor time management, to have 'rushed' their answers – missing out on vital marks.

If, having underlined the **topic and instruction keywords** of all the questions on the paper, you fell relatively comfortable with Question 1, you might decide to attempt it early and get it out of the way. If you feel less confident, you may prefer to start with your **strongest question** from Section B, to boost your confidence and recall.

In this paper, Question 1 is fairly straightforward – if you remember your reading on counselling, which offers the bulk of the marks. Parts (a), (b) and (c) cover a range of counselling issues (role, skills, advantages) and parts (d) and (e) are mainstream motivation topics. The details of the scenario are sufficient (and obvious) enough to enable you to relate your answers to the case study organisation, as required. However, if you are unsure of any of the higher-mark parts (such as part (b)), you might want to boost your confidence by tackling one or two Section B questions first.

Tackling Section A

Remember to spend no more than **72 minutes** in total on Section A. Allowing 5 minutes to read the scenario through carefully, parts (b) and (d) should take you about 24 minutes each; parts (a) and (c) about 5 minutes each; and part (e) about 8 minutes.

The most important things to bear in mind in this section are:

- Have you correctly identified the theory or model being targeted?
- Have you related your answer to the details provided in the scenario, in the *specific way* in which you were asked to do so? Note that the examiner has specifically put the name of the organisation (Bailey's) into every question part, to emphasise this requirement!

Choosing Section B questions

The Section B questions are fairly straightforward, although they require you to apply some detailed knowledge of specific authors (eg Question 2 on Drucker) and commonly-confused terminology (eg Question 5 on Theory X and Y). Your 'least favourite' or 'weakest' Section B question will, however, depend mostly on your revision: which topics you have covered and remembered most strongly. Question 2 is particularly challenging, as it requires you to remember a specific classification of objectives.

Tackling Section B

Tackle your stronger questions first – but **don't** be tempted to take longer on them than the **27 minutes** allocated for each. You can't get *more* than 15 marks for a question, however long you spend polishing your answer – and if you finish on question short, because you run out of time (or don't like your fourth question), you automatically *lose* 15 marks!

Even if you are struggling with your fourth question, leave yourself time to give it some thought and do an answer plan, which may jog your memory. At the very least, an answer plan will give the examiner some indication of your having thought the topic through.

Question 1

Text References. Material for this answer can be found in Chapter 15 (counselling) and Chapter 13 (job design and pay as motivators).

Top tips. Like any scenario question, the important thing is to focus on what *theory* is required by each question part, and how far it is related (or can be related) to the specific circumstances of the scenario.

In parts (a) – (c), note the topic key words: 'role', 'skills' and 'three advantages'. This is essential to help you organise your material! The bulk of the marks is available for part (b), so that's where you need to devote your time. If you don't remember a list of counselling skills, think carefully through the process and jot down what is involved: forming a relationship (what kind?), questioning (what kind?), listening (what kind?), working with the organisation – and so on.

Part (d) is straightforward in its theory – but you will need to put some effort into applying it to Bailey's specific situation (as specifically required): don't waste time formatting your answer as a memo or report, though, as you haven't been asked to do so.

Part (e) needs careful interpretation: it is asking you to give five reasons why financial rewards 'work' as motivators. Don't waste time and marks giving the counter-argument (limitations of pay as a motivator).

Easy marks. All the question parts are, at heart, more or less straight bookwork, and should furnish a good base of marks: part (d), in particular, should net you 15 easy marks (as long as you get your terminology the right way round). You do need to remember to keep referring your answer to the scenario at Bailey's, though, in order to fulfil the question requirements.

Marking scheme

			Marks
(a)	Definition of the role of the external counsellor	(Up to 3 marks)	3
(b)	Description of the skills of the external counsellor	(Up to 14 marks)	4
(c)	Three advantages of counselling	(1 mark each)	1
(d)	Explanation and usefulness of:		
	(i) Job rotation	(Up to 5 marks)	5
	(ii) Job enlargement	(Up to 5 marks)	5
	(iii) Job enrichment	(Up to 5 marks)	5
(e)	Reasons why financial rewards may be considered to improve motivation (1 mark each)	(Up to 5 marks)	5
			40

(a) **Role of the external counsellor**

The role of a counsellor is to relate and respond to another person (a 'client') so that that person is helped to explore his thoughts, feelings and behaviour with the aim of reaching a clearer understanding.

The role of an *external* counsellor in a work place setting is that of professional counsellor/helper. Counsellors will contract formally with Bailey's (as the funding client) and informally with each counsellee (as clients of the process) to enter into a counselling relationship, usually for a defined period, for the purposes of offering guidance, support and help in problem-solving in work-related, personal and family issues.

(b) **Skills of the external counsellor**

Because the role of counsellor (as opposed to coaching or other forms of developmental intervention) is to help the client to help himself, a particular skill set is required.

(i) Counsellors need to be **observant** and **knowledgeable** about psychology and behaviour, in order to notice and correctly interpret signals which may indicate a problem: the client may not be able clearly to identify or express what the problem is (particularly among unskilled labourers such as Baileys employs).

(ii) Counsellors need to be **sensitive** to beliefs and values which may be different from their own, so that they can exercise non-judgement, see things from other perspectives, allow the sessions to proceed at the client's pace – and refrain from giving inappropriate advice.

(iii) Counsellors need to be both **empathetic** (attempting to see the problem from the other person's point of view, and reflecting their understanding back to the other person so that they feel heard) – and yet also **impartial** (refraining from judging or giving advice unnecessarily). This combination of skills is empowering to disempowered clients like the Bailey's employees.

(iv) Counsellors also need a range of 'micro' skills in supportive communication, including:

- Establishing **rapport and trust**
- **Active listening**: to encourage the client to talk (eg by attentive behaviour and giving supportive feedback) and to demonstrate that they are genuinely trying to understand the client's point of view (eg by reflecting back what they think they are hearing). This may be particularly valuable in an atmosphere of poor motivation and suspicion, such as currently prevails at Baileys: it may be important for employees simply to feel heard.
- Using different **questioning styles**: to encourage clients to speak; to think more deeply or clearly (probing and challenging); and to check their own understanding. Challenging, for example, may be required to break through negative stereotypes of conflicting departments, while probing may be required to encourage clients to talk about sensitive issues such as fear of redundancy or family problems.
- Using **body language** (to convey attentiveness, interest support) and interpreting the client's body language accurately (in order to explore underlying feelings).

(v) External counsellors also require a range of skills in the management of their **professional practice**: time management, negotiation and relationship management with the contracting client (in this case, Baileys), the management of confidential information and so on.

(c) **Advantages of counselling for Baileys**

There are likely to be three key advantages to Baileys of initiating a programme of individual counselling for its employees.

(i) Employee **adjustment, satisfaction and motivation** will benefit from the experience of being listened to (as confirmed by Elton Mayo's classic Hawthorne experiments), as well as from any work or non-work problem-solving that is achieved in the sessions. This may translate into lower employee turnover and enhanced performance.

(ii) Better **understanding** of problems, and the development of coping and **communication skills** through the process, should impact on inter-personal and inter-group conflict. This may aid co-ordination and performance at Baileys.

(iii) The process will show **commitment** to employee well-being, which has perhaps been lacking at Baileys. This will enhance employee morale and Baileys' reputation as an employer, enabling it to attract and retain quality staff. At the same time, it will make it more **socially responsible**, as it supports staff through job insecurity and possible redundancies.

(d) **Job design as a motivator**

Some of Baileys' morale problems are directly attributable to poor job design: it is recognised that the work is repetitive and boring, with little challenge or opportunity for innovation. Factors such as skill variety, task identity and significance, autonomy and feedback have been shown to be 'core dimensions' of work which contribute to job satisfaction. Baileys should therefore focus on job re-design to build such factors (which Herzberg identified as 'motivator' factors) into their production jobs.

(i) **Job rotation** is the planned transfer of staff from one job to another: a 'sequential' extension of the job. This can add the motivating factor of task variety: reducing the monotony, repetition and boredom which are problems at Baileys. It can also be seen as a form of training: individual gain wider experience by rotating to different positions. This would add challenge to the work – and might also increase cross-functional understanding and co-operation (if employees rotated to different departments).

(ii) **Job enlargement** is the attempt to widen jobs by increasing the number of operations in which the job holder is involved: a 'horizontal' extension of the job. This increases task variety and reduces repetition. Tasks which span a larger part of the total production process should also reduce boredom and add to task meaning and significance. Enlarged jobs might also be regarded as having higher status, giving some degree of career progression for long-serving employees.

(iii) **Job enrichment** is planned action to build greater responsibility, breadth and challenge of work into a job: it is a 'vertical' extension of the job, akin to modern ideas of empowerment. A job may be enriched by greater decision-making responsibility, more discretion, participation and performance feedback – all core dimensions of job satisfaction, which is currently lacking at Baileys. Although the link between job satisfaction and motivation is not clear, Herzberg argued that motivation *only* comes from factors in the job itself.

(e) **Financial rewards as a motivator**

The main source of competitive advantage for Baileys has been low production costs based on low pay. It is therefore important to justify any use of financial rewards and incentives on the basis of improved motivation and performance. Herzberg identified financial rewards as a 'hygiene' factor rather than a motivator factor. However, they may be argued to improve motivation in the following ways.

(i) Employees need enough income to live. Particularly for an unskilled workforce in a declining business, there is likely to be an instrumental orientation: workers will put up with deprivations at work in order to gain the monetary rewards they require (as found by Goldthorpe *et al*).

(ii) Monetary rewards can be converted into a wide range of other satisfactions: they can be applied to all employees at all levels, and to all needs that employees may have (regardless of where they are on Maslow's hierarchy, for example).

(iii) Monetary rewards are a consistent measure of value or worth. Higher pay therefore offers status and recognition, and implies achievement (eg in a system of performance-related pay or bonuses): these are motivator factors.

(iv) Monetary incentives can explicitly be offered for defined levels of performance (whether through piecework or performance-related bonuses), to complement other HR initiatives in securing effort and commitment.

(v) As a hygiene factor, monetary reward is a source of *dis*-satisfaction and de-motivation, if not perceived as adequate and equitable: it is, therefore, inevitably a motivation issue.

Question 2

Text References. Material for this answer can be found in Chapter 6 (Drucker's multiple objectives).

Top tips. This is a challenging question, simply because – although Drucker is mentioned in the syllabus – this is a detailed model which you might not have revised in detail. You couldn't waffle an answer to this question, either: you could only gain as many marks as you remembered Drucker's classifications.

Perhaps the top tip for a question like this is to know when a question is a good candidate for being left alone!

Easy marks. There aren't many easy marks here. The question stem may have given you enough to go on for a 1-mark introduction on the need for multiple objectives. You could probably also get 2 marks for stating and explaining profitability (also given to you by the question stem). If you really had to answer this question, and were desperate for marks, you'd have to guess at some of the other objectives. Some might come easily enough: market share, innovation, corporate social responsible or productivity, say...

Marking scheme

		Marks
Explanation of the eight classifications of objectives	(Up to 15 marks)	15

Drucker's classification of eight organisational objectives

Peter Drucker argued that 'to manage a business is to balance a variety of needs and goals... The very nature of business enterprise requires multiple objectives'. He suggested that objectives are needed in eight key areas of business.

(a) **Market standing**: market share, customer satisfaction, the size of the organisation's product range or portfolio and its distribution resources. This reflects the organisation's ability to compete within its target market: it is an essential measure of competitive performance.

(b) **Innovation**: the ability to generate and develop new ideas, products and processes, and the speed with which they can be deployed for competitive advantage (eg time to market of new products/services). This is essential for future strategic development and growth.

(c) **Productivity**: meeting output or contribution targets for input resources. This reflects the efficiency and effectiveness with which organisational resources are used to contribute value.

(d) **Physical and financial resource**: the efficient use (minimising waste) of limited resources (including people, space, materials, plant and equipment – as well as finance).

(e) **Profitability**: a measure of effectiveness (in terms of value creation or the relationship of inputs to outputs), which integrates cost behaviour and revenue performance measures for the whole organisation. Profitability is also a source of re-investment to the business (through retained profits), and a means of attracting fresh capital investment from shareholders.

(f) **Managerial performance and development**: managerial effectiveness in developing strategy, meeting objectives and creating culture; and the development of managers for continuity (managerial succession). This is crucial for the future direction of the enterprise.

(g) **Worker performance and attitude**: labour productivity, stability (the controlling of labour turnover), motivation and morale, development of skills and so on. Labour is a key organisational resource, and must be acquired, developed and deployed systematically – as with other resources.

(h) **Public responsibility** (often called corporate social responsibility): sustainable and ethical policies in relation to environmental protection, community impacts and involvement, labour conditions, ethical trading and so on.

Question 3

Text References. Material for this answer can be found in Chapter 7 (recruit or promote? and recruitment consultants).

Top tips. This is a friendly question, covering mainstream topic areas in a highly structured way. The topic keywords are explicit ('internal promotion', 'external recruitment', 'recruitment consultants') so you should have no trouble interpreting what is required. Just make sure you have read them carefully: give the *advantages* of both promotion and recruitment – not the advantages and disadvantages of one or the other, for example.

Easy marks. This is more or less straight bookwork, so all the marks are easy if you approach your answer in a systematic way. If you're in any doubt of your ability to make five points for each question part, you can probably rely on 1 mark's worth by defining your terms.

Marking scheme

			Marks
(a)	Description of the advantages of internal recruitment (1 mark for each relevant point)	(Up to 5 marks)	5
(b)	Description of the advantages of external recruitment (1 mark for each relevant point)	(Up to 5 marks)	5
(c)	Description of five factors (1 mark each)	(Up to 5 marks)	5
			15

(a) **Advantages of internal promotion**

Internal promotion is a deliberate policy of willingness to promote suitable internal candidates to positions: it reflects a clear career ladder and succession within the organisation. The advantages of such a policy are as follows.

(i) It enables the organisation to develop skills and attributes that may be scarce (and therefore expensive to obtain) in the external labour market, including organisation-specific knowledge and expertise.

(ii) It is relatively cost-effective, because selectors will be familiar with an internal promotee and his or her capabilities.

(iii) It reduces induction times, and related costs, because the promotee has already worked within the organisation and will be familiar with its culture, structures, systems and procedures, objectives and other personnel.

(iv) It demonstrates the organisation's willingness to recognise individual potential and develop careers, which may build morale and commitment (and avoid resentments).

(v) It supports systematic succession planning, which maintains managerial continuity and individual performance improvement over time.

(b) **Advantages of external recruitment**

External recruitment is a policy of filling job vacancies through recruitment activities in the external labour market. The advantages are as follows.

(i) It enables the organisation to acquire skills and attributes that may not be available within the organisation (and would take too long to develop).

(ii) It enables the organisation to gain employees, if the demand for labour is growing, or there is a need to keep pace with employee turnover.

(iii) It supports innovation and competition: new people may bring wider views, fresh ideas and experience in competitor firms.

(iv) It supports organisational learning, flexibility and cultural change: external recruits are more likely to be able to question and challenge the status quo.

(v) It is socially responsible in creating additional employment and links to the community (eg through school/university recruitment).

(c) **Factors in the decision to use recruitment consultants**

The outsourcing decision will depend on factors including:

(i) The level of expertise, specialist knowledge and contacts which the consultant can bring to the process (eg in compliance with equal opportunities legislation or interviewing/assessment skills)

(ii) Whether such a level of expertise is available within the organisation (with added advantages of control, familiarity and cost saving)

(iii) The need for impartiality in selection, which can only be filled by an outsider: otherwise, the organisation may simply clone existing skills and personality types, and not recruit new blood.

(iv) Whether there is time available for the consultants to learn about the organisation and its requirements, so that candidates are compatible both with skill/job requirements and organisational style or cultural values.

(v) The cost of using consultants, compared to the costs of conducting the process in-house.

Question 4

Text References. Material for this answer can be found in Chapter 11 (the appraisal interview, and barriers to effective appraisal).

Top tips. You need to read the topic key words carefully in order to answer the question accurately. First of all, note that the question is about appraisal *interviews*: not appraisal techniques or criteria. Second, for part (b) you need to connect 'three approaches to conducting the appraisal interview' to the work of Maier: once you have done this, the question falls into place. (If you didn't know Maier, you could earn marks with three similar ideas: judgemental, coaching and problem-solving, say – but this would be hard work...)

Similarly, the phrase 'barriers to effective appraisal' might helpfully have connected with the work of Lockett, which you could use as a framework for your answer (as we have done) – but you could equally well find five similar barriers, using your own terminology.

Easy marks. If you remembered Maier and Lockett, the bulk of the marks are obtainable by simply outlining their models concisely and accurately. If not, plenty of marks are still available using common sense – but you would have to work harder to describe your approaches/barriers and distinguish clearly between them.

Marking scheme

			Marks
(a)	Description of the three interview approaches	(Up to 5 marks)	5
(b)	Description of the five main barriers (2 marks each)	(Up to 10 marks)	10
			15

(a) **Approaches to appraisal interviews**

Three approaches to appraisal interview, identified by Maier *(The Appraisal Interview)* are as follows.

(i) The **tell and sell** style. The manager tells the subordinate how (s)he has been assessed, and then tries to 'sell' or gain acceptance of the evaluation and any improvement plan. This is essentially judgemental and directive: it requires unusual human relations skills to convey constructive criticism in an acceptable manner, and to motivate change.

(ii) The **tell and listen** style. The manager tells the subordinate how (s)he has been assessed, and then invites a response. The assessor does not dominate discussion throughout, but adopts a coaching or counselling orientation: gathering employee feedback and ideas for improvement.

(iii) The **problem-solving** style. The manager adopts a coaching/helping orientation: the discussion is centred not on the assessment, but on the employee's work problems and potential. The employee is encouraged to think solutions through and to commit to the recognised need for personal improvement. This encourages proactive, creative thinking.

(b) **Main barriers to effective appraisal interviewing**

Lockett *(Effective Performance Management)* helpfully classified barriers to effective appraisal, which can be applied to the interview part of the process, as follows.

(i) The interview may be perceived as a **confrontation**: a show down or clearing of the air, where there have been performance or inter-personal problems. There is likely to be a lack of agreement (and further conflict) about the assessment and improvement needs. Feedback may be subjective, exaggerated or negatively delivered.

(ii) The interview may be perceived as **judgement**: a one-sided process in which the manager acts as judge and jury. This puts the subordinate on the defensive, creating resistance to change: it can damage relations between the manager and subordinate, and wastes opportunities for employee feedback and collaborative problem-solving.

(iii) The interview may be perceived as **chat**: vague positive affirmations and reviews of the year, without purpose or outcomes. This leaves issues unresolved, and wastes an opportunity for improvement planning.

(iv) The interview may be perceived as **bureaucracy**: a pointless form-filling exercise to satisfy the HR department. It underlying purpose, improving individual and organisational performance, is forgotten.

(v) The interview may be perceived as a purely retrospective, one-off event: as **unfinished business** (a 'wrap up' of the past year's unresolved performance issues) or as an **annual event**. Appraisal should be part of an on-going, future-focused process of performance management.

Question 5

Text References. Material for this answer can be found in Chapter 13 (content theories of motivation, and choosing a motivational approach).

Top tips. This is a classic question, focusing on common pitfalls of mixed-up terminology and inaccurate quoting of theories.

The pitfall in part (a) is (we hope, obviously) the potential to confuse content theory with process theory. If you have revised attentively, you should be able to explain content theory and give several named examples (which the examiner always appreciates, if done correctly!)

The pitfall in part (b) is simply getting Theory X and Y the wrong way round, although the more subtle mark-loser would be misinterpreting the theories to describe actual types of people (rather than managerial assumptions about people). Another mark-waster would be discussing the (unrelated) Theory Y, when not asked to do so.

Easy marks. If you've done your reading in motivation theory, these should all be easy marks: it should be possible to get full marks for this question. If you find yourself struggling for 5 marks' worth on each of Theory X and Y, try to earn the marks available for explaining McGregor's model as a whole.

Marking scheme

				Marks
(a)	Explanation of content theory		(Up to 5 marks)	5
(b)	(i)	Explanation of Theory X	(Up to 5 marks)	5
	(ii)	Explanation of Theory Y	(Up to 5 marks)	5
				15

(a) **Content theory**

Content theories of motivation address the question: '*What* are the things that motivate people?' They assume that human beings have an innate set of needs or desired outcomes, which may vary over time and according to circumstances. They argue that people are motivated by the innate drive to satisfy those needs: a need, once satisfied, ceases to motivate behaviour.

Content theories are essentially prescriptive approaches, because they assume that all human beings share broadly the same innate needs: the satisfactions that can be offered (eg by a work organisation) can be classified, standardised and optimised.

Need theories (such as Maslow's hierarchy of needs and Herzberg's two-factor theory) are of this type.

Content theories are contrasted with 'process theories', which examine *how* people become motivated: the process through which outcomes become desirable and are pursued by individuals.

(b) **McGregor's Theory X and Theory Y**

Douglas McGregor suggested that a manager's approach to motivating people depends on the assumptions (s)he makes about people at work, and what 'makes them tick'. He identified two extreme sets of assumptions (not actual types of people) at each end of a continuum.

Theory X is the assumption that most people dislike work and responsibility and will avoid both if possible. Because of this, most people must be coerced, controlled, directed and/or threatened with punishment in order to get them to make an adequate effort. Managers who operate according to these assumptions will tend to supervise closely, apply detailed rules and control, and use 'carrot and stick' motivations.

Theory Y is the assumption that physical and mental effort in work is as natural as play or rest. The ordinary person does not inherently dislike work: according to the conditions, it may be a source of satisfaction or dissatisfaction. The potentialities of the average person are rarely fully used at work, but people can be motivated to seek challenge and responsibility in the job, if their goals can be integrated with those of the organisation. A manager with this sort of attitude is likely to be a consultative, facilitating leader, using positive feedback, challenge and responsibility as motivators.

Theories X and Y tend to be self-fulfilling prophecies: employees treated as if Theory X were true will begin to behave accordingly, while those treated as if Theory Y were true – being trusted to take on more responsibility – are more likely to rise to the challenge.

Question 6

Text References. Material for this answer can be found in Chapter 15 (direction of communication flows) and Chapter 3 (informal organisation).

Top tips. Part (a) looks straightforward at first glance, because you should recognise the concept of downward, upward and lateral channels of communication. However, note that you are required to explain the *purposes* of each: what they are used for, or what advantage they offer the organisation. The concepts of 'direction', 'participation/feedback' and 'co-ordination' should set you on the right track...

Part (b) is challenging, because it is not common to distinguish in this way between 'the grapevine' (which is an informal communication channel) and 'rumour' (which is a type of communication, often transmitted via the grapevine). Having said that, though, we have already given a point of entry to a valid answer! Structure your argument carefully to ensure that you have contributed 6 marks' worth.

Easy marks. There are straightforward marks in part (a), starting with definition of the terms, plus the key purposes/advantages which should come easily to mind. You should be able to get 2-3 marks for explaining the grapevine – and at least 1 mark on 'rumour' using your common sense. Tackle each part in turn to ensure that you get all the basic marks available.

Marking scheme

			Marks
(a)	Brief explanation of the purposes of three main channels.		
	(i) Downwards	(Up to 3 marks)	3
	(ii) Upwards	(Up to 3 marks)	3
	(iii) Lateral or horizontal	(Up to 3 marks)	3
(b)	Brief explanation of two types of informal communication (up to 3 marks each)	(Up to 6 marks)	6
			15

(a) **Formal communication channels**

The formal communication channels of an organisation generally flow in three directions. Although traditionally, downward communication has dominated, organisational flexibility and learning has placed increasing emphasis on upward and lateral communication.

(i) **Downward communication** takes the form of instructions, briefings, rules and policies, announcement of plans and so on, from superior to subordinate. Its primary purpose is direction and control: expressing the goals and processes of the organisation, so that top-level strategies 'flow down' to lower levels and are put into action.

(ii) **Upward communication** is rarer – but very important for the organisation. It takes the form of reporting back, feedback, suggestions and so on from subordinates to superiors. In a bureaucratic organisation, its main purpose will be control (feedback on results and deviations from plan to allow corrective action). In a more flexible learning organisation, it will have the additional purpose of involving employees in decision-making and taking advantage of front-line knowledge and expertise in developing strategies.

(iii) **Horizontal or lateral communication** takes place between peers or peer groups at the same level of the organisation – often across functional boundaries (or vertical barriers). Its key purpose is co-ordination, but it also performs valuable functions in supporting information-sharing, ideas-creation and learning; and increasing flexibility and speed of response to customer demands (typically also enhancing customer service).

(b) **Informal communication channels**

Informal networks of communication inevitably exist alongside formal channels, as part of the informal organisation. Unlike formal channels, they are loosely structured, flexible and spontaneous.

The **grapevine** comprises the informal communication channels, which by-pass the formal reporting channels and routes. Research shows that grapevines thrive even when there is healthy information-flow through formal channels, because they reflect diverse informal contacts and relationships – and the opportunity to exchange 'non-official' information. The grapevine spreads information much faster than formal channels. It is also notoriously inaccurate and can carry gossip, rumour and unchecked assumptions, which can be morale-damaging. For this reason, managers often seek to harness the grapevine by feeding accurate or motivational information into it.

Rumours are one category of information carried by grapevines. They consist of unverified information, passed swiftly and unchecked from one person to another – and therefore often increasingly exaggerated or confused. Rumours can be extremely damaging to morale (eg in the case of an untrue statement about forthcoming redundancies): managers often seek to eliminate rumour by ensuring that accurate information is supplied as early as possible.

ACCA
Examiner's answers

Part 1 Examination – Paper 1.3 **June 2006 Answers**
Managing People

1 All organisations of whatever size need to understand and address the issues of the relationship between various levels of management, especially the nature, source and limitations of authority, responsibility and delegation. Understanding responsibility, delegation and authority is fundamental to the practice of management. Professional accountants should be able to show an understanding of the problems and challenges associated with these concepts of management. Students are not expected to remember definitions verbatim, but they are expected to show an understanding of the inherent logic contained in these concepts, and to demonstrate a clear distinction between the two main concepts of authority and responsibility.

(a) There are many explanations of what managers do. The most widely understood approach is that of Henri Fayol, who said that managers perform five duties, to forecast and plan, to organise, to command, co-ordinate and control. Managers are ultimately responsible for the efficient use of the organisation's resources and are accountable to the organisation's owners. At Flavours Fine Foods, the owners (the Jones brothers) must recognise this reality and allow the managers to manage.

It used to be said that a manager did his or her job by getting others to do theirs. In many ways this sums up the role of the supervisor. However, management must ensure that supervisors understand organisational objectives and must make clear the powers and limits of the supervisors' authority. Supervision is an important and integral part of the task and process of management.

The role of the supervisor is critical because of direct contact with and responsibility directly for the work of others. The supervisor is unique; he or she is the *interface* between management and the workforce and is the direct link between the two, being in direct physical contact with non-managers on a frequent basis. Supervisors are in the front line of management and see that others fulfil their duties, resolve problems first hand and often quickly, direct the work of others and enforce discipline. In addition, they often must have direct knowledge of health, safety and employment legislation and have authority for negotiation and industrial relations within the department.

(b) **(i)** RESPONSIBILITY is the liability of a person to be called to account for their actions and results, and is therefore an obligation to take some action to discharge that responsibility. Unlike authority, responsibility cannot be delegated. There is however some discussion on the extent to which this statement is true: the idea that responsibility cannot be delegated is too simplistic. Any task contains an element of responsibility. It is the idea of accountability and the *direction* of responsibility that is the relevant concept and is the problem at Flavours Fine Foods; ultimate responsibility resides with the owners. It is self evident that it is impossible to exercise authority without responsibility because this could lead to problems of control and therefore undesirable outcomes for the organisation. However, the superior (the owner) is always ultimately responsible for the actions of his or her subordinates. The key element here is the recognition of discretion by virtue of the person's position. This underlines the doctrine of absolute responsibility; the superior is always ultimately accountable.

(ii) AUTHORITY is the scope and amount of discretion given to a person to make decisions by virtue of the position held within the organisation. The authority and power structure of an organisation defines the part each member of the organisation is expected to perform and the relationship between the organisation's members so that its efforts are effective. The *source* of authority may be top down (as in formal organisations) or bottom up (as in social organisations and politics). In the scenario, authority is from the top and should be delegated downwards.

(iii) DELEGATION is giving a subordinate the discretion to make decisions within a certain, defined sphere of influence. Therefore the superior must possess the authority to delegate. The key element here is discretion and the level of authority within a specific sphere which is behind the problems at Flavours Fine Foods. Authority should be clearly delegated as appropriate to the managers and, through them, to the supervisors.

(c) **(i)** Without delegation, formal organisations could not exist. Without allocation of authority, responsibility and delegation, a formal organisation cannot be effective. They are critical aspects. Managers must delegate because of the size and complexity of the organisation (certainly an issue for Flavours Fine Foods). Delegation can help overcome the physical and mental limitations of staff, managers and supervisors and it allows management to attend to other matters since routine tasks and decision making can be passed down. However, superiors must call subordinates to account and co-ordinate their activities.

(ii) Effective delegation can be achieved by assigning agreed tasks to the subordinate, ensuring that resources are allocated and by specifying expected performance levels and ensuring that they are understood. In addition, it is necessary to ensure that the subordinate has the ability and experience to undertake the tasks by maintaining frequent contact and ensuring that the subordinate has authority to do the job. Sufficient authority must be delegated to fulfil the task. This authority in turn may be specific or general; the scenario suggests that the authority of the managers and supervisors is specific. The subordinate should not refer decisions upwards, and the superior should not expect this. In addition there should be no doubts over boundaries; they must be clearly defined as to who holds what authority and who accounts to whom. Therefore there must be clarity as to departmental functions and individual authority, which is at the root of the problem at Flavours Fine Foods.

(iii) Problems with delegation are threefold. Firstly, reluctance from managers who are afraid of losing control, who fear that subordinates may carry out the work badly and who are resentful of subordinate development. Secondly, there is the problem of lack of confidence, lack of self confidence in the manager and often a lack of confidence in the subordinates. Thirdly, there are problems of trust; that is the amount of trust the superior has in the subordinate and the trust that the subordinate feels the superior has in him or her.

(iv) Problems with delegation can be overcome by careful selection and training, an open communication system, the establishment of an appropriate control system and a system that rewards effective delegation.

2 All organisations of whatever size have to work in a co-ordinated way to ensure that the objectives laid down are achieved. However, for effective co-ordination to take place, the structure must be correct and understood. Very often, managers know the structure but cannot explain its significance or appropriateness.

(a) The structure of an organisation is often depicted as a chart. The structure explains the communication pattern, the linking mechanism between departments, tasks and individuals, the co-ordinating mechanism that ensures the entire organisation is working toward the same objective, and who is in control of the organisation's activities and at what level in the organisation.

(b) The **strategic apex** is the highest level of the organisation and is therefore the highest level of management. This part ensures that the organisation's mission is followed and manages the relationship with the environment.

The **operating core** is the part that represents the productive activity of the organisation, gathering inputs and, through conversion, turns them into outputs.

The **middle line** represents that part of the organisation where the middle managers operate. The role of this part is to turn the instructions of the strategic apex into activities for the operating core.

The **technostructure** includes the staff who provide a technical or supportive activity but which are not a part of the core activities. This part of the organisation includes the engineering, accounting and human resource departments.

The **support staff** carry out the ancillary activities that are neither part of the core nor the technostructure. Support staff have no role in the direct activities of the organisation: these activities include catering and public relations.
(Students may draw the appropriate diagram)

3 The interview is extensively used for the selection of new employees and in many cases is the only method of selection. However, interviews have been criticised for failing to identify appropriate candidates suitable for the organisation. It is essential therefore that professional accountants recognise both the problems and opportunities that the formal selection interview presents.

(a) The purpose of the selection interview is to find the best possible person for the position who will fit into the organisation. Those conducting the interview must also ensure that the candidate clearly understands the job on offer, career prospects and that all candidates feel that fair treatment has been provided through the selection process.

In addition, the interview also gives the opportunity to convey a good impression of the organisation, whether the candidate has been successful or not.

(b) **(i)** The **face to face** interview is the most common form of interview. In this situation the candidate is interviewed by a single representative of the employing organisation.

The advantages of such interviews are that they establish an understanding between the participants, are cost effective for the organisation (only one member of the organisation's staff is involved) and, because of the more personal nature, ensure that candidates feel comfortable.

The disadvantages are that the selection interview relies on the views and impression of a single interviewer that can be both subjective and biased. In addition, the interviewer may be selective in questioning and it is easier for the candidate to hide weaknesses or lack of ability.

(ii) **Panel** interviews are often used for senior appointments and consist of two or more interviewers.

The advantages of such interviews are that they allow opinion and views to be shared amongst the panel. They provide a more complete and coherent approach, hence problems of bias inherent in face to face interviews can be reduced. They may also be appropriate where an individual with specialist or technical skills has to support the interviewer in relation to assessing the technical competencies of the interviewee.

The disadvantages are that panel interviews can be difficult to control, interviewers may deviate or ask irrelevant questions and they can be easily dominated by a strong personality who is able unduly to influence others. In addition, such interviews can often result in disagreement amongst the panel members.

4 All organisations need appropriately trained employees. Due to the nature of modern business, especially the professions, much of this training is internal and often on a one to one basis. Accountants as managers should therefore be able to understand the different approaches to training and which of them is the most appropriate and cost effective for the training requirements of the organisation.

(a) **Computer based** training can be inexpensive and is based upon user friendly interactive computer programs designed to enable trainees to train on their own and at their own pace.

(b) **Coaching** involves the trainee being assisted by another, experienced employee. It is a specialised, systematic learning programme based on communication, defined targets and continuous learning. It encourages constructive feedback between the trainee and trainer.

(c) **Mentoring**, not to be confused with coaching, involves training on a wider range of activities, often aimed at career development of employees at supervisory or management level. The trainee is provided with a development programme and is under close supervision. The mentor should not be the trainee's immediate supervisor or manager.

(d) **Job rotation** is an important training method and is often also seen as a means of motivation. It involves moving the trainee from one job to another and is therefore more suitable for lower level employees. The trainee is required to do different jobs in logical succession, thus broadening experience and gaining a picture of the organisation's wider activities.

(e) **Job instruction** is a one to one method of training through which the trainee is shown how to fulfill a task and then allowed to get on with that task. It is a systematic approach to training involving immediate supervision and by allowing the trainee to complete the task is a cost effective way of training.

5 The way in which managers' duties are undertaken can significantly influence the satisfaction that employees derive from their work. Abraham Maslow suggested that individuals have a hierarchy of personal needs which are identifiable, universally applicable and can be satisfied in the workplace. Understanding this concept provides guidance to management as to the appropriateness of motivational techniques.

(a) Maslow's theory of motivation is a **content** theory. Its basic idea is that each individual has a set of needs which have to be satisfied in a set order of priority.

Maslow suggested that individuals have five needs:

Self-actualisation
(or self fulfilment)

Esteem needs
(or ego)

Social needs

Safety needs

Physiological needs

These needs are arranged in a hierarchy of importance and movement is upwards, from physiological needs to self-actualisation. Any individual will always want more; each need must be satisfied before the next is sought. However – and critically so far as motivation in the workplace is concerned – *a satisfied need is no longer a motivator.*

The theory is usually presented in the shape of a triangle, with physiological needs at its base and self-actualisation at its apex. The triangle shape has a clear significance. As an individual moves up toward the apex, the needs thin out, that is physiological needs are far greater than self-actualisation needs. For many individuals, reaching social needs is often the highest need to be satisfied. The theory is sometimes presented as a staircase; again with self-actualisation at the top. This second diagrammatic form reflects the application of the theory to more modern situations, where it can reasonably be assumed that those within the organisation have already achieved physiological and safety needs. For such individuals, social and esteem needs may well be greater.

Physiological needs are the basic survival needs which, although part of the theory, probably have less relevance today. These needs are usually seen as food, shelter (which is sometimes noted as a safety need), warmth and clothing.

Safety needs are the desire for security, order, certainty and predictability in life and freedom from threat.

The above two so-called 'lower order needs' dominate until satisfied.

Social needs are the gregarious needs of mankind, the need for friendship, relationships and affection. This is often seen as the desire to be part of a family.

Esteem needs are the desire for recognition and respect, often associated with status, especially in the modern world.

Self-actualisation (self fulfilment) is the ultimate goal. Once this state is achieved the individual has fulfilled personal potential.

However, later work by Maslow has suggested that there are two additional needs; **freedom of enquiry** (free speech and justice) and **knowledge** (the need to explore and learn). These additional needs are a further development of social needs and recognise the changing nature of modern life.

(b) This theory is based on the idea that the goals of the individual and the organisation can be integrated and that personal satisfaction can be achieved through the workplace. It also assumes that individuals will achieve self-actualisation through their role in assisting the organisation to achieve its objectives. It follows therefore that work is the principal source of satisfaction.

The theory's practical application is that managers should recognise that subordinates' needs are always evolving and increasing, so continued attention to increasing the employees' personal development, opportunities for advancement and recognition of achievement are essential to keep them motivated.

6 To get the best out of people, managers need to have effective communication skills. Professional accountants as managers need to understand the difference between aggressive and assertive behaviour. Often an exchange of communication can be interpreted as a belligerent response from an employee. However, a slight difference in approach can communicate different feelings and achieve a more positive result.

(a) **Aggressive behaviour** is competitive and directed at defeating someone else. It is standing up for oneself at the expense of other people. It is defending one's rights but doing so in such a way that violates the rights of other people. Aggressive behaviour ignores or dismisses the needs, wants, opinions, feelings or beliefs of others.

Characteristics of aggressive behaviour include excessive 'I' statements, boastfulness, and the individual's opinions expressed as fact, threatening questions or postures from the individual, sarcasm and other throw-away remarks and a constant blaming of others.

Aggressive behaviour can be self defeating. It may cause such antagonism in the others in the organisation that they will refuse to co-operate or work with the person showing aggressive behaviour.

(b) **Assertive behaviour** on the other hand is based on equality and co-operation. It involves standing up for one's own rights and needs but also respects the rights and needs of others. It is not overbearing or aggressive but can be described as clear, honest and direct communication.

Assertive individuals defend their rights in a way that does not violate another individual's rights. They express their needs, wants, opinions, feelings and beliefs in direct and appropriate ways.

Characteristics of assertive behaviour include statements that are short, clear and to the point, distinctions made between fact and opinion, suggestions weighted with advice and evidence. Constructive criticism is the norm and offered without blame or assumptions. Questions to establish the wishes, opinions and thoughts of others are used as ways of getting around problems. There are no 'ought' or 'should' conditions, the first statement is often held, the individual's own feelings are expressed and not those of others. Assertive behaviour can be successful if it displays a willingness to deliver a mutual compromise as an aid to achieving a clear objective.

Part 1 Examination – Paper 1.3
Managing People

June 2006 Marking Scheme

1 (a) Explanation of the differences between the manager and supervisor
Five marks for the manager
Eight marks for the supervisor
(One mark for a specific reference to the *interface* role) Up to 13 marks

(Maximum for part (a) 13 marks)

(b) Explanation of:
(i) responsibility Up to 4 marks
(ii) authority Up to 3 marks
(iii) delegation Up to 3 marks

(Maximum for part (b) 10 marks)

(c) Explanation of:
(i) the need for delegation Up to 3 marks
(ii) achieving effective delegation Up to 6 marks
(iii) problems with delegation Up to 4 marks
(iv) how to overcome problems Up to 4 marks

(Maximum for part (c) 17 marks)

(Total for question 40 marks)

2 (a) Description of the term 'organisational structure.'
(One mark per factor identified) Up to 5 marks

(Maximum for part (a) 5 marks)

(b) Explanation of Mintzberg's five organisational components.
(Two marks per component) Up to 10 marks

(Maximum for part (b) 10 marks)

(Total for question 15 marks)

3 (a) Explanation of the purpose of the selection interview
(One mark per factor identified) Up to 4 marks

(Maximum for part (a) 4 marks)

(b) Explanation of the advantages and disadvantages:
(i) The face to face interview Up to 6 marks
(ii) The panel interview Up to 5 marks
(in each case, one mark per factor)

(Maximum for part (b) 11 marks)

(Total for question 15 marks)

4	**(a)**	Explanation of computer based training	Up to 3 marks
			(Maximum for part (a) 3 marks)
	(b)	Explanation of coaching	Up to 3 marks
			(Maximum for part (b) 3 marks)
	(c)	Explanation of mentoring	Up to 3 marks
			(Maximum for part (c) 3 marks)
	(d)	Explanation of job rotation	Up to 3 marks
			(Maximum for part (d) 3 marks)
	(e)	Explanation of job instruction	Up to 3 marks
			(Maximum for part (e) 3 marks)
			(Total for question 15 marks)
5	**(a)**	Explanation of Maslow's theory (Two marks per step)	Up to 10 marks
			(Maximum for part (a) 10 marks)
	(b)	Application of the theory	Up to 5 marks
			(Maximum for part (b) 5 marks)
			(Total for question 15 marks)
6	**(a)**	Explanation and examples of aggressive behaviour	Up to 8 marks
			(Maximum for part (a) 8 marks)
	(b)	Explanation and examples of assertive behaviour	Up to 7 marks
			(Maximum for part (b) 7 marks)
			(Total for question 15 marks)

Part 1 Examination – Paper 1.3
Managing People **December 2006 Answers**

1 One of the many skills that managers are called upon to use is counselling. Situations often arise in the workplace where particular and careful people-centred skills are required. It is important that managers understand exactly what counselling involves and the delicate skills involved. In addition, many problems identified by counselling can be resolved through appropriate methods of motivation. Widening and deepening interest in the organisation and its many tasks and departments is a tried and tested method for motivating employees. However, financial rewards remain a strong and important motivator.

(a) The external counsellor's role must be as 'a person who takes on the role of counsellor and agrees explicitly to offer time, attention, advice, guidance and support to another person (or persons) temporarily in the role of client'.

(b) It is clear that many of the problems at Bailey's that have led to the unhappy atmosphere lend themselves to resolution through the neutral and non-judgemental approach offered by the appointment of external counsellors. The counsellor must be in a position to help the individual employee to identify problems, issues and possible solutions to the kind of problems that have manifested themselves at Bailey's: poor production, unrest, low morale and significantly, the long tradition of poor pay that is leading to employee family problems outside the factory. There is always the danger of leading the employee, so the counsellor must adopt a passive role, show interest and encourage reflection whilst allowing the employee to lead and talk around the issues. Open questions must be used to help the employee explore ideas and feelings. The counsellor must be an active listener, speaking only to clarify issues and elicit answers when appropriate. Above all, the counsellor must be impartial and this is why Bailey's has appointed outside counsellors.

Counselling skills require the ability to establish rapport with the employee, to clarify and summarise as appropriate, to ask non-specific questions, use a non-directive approach, to listen and be able to discern what is meant by what the employee says. In addition, the counsellor must allow the employee to be silent if he or she wishes to be, to allow any meeting to take place at the speed of the employee and anticipate the employee's views on the causes, which at Bailey's are many, and to allow solutions to the problems.

(c) For Bailey's the advantages of counselling as a means of understanding and addressing the problems are that it provides a confidential service to the employee to discuss problems away from and not involving management or supervision. There is no obvious human resources policy at Bailey's and counselling provides an opportunity to develop an appropriate policy from understanding individual problems.

This in turn will demonstrate organisational commitment to the employees that has been lacking in the past at Bailey's and begin the process of better performance and increase in commitment.

At another level, counselling can provide a link to other external agencies to assist with personal problems that may be deemed too specific for resolution within Bailey's.

(d) **(i)** Job rotation is the planned rotation of staff between jobs and tasks to reduce monotony and boredom and provide fresh opportunities and challenges. This could be a useful way of encouraging employees at Bailey's alongside enrichment and enlargement. Rotation would encourage better understanding between employees at Bailey's. It takes two forms, the transfer to another job after some time in an existing job and the introduction of another individual to the job being vacated, or as a form of training where individuals are moved through different jobs to learn new skills.

(ii) Job enlargement is often referred to as 'horizontal job enlargement' and is aimed at widening the content of jobs by increasing the number of operations in which the job holder is involved and is another method by which employees at Bailey's might become more involved. It reduces the level of repetition and dullness by providing a horizontal extension to activity, reducing monotony and boredom inherent in the operations at Bailey's.

(iii) Job enrichment, which is often referred to as 'vertical job enlargement', is a planned, deliberate action to build greater responsibility, breadth and challenge into the work of the individual. The emphasis is on the individual rather than the organisation, team or group. This may be a way forward for some of Bailey's employees since it provides the individual employee with the responsibility for decision making of a higher order, provides greater freedom to decide how the job or task should be undertaken, improves understanding of the entire process, encourages participation in the planning and production procedures and provides regular feedback to management – urgently needed at Bailey's.

(e) There are issues at Bailey's as a consequence of poor pay. Although non-financial motivation has an important role to play in encouraging commitment, the fact remains that financial rewards act as a strong motivating factor, especially in what has been a low pay business. Financial rewards are all encompassing and apply to all employees at all levels, are universally applicable, able to satisfy all types of need and simple to apply and understand. At Bailey's, financial rewards have a greater effect because they can provide recognition and prestige if pay is improved, are seen as the most important hygiene factor (especially in a business with a history of low pay and low morale) and are a measure of achievement against goals, especially if some form of bonus or performance related pay is introduced by the new management at Bailey's. In addition, financial rewards are a basis for satisfaction and are often used as a form of professional or social comparison outside the organisation.

2 For the complex, modern business, the view that the single objective of business is to make a profit is regarded by many writers as simplistic. Peter Drucker has argued that for a business to be successful, it must address a number of objectives.

Drucker was one of the first writers to identify the dangers of the single objective of profit maximisation. Concentrating on a single objective (invariably profit) is not only unproductive but potentially harmful to the organisation and can endanger the survival of the business and seriously undermine its future. He argues that business organisations have in fact eight objectives, all of which must be addressed concurrently. These eight objectives are particularly relevant to management, bringing together as they do the need to address all the issues with which the organisation is concerned.

Market standing is the need to identify and maintain market share and to ensure the development of new products to maintain share. Without market standing, no organisation can succeed.

Innovation is the need to develop and find new products and processes; no business can survive on providing the same product or service over the long term. Innovation is fundamental to understanding growth; organisations grow by developing innovative differences to their competitors.

Productivity and 'contributed value' recognises the need for efficiency and the efficient use of business resources.

Physical and financial resources is a recognition of the need to use the correct and appropriate financial resources.

Profitability. The word 'profit' does not appear, but 'profitability'. Here there are three important determinants, profitability as a measure of effectiveness (many businesses make a profit which in fact is a poor return on the effort produced), the need for profit so that the business can be self-financing and the need to attract new capital.

Manager performance and development is the explicit recognition that the business requires objectives and that management activity can be linked directly to those objectives.

Worker performance and attitude is recognition that it is vital to measure the performance of the workforce by such means as labour turnover. However, worker attitude is more difficult to measure, but should be attempted.

Public responsibility has become an issue in the twenty-first century. Any business needs to be aware that it is a part of the community within which it operates and is therefore part of a wider social system.

3 All organisations rely upon their staff for success. However, recruitment of staff can be time consuming; a drain on resources and the necessary expertise may not exist within the organisation.

(a) Internal promotion describes the situation where an organisation has an explicit policy to promote from within and where there is a clear and transparent career structure. This is typical of many professional bodies, large organisations and public services.

The advantages of internal promotion are that it acts as a source of motivation, provides good general morale amongst employees and illustrates the organisation's commitment to encouraging advancement. Recruitment is expensive and internal promotion is relatively inexpensive in terms of time, money and induction costs and since staff seeking promotion are known to the employer, training costs are minimised. Finally, the culture of the organisation is better understood by the individual.

(b) External recruitment describes the situation where the organisation decides to fill a staff vacancy and recruit from outside the organisation.

It may be essential if particular skills or expertise are not already available within the organisation and is necessary to restore depleted staffing levels or when for some reason the organisation urgently needs new employees. New staff members bring new ideas and novel approaches to the organisation and to the specific task, often providing experience and work methods from other employers.

(c) An organisation considering the use of external recruitment consultants would make its decision upon the availability, level and appropriateness of expertise available within the host organisation and its likely effectiveness, together with the cost of using consultants set against the cost of using the organisation's own staff. The organisation should consider the level of expertise required of potential employees and therefore the appropriate knowledge required of the consultants and the need for impartiality or security which may be of particular importance for some organisations. In addition, the views of internal staff as to the likely effect of using outside consultants must be considered, as is the effect the use of consultants might have on the need to develop expertise within the organisation.

4 Appraisal systems are central to human resource management and understanding the difficulties of such schemes and the correct approach to them is necessary if the appraisal process is to be successful and worthwhile.

(a) The manager conducting the interview might base it on one of three approaches.

The *Tell and Sell* Method. The manager explains to the employee being appraised how the appraisal assessment is to be undertaken and gains acceptance of the evaluation and improvement plan from the employee. Human resource skills are important with this approach in order for the manager to be able to provide constructive criticism and to motivate the employee.

The *Tell and Listen* Method. The manager invites the employee to respond to the way that the interview is to be conducted. This approach requires counselling skills and encouragement to allow the employee to participate fully in the interview. A particular feature of this approach is the encouragment of feedback from the employee.

The *Problem Solving* Method. With this method the manager takes a more helpful approach and concentrates on the work problems of the employee, who is encouraged to think through his or her problems and to provide their own intrinsic motivation.

(b) The appraisal system should be well constructed and fair to both the individual and the organisation. However, there are a number of barriers, often because employees see the appraisal as one or more of the following:

Confrontation due to lack of agreement on performance, badly explained or subjective feedback, performance based on recent events or disagreement on longer term activities.

Judgement, the appraisal is seen as a one sided process based entirely on the manager's perspective.

Chat is the worst of all worlds. The appraisal interview is seen as an informal, loosely constructed and badly managed conversation without purpose.

Unfinished business is when the appraisal is not seen as part of a continuing process of performance management.

An annual event when the appraisal is seen as largely irrelevant and simply an event to set annual targets that quickly become out of date.

A system of *bureaucracy* based on forms devised solely to satisfy the organisation's human resources department so that its main purpose, that of identifying individual and organisation performance and improvement, is forgotten.

5 The way in which managers treat their employees can significantly influence the satisfaction that the employees derive from their work and thus the overall success of the organisation. Understanding the importance of motivation is therefore an important management skill.

(a) Content theories address the question '*What* are the things that motivate people?'

Content theories are also called need theories (because they concentrate on the needs fulfilled by work) and are based on the notion that all human beings have a set of needs or required outcomes, and according to this theory, these needs can be satisfied through work. The theory focuses on what arouses, maintains and regulates good, directed behaviour and what specific individual forces motivate people. However, content theories assume that everyone responds to motivating factors in the same way and that consequently there is one, best way to motivate everybody.

(b) Douglas McGregor has suggested that the managers' view of the individuals' attitude to work can be divided into two categories, which he called Theory X and Theory Y. The style of management adopted will stem from the view taken as to how subordinates behave. However, these two typologies are not distinct; they do in fact represent the two ends of a continuum.

(i) Theory X is based on traditional organisational thinking. It assumes that the average person is basically indolent and has an inherent dislike of work which should be avoided at all costs. The individual lacks ambition, shuns responsibility, has no ambition and is resistant to change. This theory holds that the individual seeks only security and is driven solely by self-interest. It follows that because of this dislike of work, most have to be directed, controlled, organised or coerced. Management is based on fear and punishment and will have an exploitative or authoritarian style. This reflects the thinking of the classical school of management, based on a scientific approach, specialisation, standardisation and obedience to superiors.

(ii) Theory Y is at the opposite end of the continuum and reflects a contemporary approach to motivation, reflecting growth in professional and service employment. It is based on the idea that the goals of the individual and the organsiation can – indeed should – be integrated and that personal fulfilment can be achieved through the workplace. It assumes that for most people, work is as natural as rest or play and employees will exercise self-discipline and self-direction in helping to achieve the organisation's objectives. Physical and mental effort at work is perfectly natural and is actively sought as a source of personal satisfaction.

In addition, the average employee seeks and accepts responsibilty and creativity. Innovative thinking is widely distributed amongst the whole population and should therefore be encouraged in the work situation.

The intellectual ability of the average person is only partly used and should be encouraged and thus individuals are motivated by seeking self-achievement. Since control and punishment are not required, management therefore has to encourage and develop the individual. However, the operation of a Theory Y approach can be difficult and frustrating, time consuming and sometimes regarded with suspicion.

6 There are many forms of communication within an organisation, both formal and informal. Formally communicated information often flows in one of three main directions: downwards, upwards and lateral. However, all organisations also have informal communication channels and management must understand their importance.

(a) Formal communicated information flows in three main directions.

(i) *Downwards*. This form of communication is often the one most easily recognised and understood. The purpose of downward communication is to give specific directives, to provide information about procedures and practices and to provide information about work practices. It also serves to tell employees about their performance and provides information on organisational and departmental objectives.

(ii) *Upwards* communication is generally non-directive in nature and often takes two forms: personal problems or suggestions and/or technical feedback as part of the organisation's control system.

(iii) *Lateral or horizontal*. Traditional communication assumes a hierarchical structure with only vertical communication, however horizontal communication has become important and necessary in less formal organisations. It takes the form of coordination with departmental managers or supervisors meeting regularly, problem solving with department members meeting to resolve an issue or information sharing and it also describes interdepartmental sharing of ideas or conflict resolution where there is a need to resolve interdepartmental friction.

(b) The *grapevine* and *rumour* are the two main types of informal communication.

The *grapevine* is probably the best known type of informal communication. All organisations have a grapevine and it will thrive if there is lack of information and consequently employees will make assumptions about events. In addition, insecurity, gossip about issues and fellow employees, personal animosity between employees or managers or new information that has not yet reached the formal communication system, will all drive the grapevine.

Rumours are the other main informal means of communication and are often active if there is a lack of formal communication. A rumour is inevitably a communication not based on verified facts and may therefore be true or false. Rumours travel quickly (often quicker than both the formal system and the grapevine) and can influence those who hear them and cause confusion, especially if bad news is the basis of the rumour. Managers must ensure that the formal communication system is such that rumours can be stopped, especially since they can have a serious negative effect on employees.

Part 1 Examination – Paper 1.3
Managing People — **December 2006 Marking Scheme**

1 **(a)** Definition of the role of the external counsellor. (Up to 3 marks)
(Maximum for part (a) 3 marks)

(b) Description of the role and skills of the external counsellor. (Up to 14 marks)
(Maximum for part (b) 14 marks)

(c) Brief description of three advantages to Bailey's of counselling (one mark each). (Up to 3 marks)
(Maximum for part (c) 3 marks)

(d) Explanation and usefulness of:

(i) job rotation (Up to 5 marks)

(ii) job enlargement (Up to 5 marks)

(iii) job enrichment (Up to 5 marks)
(Maximum for part (d) 15 marks)

(e) Five reasons why financial rewards could be considered to improve motivation (one mark each). (Up to 5 marks)
(Maximum for part (e) 5 marks)

(Total for question 40 marks)

2 Explanation of the eight classifications of objectives. (Up to 15 marks)

(Total for question 15 marks)

3 **(a)** Description of the advantages of internal recruitment (one mark for each relevant point). (Up to 5 marks)
(Maximum for part (a) 5 marks)

(b) Description of the advantages of external recruitment (one mark for each relevant point). (Up to 5 marks)
(Maximum for part (b) 5 marks)

(c) Description of five factors (one mark each). (Up to 5 marks)
(Maximum for part (c) 5 marks)

(Total for question 15 marks)

4 **(a)** Description of the three interview approaches. (Up to 5 marks)
(Maximum for part (a) 5 marks)

(b) Description of the five main barriers (two marks per barrier). (Up to 10 marks)
(Maximum for part (b) 10 marks)

(Total for question 15 marks)

5 **(a)** Explanation of content theory. (Up to 5 marks)
(Maximum for part (a) 5 marks)

(b) **(i)** Explanation of Theory X. (Up to 5 marks)

(ii) Explanation of Theory Y. (Up to 5 marks)
(Maximum for part (b) 10 marks)

(Total for question 15 marks)

6 **(a)** Brief explanation of the main purposes of the three main formal communication channels:

(i) Downwards (Up to 3 marks)

(ii) Upwards (Up to 3 marks)

(iii) Lateral or horizontal (Up to 3 marks)

(Maximum for part (a) 9 marks)

(b) Brief explanation of the two types of informal communication (up to 3 marks each) (Up to 6 marks)

(Maximum for part (b) 6 marks)

(Total for question 15 marks)

Review Form & Free Prize Draw – Paper 1.3 Managing People (1/07)

All original review forms from the entire BPP range, completed with genuine comments, will be entered into one of two draws on 31 July 2007 and 31 January 2008. The names on the first four forms picked out on each occasion will be sent a cheque for £50.

Name: ______________________ **Address:** ______________________

How have you used this Kit?
(Tick one box only)

☐ Home study (book only)
☐ On a course: college ______________
☐ With 'correspondence' package
☐ Other ______________

Why did you decide to purchase this Kit?
(Tick one box only)

☐ Have used the complementary Study Text
☐ Have used other BPP products in the past
☐ Recommendation by friend/colleague
☐ Recommendation by a lecturer at college
☐ Saw advertising
☐ Other ______________

During the past six months do you recall seeing/receiving any of the following?
(Tick as many boxes as are relevant)

☐ Our advertisement in *Student Accountant*
☐ Our advertisement in *Pass*
☐ Our advertisement in *PQ*
☐ Our brochure with a letter through the post
☐ Our website www.bpp.com

Which (if any) aspects of our advertising do you find useful?
(Tick as many boxes as are relevant)

☐ Prices and publication dates of new editions
☐ Information on product content
☐ Facility to order books off-the-page
☐ None of the above

Which BPP products have you used?

Text	☐	*Success CD*	☐	*Learn Online*	☐
Kit	☑	*i-Learn*	☐	*Home Study Package*	☐
Passcard	☐	*i-Pass*	☐	*Home Study PLUS*	☐

Your ratings, comments and suggestions would be appreciated on the following areas.

	Very useful	*Useful*	*Not useful*
Passing ACCA exams	☐	☐	☐
Passing 1.3	☐	☐	☐
Planning your question practice	☐	☐	☐
Questions	☐	☐	☐
Top Tips etc in answers	☐	☐	☐
Content and structure of answers	☐	☐	☐
'Plan of attack' in mock exams	☐	☐	☐
Mock exam answers			

Overall opinion of this Kit *Excellent* ☐ *Good* ☐ *Adequate* ☐ *Poor* ☐

Do you intend to continue using BPP products? *Yes* ☐ *No* ☐

The BPP author of this edition can be e-mailed at: nickweller@bpp.com/learningmedia

Please return this form to: Nick Weller, ACCA Publishing Manager, BPP Learning Media Ltd, FREEPOST, London, W12 8BR

Review Form & Free Prize Draw (continued)

TELL US WHAT YOU THINK

Please note any further comments and suggestions/errors below.

Free Prize Draw Rules

1 Closing date for 31 July 2008 draw is 30 June 2008. Closing date for 31 January 2008 draw is 31 December 2007.

2 Restricted to entries with UK and Eire addresses only. BPP employees, their families and business associates are excluded.

3 No purchase necessary. Entry forms are available upon request from BPP Learning Media Ltd. No more than one entry per title, per person. Draw restricted to persons aged 16 and over.

4 Winners will be notified by post and receive their cheques not later than 6 weeks after the relevant draw date.

5 The decision of the promoter in all matters is final and binding. No correspondence will be entered into.